blues*Speak*

DISCARD

BLUES *Speak*

The Best of the *Original Chicago Blues Annual*

Edited by Lincoln T. Beauchamp Jr.

University of Illinois Press
Urbana and Chicago

© 2010 by the Board of Trustees
of the University of Illinois
All rights reserved
Manufactured in the United States of America
1 2 3 4 5 C P 5 4 3 2 1
♾ This book is printed on acid-free paper.

Frontispiece: L. Beauchamp; background painting, *Tenochtitlan*, by Oscar Romero. Photo by Joan Hackett.

Library of Congress Cataloging-in-Publication Data

BluesSpeak : the best of the Original Chicago Blues Annual / edited by Lincoln T. Beauchamp Jr.

p. cm.

Includes index.

ISBN 978-0-252-03440-4 (cloth : alk. paper) —

ISBN 978-0-252-07692-3 (pbk. : alk. paper)

1. Blues (Music)—Illinois—Chicago—History and criticism.

2. Blues musicians—Illinois—Chicago. I. Chicago Beau, 1949-

II. Original Chicago Blues Annual.

ML3521.B65   2009

781.64309773'11—dc22   2009019585

To my greatest inspiration, my parents,
Betty and Lincoln Sr.,
and to all of my children and their mothers.

Special thanks and praises to my dear friend, Jim Conley,
who provided music, light, cane, and humor.

For Memphis Slim and Archie Shepp,
whom I met at the crossroads,
and they showed me the way.

For the Art Ensemble of Chicago:
Famoudou, Roscoe, Lester, Joseph, Malachi,
who since the beginning have steadfastly supported my every endeavor.

Praise be unto the Ancestors,

—LET THEIR STORY BE KNOWN!

Contents

Acknowledgments ix
Introduction xi

FROM THE *ORIGINAL CHICAGO BLUES ANNUAL*, ISSUE NUMBER 1
Interview with Koko Taylor   *Guy "Doc" Lerner*   3
Interview with Eddie Boyd   *L. "Chicago Beau" Beauchamp*   9
Interview with Famoudou Don Moye   *L. "Chicago Beau" Beauchamp*   13
Interview with Big Daddy Kinsey   *Jacques Lacava*   17
The Blues Reality of Maxwell Street   *Davis Whiteis*   22
Southern Sound: A Brooding under Blood   *Eugene B. Redmond*   26

FROM THE *ORIGINAL CHICAGO BLUES ANNUAL*, ISSUE NUMBER 2
Interview with Pinetop Perkins   *L. "Chicago Beau" Beauchamp*   29
Welcome Home Luther   *Jacques Lacava*   37
The Bean and The Newk   *Hart Leroy Bibbs*   39
A Gun in the Hand Is Worth . . .   *Kalamu Ya Salaam*   42
They Say the Hoochiecoochie Man Done Up an Gone   *Quincy Troupe*   43
Funky-Grace (From the Hero Series)   *Eugene B. Redmond*   44

FROM THE *ORIGINAL CHICAGO BLUES ANNUAL*, ISSUE NUMBER 3
Interview with Lester Bowie   *L. "Chicago Beau" Beauchamp*   47
Interview with Bruce Iglauer   *L. "Chicago Beau" Beauchamp*   54
A Few Words from a Chicago Blues Mama   *Deitra Farr*   62
The Blues Aesthetic   *Kalamu Ya Salaam*   65
I, the Blues   *L. "Chicago Beau" Beauchamp*   70

FROM THE *ORIGINAL CHICAGO BLUES ANNUAL*, ISSUE NUMBER 4
Interview with Junior Wells   *L. "Chicago Beau" Beauchamp*   73
J. B. Hutto and Lil' Ed Williams   *David Witter*   80
The Blue Bayou   *Julio Finn*   83
Bebop Blues   *James Otis Williams*   88
Blues Bar Poem   *Julie Parson Nesbitt*   89
A Photo Salute to Blues Greats   *Barbara Barefield*   90

FROM THE *ORIGINAL CHICAGO BLUES ANNUAL*, ISSUE NUMBER 5
Interview with Billy Boy Arnold   *L. "Chicago Beau" Beauchamp*   97
Interview with Herb Kent   *L. "Chicago Beau" Beauchamp*   109
The Blues Are a People Who Are
Finally Going to Take Care of Business   *David Whiteis*   117

FROM THE *ORIGINAL CHICAGO BLUES ANNUAL*, ISSUE NUMBER 6
Interview with Chicago Beau   *Julio Finn*   123
Interview with E. Parker McDougal   *L. "Chicago Beau" Beauchamp*   131
Blues for Zazen   *Joseph Jarman*   136

FROM THE *ORIGINAL CHICAGO BLUES ANNUAL*, ISSUE NUMBER 7
Interview with Johnny Shines   *L. "Chicago Beau" Beauchamp*   139
Interview with Barry Dolins   *L. "Chicago Beau" Beauchamp*   142
Juke Joint Voices   *James Otis Williams*   146
Art Ensemble of Chicago   *Mike Hennessey*   149
Now Mother of Time   *Hart Leroy Bibbs*   152

Afterword   153
Contributors   155
Index   159

Acknowledgments

Enormous thanks to my wife Dooney, for your love and encouragement while I was working on this project, and beyond.

There are a few people who worked on or behind the scenes who helped shape *OCBA*. My deepest gratitude to A.-C. McGraw, Jacob Russell, Eric Shropshire, Felix Wohrstein, Lowell Thompson, Joan Hackett, Bernadette Dunn, Floyd Webb, Herb Walker, Willie Kent and the Gents, Peter Raczkiewicz, Leigh Jones, Honorée Dakar McGraw Beauchamp, Jessica K. Carter, Beguine Beauchamp, Pete Crawford, Massimo Palmas, Halldor Bragason, Guðmundur Peterson, Julia Svensdottir, Hilmar Hilmarson, Russell Prince Arnold, Daniele Bombasarro, Erin Fahey, Annette Briton, Howard Watkins, Jim Dale, Sylvie Dale, Val Davis, Clare Schapiro, Milly Hurlimann, Jean Marie Robbins, DonAlonzo Beauchamp, Big "Golden" Wheeler, Thomas Harris, Isamu Suzuki, Maite Battini, Kathy Tyler, Ajaramu, Bernard McDermot, Kathy Rago, Robin Gould, Norio Myabyashi, Micheline Harvey, Lise Malo, Raquel Irving, Jackie Fields, Mark Worden, Rosanna Casanno, Sharon Kringle, Greg Davis, Clarence Wheeler, Harold Bradley, Gabriel Kleinschmidt Promotions, Jonas Blues Band, Luca O'Neill, and Raffi Marat O'Neill.

Special recognition to Carrie Holt for her unswerving loyalty, professional insight, huge soul, and grand sense of humor. Without you, Carrie, the road would have been a lot rougher, and we may not have made it through.

Introduction

The four of us, my mother, my father, my older sister, and I, lived in one room in a "House of Blues" located at 855 East Oakwood Boulevard near Cottage Grove Avenue on Chicago's South Side until I was three years old. The landlady, Mrs. Terrell, who was entrusted with caring for me from time to time, ran a "numbers" operation on the first floor. She received local "runners" and others associated with "the game" by day and a variety of friends at night, including musicians. There was always activity and chatter about betting: Who won? How much? What are the odds?

I was not quite the height of Mrs. Terrell's kitchen table, which was where much of the daytime activities occurred. My toddler's vantage point yielded an incredibly surreal montage of men, women, and the accoutrements of their daily activities: playing cards, the *Daily Racing Forum,* white "policy" tickets printed with purple or green ink, liquor bottles, cigarettes, and cigars with fancy bands that were usually given me to play with. Sometimes at the table sat women wearing fancy plumed hats with face nets. They wore beautifully printed dresses and smoked cigarettes in ornate cigarette holders: inhaling, exhaling, gesturing, and accentuating every utterance. The men who always seemed to be standing and swaying to Bebop or Blues on the record player were clad in double-breasted suits, Stacy Adams shoes with white stitching, diamond stick pins, and hats by Stetson or Dobbs. My child eyes would scan upward under the kitchen table from the partially removed high-heel shoes dangling on the toes of the ladies, to clearly visible ebony thighs and perfumed undergarments and then farther up to the cigar-smoking men with betting tickets slipped into their hat bands. The miasma of smoke, perfume, and alcohol dominated my senses, stimulated my desire to know more, and teased my imagination.

In 1952, at the age of forty-nine, my father's, Lincoln Sr.'s, hard work and perseverance began paying off. Times were difficult after World War II. For a Black man trying to start a law practice in Chicago, the obstacles were nearly as difficult as were those where he came from: a tenant farm near the town of Rusk in east Texas. We moved into a *real* apartment at 848 East Fortieth Street, just two blocks from Mrs. Terrell's. The Blue Flame Blues Club, Two Gun Pete's joint, and the notorious Green Gables Hotel were all within walking distance down Oakwood Boulevard heading east past Mrs. Terrell's toward Lake Park Avenue. We lived in Bluesville, and I heard and lived the blues every day.

Often after school or on Saturdays I would sit in the waiting room of my father's law office located at Forty-seventh Street and South Park Way (now Martin Luther King Drive). It was situated flush against and up above the Regal Theatre, the premier music venue in Black Chicago. In the waiting room, I would sometimes chat with clients, and on occasion pianists Ahmad Jamal and Lafayette Leak, both of whom my father represented, would be there. I was intrigued by their stories from two different sides of Black music: Ahmad in Jazz and Lafayette in Blues. They were both clever, creative, famous, and sharp dressers; I imagined myself one day to be somewhat like them, living in a music world.

In 1961, I was present at the grand opening of Ahmad Jamal's club/restaurant, Ahmad Jamal's Alhambra. It was an unforgettable evening that exposed me to Jamal's musical genius, a million dollar ambiance that I have rarely seen in a nightclub since, with five-star service and dining. Ahmad Jamal was living his dream; and even though I was quite young, he was having an influence on mine.

A few years later when I was seventeen, I met Muddy Waters. Little Billy Boy, brother of Billy Boy Arnold, now Julio Finn, and I would show up at his gigs almost anywhere in the country, as we were kind of itinerant musicians at the time. One night in Boston from the dressing room of the Jazz Workshop nightclub, Muddy shouted, "Hey Bo!" When he said this, his man Friday/bodyguard and I both went to see what he wanted. Muddy said, "Every time I call, both y'all gets up. Young Bo, I'm going to call you Chicago Bo, so y'all don't be getting messed up." That is how I became Chicago Beau. Muddy never knew I was Beauchamp, hence Beau, but "Chicago Beau" was perfect, and the name stuck. Muddy started introducing me as Chicago Beau. In 1967 in Boston at Wally's Lounge on Massachusetts Avenue, I did my first gig as Chicago Beau with organist Hopton Johnson, but I consider the real beginning of my music career to be August 16, 1969, in Paris, when Archie Shepp invited me to play on his session, titled Blasé.

And then there were books. My mother surrounded me with books and read to me incessantly when I was a child. In our new apartment a small library developed. My father bought multiple volumes of the Harvard Classics and the *Encyclopaedia Britannica*. My mother bought books weekly: Sterling Brown, Richard Wright, Zora Neale Hurston, Albert Camus, and many more. So I would not get hurt, she often cautioned me not to appear too smart around White people, because where she had come from in rural Kentucky, whites did not like "uppity" educated Negroes. I was always thinking of books and music. Sometimes while I was reading I would have a beat going in my mind, patting my food to the rhythm of the words. I probably would not have done that if headphones or iPods had been around in those days.

I have had the good fortune to meet several writers that I admired greatly, among them Alejo Carpentier. I met Alejo in Paris in 1969 when he was cultural attaché at the Cuban embassy. Occasionally we would spend afternoons together strolling Avenue Foch, smoking cigars, and talking—perhaps about his literacy accomplishments in Cuba, music, or life in general. He gave me the rights to publish some previously unpublished and not yet translated works of his, which unfortunately, due to my age (twenty at the time) and lack of resources, I was never able to do. However, I did vow to myself that one day, when I was ready, I would publish some of his work. That occurred in *Literati Chicago* number 2 where I published an excerpt from his novel, *A Kingdom of this World*.

For years I had wanted to be a publisher of books and magazines. Initially I was inspired by W. E. B. DuBois's magazine *The Crisis* and John H. Johnson, publisher of *Ebony* and *Jet* magazines, who struggled in the beginning and eventually overcame numerous hurdles to become the leading Black publisher in the United States. I greatly admired the *Paris Review* with its broad content, and it served partially as a model for my first magazine venture, *Literati Chicago*, which I founded in 1988 and evolved into *Literati Internazionale*.

Literati reflected my heritage and long interest in creating a publication that would present multiculturalism in literature to a broader audience beyond the journals section of university bookstores. One way to achieve this was to establish a circle of editorially like-minded people that included A.-C. McGraw, Eugene B. Redmond, Marta Nicholas, and Jacob Russell. Promotionally to be more accessible, we put on *Literati* celebrations that included music, poetry reading, and other entertainment. Besides conventional worldwide distribution, magazines were sold at music events such as Chicago's Jazz and Blues Festivals, the Spoleto Festival, the Montreal Jazz Festival, and book fairs in Chicago, around the United States, and abroad. Magazines were also donated to schools and cultural institutions.

Contributing writers and artists came from diverse backgrounds, some being well established and others emerging. Among them were Alejo Carpentier, Margaret Walker, Sterling Plumpp, Janis Mirikitani, Gwendolyn Brooks, Ishmael Reed, Jean-Joseph Rabearivelo, Henry Dumas, J. P. Donleavey, Jessica Hagedorn, Dennis Brutus, Sharese Locke, Tamara Madison, Shyvette, Pinkie Gordon Lane, Jibari Asim, Amir Bey, Gabriel Koren, Julie Parson, Henry Miller, and nearly ninety others.

The support for *Literati* was as diverse as its content. I created a category of support called Graphic Endorsement and a circle of supporters called Associates of *Literati Chicago*. Among the Associates were the Art Ensemble of Chicago, Blues entrepreneurs, a legal team, and individuals and businesses completely removed from literature but interested in the *Literati* concept of accessibility. There was also financial participation from granting organizations and Southern Illinois University at Edwardsville for the 1991 issue. I danced on a tightrope suspended between quasi commercialism and the not-for-profit route in an attempt to support the publication; however, it would be the need for cash flow that would be the deciding factor in suspending the *Literati* project in 1991 and moving vigorously forward with a new idea, the *Original Chicago Blues Annual* (*OCBA*), which I founded in 1989.

OCBA offered possibilities on a larger scale than *Literati*. Within its pages I could present much that I had planned for *Literati* and more because its platform was Blues as the root impetus of music, literature, art, and lifestyle. Blues as music is the root of Jazz, Rhythm and Blues, Rock, Country, and most other popular Western music. Blues as a condition shares the same reasons for coming into existence as do the cultures of nearly all peoples of the African diaspora whose ancestors encountered Europeans: brutal dis-Africanization by Christians that separated Africans from their religions, customs, and families, especially in the United States; slavery; colonialism; poverty; racism; and four hundred years of dehumanizing disenfranchisement.

One of the concepts of *OCBA* was to remove artists from under the microscope of critics. There are no record reviews, performance reviews, or gossip written by individuals whose backgrounds and lifestyles rarely, if ever, touched the lives of Black people. However, there were regular contributions from individuals from diverse backgrounds who displayed a true passion and love for the music and sensitivity toward the lives and history of those who play it. David Whiteis, Jacques Lacava, Guy Lerner, David Witter, and Isio Saba are among those people.

Overall, *OCBA* was rooted in communication from the source: artists speaking their minds in their own language as contributing writers, poets, interviewers, and interviewees, without the insult of having their art and lives dissected, which is the tendency of many music writers and critics.

As *OCBA* editor and as an artist, I am interested in the source and the now, no matter how one gets there: Muddy Waters, John Coltrane, Bessie Smith, Sister Rosetta Tharpe, Gaspar Yanga, Mancandal, Nelson Mandela, Robert Nesta Marley, and the millions of other African progeny—same root, same pain.

Another element of *OCBA* was to be inclusive of people from other cultures who love and are inspired by the Blues. To achieve this goal, *OCBA* published some articles in Italian, Spanish, French, and Yoruba. The result was the creation of long-term cultural and business relationships with individuals and organizations in France, Italy, Sardinia, Iceland, Argentina, Spain, Senegal, and Japan. *OCBA* and its parent company, Straight Ahead Productions, coproduced concerts in Sardinia with promoter Isio Saba, and I partnered with Icelandic (Platonic Records) and Japanese (DIW Records) recording companies to produce CDs of Valerie Wellington, Billy Boy Arnold, Junior Wells, Pinetop Perkins, Jimmy Dawkins, and Shirley King among many. Internationally, *OCBA* became highly respected for its *roots to the source* delivery and global inclusion. The message *is* in the music.

The Blues was enjoying popularity similar to the 1960s during the 1980s and up through the mid-1990s. The Chicago Blues scene was vibrant, with numerous new Blues venues coming into existence as well as recording companies, with both major and independent labels joining the field of Blues businesses. The 1991 *OCBA* Resource Directory listed nearly 150 venues that featured Blues and/or Jazz on a regular basis or from time to time and more than 160 active musicians and bands. Today, the number of musicians is about the same, but the number of venues has dropped to less than fifty. When I asked Pete Crawford, co-owner of the famed B.L.U.E.S., etc. nightclub, why he closed the club in 1996, he said, "The club had outlived its usefulness, and the economics of the music environment was no longer supportive."

By 1995, small record labels were starting to feel the pressure from bigger companies. Some of them licensed their catalogs to the larger companies because they could not compete. Some big box stores were also distributors and begin selling compilations at very low prices. This meant that listeners could spend little and get a lot of music. Well-known, established record stores began folding nationwide. New technology made what we were about more accessible: CD burning, downloads, pay-per-view, and information on the Internet began inflicting a strain on more conventional concepts. Things were changing quickly in the music business, and things were changing for businesses that supported music. Some of our more generous sponsors like Alitalia Airlines of Italy completely closed up shop in Chicago and other cities in the United States, citing rising operating costs and other issues that caused them to scale back on cash outlay. The state of Illinois, which had generally maintained a presence in the *OCBA* and other small-press, cultural, and minority publications, turned its advertising over to an advertising agency that turned a cold shoulder to nonmainstream print media and directed the state's ad budget toward the big players. I perceived this as an attack by the ad agency on minorities in print media because how many Blacks and other minorities own satellites, television networks, and radio stations?

For seven years, *OCBA* had been a major part of the Chicago Jazz, Blues, and literary communities and extended itself outward to connect with people globally. By 1995, I felt that my work, and that of those around me who had displayed unfaltering confidence in the *OCBA* project and contributed so much to its identity, had come to a close.

The final issue that featured the Art Ensemble of Chicago was a fitting tribute and farewell. Twenty years ago when I had the idea for *Literati Chicago*, and later the *Original Chicago Blues Annual,* Famoudou Don Moye, Lester Bowie, Malachi Favors Maghoustus, Roscoe Mitchell, and Joseph Jarman were the first to step up, endorse, and offer financial and moral support for the projects.

This is the best of the *Original Chicago Blues Annual,* and it has been made possible because of what is written here, and more. Enjoy.

(top) **Left to right:** Producers Isio Saba and Rocco di Napoli at a Roberto Murolo and Chicago Beau recording session, 1992, Naples, Italy. Photo by L. Beauchamp.

(bottom) **Left to right:** L. Beauchamp, Julio Finn, and Eric Fienblatt at Café La Palette, Paris, France, 1993. *OCBA* archive photo.

(top) **H. J. the DJ broadcasting from Chicago's Kennedy-King College on WKKC radio station, 1989.** Photo by L. Beauchamp.

(bottom) **Philadelphia Jerry Ricks onstage in Washington, DC.** *OCBA* archive photo.

(top) **Left to right: Big "Golden" Wheeler, Larry Frazier, Clarence Wheeler, and Ed Wilkerson Jr. performing at Club Lower Links in Chicago on the occasion of the** *Literati Chicago* **second anniversary dinner party. Photo by L. Beauchamp.**

(bottom) **Jimmy Johnson in Montreal, Quebec, 1994. Photo by L. Beauchamp.**

(top) **Left to right: Snooky Pryor, Herb Walker, and Pinetop Perkins in San Remo, Italy, 1993. Photo by L. Beauchamp.**

(bottom) **Smokey Smothers at the Southside Garage, 1992. Photo by L. Beauchamp.**

(top) **Carl Trambley, Quebec City, Quebec, 1995. Photo by L. Beauchamp.**

(bottom) **Left to right: "Blue Ice" Bragason, Johnny Johnson, and Julia Svensdottir at Montreal Blues Nights, Montreal, Quebec, 1995. Photo by L. Beauchamp.**

(top) L. "Chicago Beau" Beauchamp, guest chef at Club Jazz, Reykjavik, Iceland, 1992. *OCBA* archive photo.

(bottom left) Jim Conley performing at Blue Ice, record release party, Moosehead Bar and Grill, Chicago, 1991. Photo by L. Beauchamp.

(bottom right) Guðmundur "Gummi" Peterson performing in Akranes, Iceland, 1991. Photo by L. Beauchamp.

(top) Arlo Guthrie, Paradisa, L. "Chicago Beau" Beauchamp, Daniele Bombasaro, Alex Britti, and Isio Saba dining at Francesca, Rome, Italy, 1998. *OCBA* archive photo.

(bottom) Quincy Troupe, Harlem, New York, 1989. Photo by Eugene B. Redmond.

(top) **Johnny Twist in his record store, Twist Records, Chicago, 1992.**

(bottom) **Left to right: Sunnyland Slim and Eugene B. Redmond, Chicago Blues Festival, 1989. Photo by L. Beauchamp.**

(top) **Concert producer Hilmar O. Hilmarson, Reykjavík, Iceland, 1991. Photo by L. Beauchamp.**

(bottom) **Julio Finn and the Hoodooettes Gabonais. Left to right: Julio, Aleka, Lilly, and Decky. Photo by L. Beauchamp.**

(top left) **Billy Branch performing at B.L.U.E.S., Chicago, 1992. Photo by L. Beauchamp.**

(top right) **Lucky Peterson performing at the Second Annual Sardegna Blues Festival, 1993, Arbatax, Sardinia. Photo by L. Beauchamp.**

(bottom) **Valerie Wellington and Rico McFarland performing at Moosehead Bar and Grill, Chicago, 1990. Photo by L. Beauchamp.**

(top) **Left to right: Sydney James Wingfield and Pete Crawford standing in front of Pete's Blues club, B.L.U.E.S., etc., Chicago, 1992.**

(bottom) **Andrea Gylfadottir performing at First Annual Sardegna Blues Festival, Arbatax, Sardinia, 1992. Photo by L. Beauchamp.**

(top) Left to right: L. Beauchamp and L. Beauchamp Sr., Blue Ice record release party, Moosehead Bar and Grill, Chicago, 1991. *OCBA* archive photo.

(bottom) L. "Chicago Beau" Beauchamp and Björk (right), Park West Chicago, 1993. *OCBA* archive photo.

(top) **Bob Stroger performing at B.L.U.E.S., Chicago, 1990.**

(middle) **Left to right: Andrea Gylfadottir and Julia Svensdottir, First Annual Sardegna Blues Festival, Arbatax, Sardinia, 1992. Photo by L. Beauchamp.**

(bottom) **Left to right: Sunnyland Slim and Pinetop Perkins, Chicago, 1991. Photo by L. Beauchamp.**

(top) **Left to right: Alvin Singleton, Roscoe Mitchell, Victoria Gonzales, Lester Bowie, and Furaha Moye, seated front, Wyndam Hotel, Atlanta, Georgia, 1989. Photo by L. Beauchamp.**

(bottom) **Solomon Burke blessing the audience, Cagliari, Sardinia, 1993. Photo by L. Beauchamp.**

(top left) Albert King performing at B.L.U.E.S., etc., Chicago, 1993. Photo by L. Beauchamp.

(top right) Jimmy Rogers performing at B.L.U.E.S., Chicago, 1991. Photo by L. Beauchamp.

(bottom) **Left to right:** Famoudou Don Moye and DonAlonzo Beauchamp, Freiburg, Germany, 1993. Photo by L. Beauchamp.

FROM THE *ORIGINAL CHICAGO BLUES ANNUAL*

Issue Number 1

After much planning, hard work, and help from colleagues and supporters, the first issue of the *Original Chicago Blues Annual* (*OCBA*) became reality. *OCBA* was introduced at the 1989 Chicago Blues Festival, and on its cover was the A.-C. McGraw painting of legendary Blues piano player and singer Sunnyland Slim, to whom the first issue was dedicated.

Interviews, articles, and essays are at the core of the literary content of *OCBA*, with many contributing writers like Eugene B. Redmond and David Whiteis maintaining a presence in *OCBA* in the coming issues.

Issue number 1 contained the first ever resources guide for Chicago Blues artists. It featured a Musicians Directory, Club Guide, and multiple listings for finding agents, recording studios, and granting organizations. This feature of *OCBA* would continue through the next five issues.

Number 1 was well received by artists and fans, so we pushed on, looking to improve and grow with number 2.

INTERVIEW WITH KOKO TAYLOR
Guy "Doc" Lerner

Koko Taylor is the Queen of the Blues. Her illustrious career has transcended race, social class, and international borders. Although at the pinnacle of her profession, Koko is often portrayed as a regular person. She credits her fans as much as herself for her success. She sees her role as a goodwill ambassador spreading the joy of the Blues. The Queen of the Blues is a title she has earned and deserves.

GUY: How does it feel to be the Queen of the Blues?

KOKO: It feels good. I feel real unique. I feel very honored, and I am very proud to be titled as the Queen of the Blues.

GUY: Do you feel you have earned this title?

KOKO: Well, I do not want to put roses on my shoulders, but my fans seem to feel that I've earned being the Queen of the Blues. Like I said, I just feel good about it.

GUY: How has the music industry changed over the time you've been associated with it?

KOKO: When I first got to Chicago, I used to sit in with different guys around Chicago's local clubs, Elmore James and Magic Sam, Junior Wells, Muddy Waters, J. B. Lenoir—you name 'um. During those years, the only clubs that we would sing in or go in or just go out for a good time—we're talking about the same clubs—and that was all Black clubs on Chicago's South Side. Oh God, this was way back somewhere in the late '60s—uhh, middle '60s. During those years, the only time somebody like myself would go up on the North Side would be because we had some other kind of job, and it wasn't singing at a club because Blacks was not performing and singing at all. The doors hadn't been open for the Blues at all on Chicago's North Side. During the years that I'm talking about now, I wasn't out here on the road traveling like I am today with my band. I would sometimes work or get an opportunity to work here or there on the weekend. Like Friday and Saturday nights, somebody might hire me to work just the weekend. I'm still talking about some little Black club on the South Side. Whenever I'd go on the North

Left to right: Koko Taylor and Willie Dixon at Buddy Guy's Legends, 1990. Photo by L. Beauchamp.

Shore/North Side, it would be that I'd be going up there to work because I also had a job that I worked every day during the week up on the North Shore. This was our income, period. This was our bread and butter. You know, Pop [Koko's husband of thirty-five years, Pop Taylor, who passed away] would work every day. He was working every day at Wilson Packing Company, and I was working, like I said, on the North Shore in different people's homes doing what they call domestic work—cleaning house, ironing clothes, taking care of people's children. And I was real good at it, too. Like I'm saying, this was the only time that I ever even went to the North Side. Then, as the years passed on—getting up into the early '70s—things started changing. I remember the first job that I got on the North Side. The first club that I ever worked in on the North Side was up on 2270 North Lincoln at the Wise Fools. I went in there with a band, and the guy that was in charge of the band was named Bob Reedy. And Bob Reedy would hire me to come up there and sing with his band. I was making like twenty sometimes twenty-five dollars a night, and if I got twenty-five dollars a night, I was real happy [Koko laughs]. That made me real proud. I mean, twenty-five dollars, I could come back home and buy, you know, quite a big amount of groceries with that. That went on and on and kept on and on.

When "Wang Dang Doodle" was recorded and hit the charts, it turned out to be a number one seller right around then. I got my band together, and I started traveling from place to place—over the road and everything. So, I could begin to see a change. Now, out on the road, things had not changed. I was still working for all-Black audiences and Black clubs. There was a lot of times that I would go out on the road and I would work in Black clubs and didn't get a dime. You know—I mean—there had been a lot of times that I had worked places, and when time come for me to get paid, they start scratching their heads and things and, and, and stuttering, you know—like making excuses like: "Well, you know, the crowd didn't turn out like I thought it was going to be, and so what I'm going to have to do, I'm going to have to give you some of your money, but you don't have to worry about it, when you get back to Chicago, I'm going to wire it to you—it will be there waiting for you, and that will be the end of it." I would never hear from them no more. But anyway, these were the kinds of things that went on out on the road. This wouldn't happen every time, but a lot of times it did happen. But all in all, speaking about the change, as the years passed by, I kept working the Wise Fools. The next club that opened up was the Kingston Mines. Then I started working the Kingston Mines very frequently. That went on for a long time. It wasn't nobody but the Wise Fools and the Kingston Mines. God Bless 'em for giving us the opportunity to come to the North Side and work.

GUY: Not only were you getting more secure paying positions, but you were also playing to White audiences on the North Side of Chicago?

KOKO: Yes, and it was strictly all White. Then as the years passed and time went on, others clubs start opening up. The third club that opened up for the Blues and for Blacks was Biddy Mulligan's, which is far north. And then, we had three clubs that we would work. It was getting real good then.

GUY: Are you now too "big" to work the clubs?

KOKO: No, I'm not too big to work the clubs now. I feel today just like I did then, except that time do bring about a change. What I'm doing now is mostly concerts. I'm doing tours with other guys. They are putting us together. For instance, I just finished a tour with Lil Ed [Lil Ed and the Blues Imperials] and Albert Collins. We did a whole West Coast tour. We worked Los Angeles, San Francisco, Portland, and Seattle. You know what I'm saying? This is mostly what I'm doing now. I'm not doing as many clubs now as I was in the past. And it is not because I'm too good to work in clubs, and it is not because I wouldn't work in clubs, and it is not because I am so high and mighty or got a big head. [It is] because I love the people at the clubs right here today just as I did then. But like I said, my work has changed. I'm doing bigger things like concert halls.

GUY: In the early '70s when you came to Chicago's North Side, what were your feelings about playing for predominately White audiences?

KOKO: I felt real good. Like I said before, I was real happy. I was proud that some more clubs—White clubs—had opened up for the Blues. It gave not only myself, but it gave other Blues people an opportunity to have other clubs to go and work. It expanded us, because during that time, we was just working Sixty-ninth Street, Seventy-ninth [Street], Forty-third [Street], and two or three clubs on the West Side. During that time, a disc jockey by the name of Big Bill Hill had a club on the West Side and called it the Copacabana Club. A lot of us would go over there and work and stuff. To be up on the North Side just gave us more room—more places to choose from to work.

GUY: What about the White audiences?

KOKO: It felt good. I liked it, and I still like it. I'm not saying that I don't like working for Blacks. What I like is to work for a mix of White and Black audiences. I had worked for White audiences before I started going to the North Side to the Wise Fools and Kingston Mines. I had worked for White audiences before, but it wasn't clubs. Like I did the Ann Arbor Blues and Jazz Festival in 1972 or '73, somewhere along in there, you know. In 1967, I did an eight-week tour over in Europe. I went to a lot of countries over there, and all I did was concert halls for all-White audiences. So I had worked for White audiences before, but there was not White clubs that were opened up for the Blues.

GUY: You have toured Europe and will be touring behind the Iron Curtain in late 1988. What is the difference between American and foreign audiences?

KOKO: I haven't been behind the Iron Curtain before. Just the word

Iron Curtain kind of scares me [Koko laughs]. I don't like the name of that. But the foreign audience is really beautiful. And you would be surprised to know that the people over there that don't speak English really get into what you're doing, enjoy the Blues, and respond to every song that I do when I'm over there. Then when I come down off the bandstand, I can't ask those same folks for a drink of water. They don't know what I'm saying. The people over here feels it, and they gets into it, too. But they respond different because by them knowing exactly what you are saying, they sometimes yell out, whistle, or get up and dance. Most of the audience over there I notice usually sit and just observe. I think that's because they want to understand just what you're saying and what you mean in each song.

GUY: Not only are you recognized internationally, but you are also recognized by all social classes as the premier woman's Blues singer. [Koko recently was on hand for the gala opening of Bloomingdale's Department Store in Chicago.] Do you consider yourself a goodwill ambassador of the Blues?

KOKO: Yes, I do. Right now, by me traveling so much and so far and going everywhere, I'm singing to all kind of people—young, old, White, Black, big, little. And everybody seems to be into it, and a lot of them that don't know nothing about the Blues is getting a good experience by listening to me from place to place. It's like I'm a teacher. I'm a teacher of the Blues. I do find myself as a role model in that way—letting people know what the Blues is all about.

GUY: Do you believe this was your destiny?

KOKO: This was how I saw it in the back of my mind years ago. Years ago I wasn't doing this, but I have always had that thought—that dream that it might happen like this one day. It feels real good, and I'm real proud of myself to spread that kind of news around all over the world. I would like to some day—this is in the back of my mind: Maybe when I get too old to travel on the road or retire, whatever, I would like to open up a little music studio just to teach some of the young people about singing—you know, and things like that.

GUY: You started your recording career with Chess Records, and you are now with Alligator. What changes have you seen in the recording industry?

KOKO: Yeah, I started with the Chess brothers and working with Willie Dixon in the studio and around his house in his basement. During this time, it wasn't like I would choose my songs or would help with choosing them or help with ideas. I didn't have no parts in that at all. I didn't have no say-so into that. They told me your job is to sing and our job is to take care of the musicians and the music and the arrangements or whatever. After I started recording for Alligator it was very different. Working with Bruce Iglauer, you know, was a real challenge. Him and I usually get together and suggest tunes, talk about tunes, and listen to them. If we be doing something that has been done before, we listen to it and think about, you know, how would this sound, how would the people react to this tune just listening to it, dancing to it, or just go out and purchase it, whatever. I'm always thinking about my fans in that way. We always put our heads together on my recordings with Alligator, and it makes a big difference because I play a big part in whatever I record. You know, I help with the arrangements and with selecting the tunes. I can put more into it like that.

GUY: *Rolling Stone* magazine has called you the "hardest working lady in show business today."

KOKO: Well, I'll agree that I put 100 percent into what I'm doing. I guess it's because I enjoy it so much myself. I am a hardworking person, and when I'm on the bandstand, it comes out, and everybody can see that I'm a hard worker because it's almost nonstop from the time that I hit the bandstand until I come down. I'm full of energy, raw power, gritty. I just like to keep on whalin'.

GUY: You have been described as a "Blues growler" and your voice as "gravelly."

KOKO: That's because my voice is heavy, and when I start singing, it just comes out just the way you hear it—rough and tough. Hey, that's why they describe me as gritty.

GUY: Lightnin' Hopkins once said: "I had the one thing you need to be a Blues singer, I was born with the Blues."

KOKO: I definitely was. I was born with the Blues, and it looks like I am going to die with them. But, it don't make no difference. I'm having a good time doing what I'm doing. I'm enjoying what I'm doing. I'm happy with what I'm doing, and you know, I have no regrets. I have nothing to look back on. Every day and every step that I make I'm going forward, and I'm looking forward to the future.

GUY: Is having the Blues essential to be a Blues singer?

KOKO: No, I don't think that. I think that a person that wants to sing the Blues—I think anybody could sing the Blues. You don't necessarily have to have lived the life, you know, and went through the struggle and hardships of life that I have to sing the Blues. There's a lot of White groups out here today singing the Blues, and I refuse to think that they is singing the Blues because they have lived the Blues or was born with the Blues. I think they are singing the Blues because they love the Blues music, and they have very good talent to sing the Blues.

GUY: You are at the pinnacle of your career, yet the money that you earn is not at the level of even the most mediocre rock-and-roll star. How do you feel about this?

KOKO: No, it hasn't been up there, and I'm not counting on it ever getting up there. But, you know, I'm just content with what I'm doing, and I'm content with the money I'm making. I don't compare my salary with nobody else's. I know that I'm not a rock singer. I could have been a rock singer. I know how to sing rock, but I'm singing the Blues because that is of my own choice. If I don't never make the money that they make, I'm just happy and content with what I do get. And I can deal with that.

GUY: Do you enjoy life on the road?

KOKO: If I did not enjoy, I would be home every day. I enjoy being out of the house and away from home. My husband, Pop Taylor, travels with me. Being out on the road, I have a chance of meeting people, seeing new faces, making friends, and going to different places, and I just enjoy that, and this is what I like about my work. Like I said, if I did not enjoy it—doing it—I would definitely stay at home, because in the first place it is not easy, it is not an easy job at all. We go out there and get in the van. I have a van sitting out there in the front [of the house]. We load up—me and the Blues Machine [Koko's band]— and we leave here headed, say, to Boston, a good 1,300 miles. Now to get in that van and sit there and ride about twenty hours from here [Chicago] to Boston, it's not no fun and it's not easy. You know, I done miss a whole night sleep at home. We done stop all up and down the highway eating out of truck stops and snack plazas. Then, when we get where we going, we checks into a hotel. I'm sleeping in a different hotel every night. I'm eating— going into restaurants—eating whatever they have on the menu. A lot of times we go into restaurants, and the waitress—all of a sudden we Black—they don't see us in there when they passing the coffee around. "Would you like more coffee—would you like for me to heat up your coffee (Koko mimics a White female voice)?" That's not easy. That's not a happy feeling. That don't happen all the time and that don't happen every day, but it do happen. It's not easy when you go to check into a hotel, and you know that you have reservations because Alligator done gave me my papers and things. And, all of a sudden, they tell you, "I don't think you have reservations here. Are you sure? When was the reservation made? Who made the reservations?" That's because we standing up in there and Black, and they don't want us in there. So they come up with all kind of excuses to keep from giving us a room there. So that's the reason why I say: If I didn't enjoy being out there, I would definitely be right here [Koko laughs emphatically].

GUY: Don't you think that you deserve better, like flying to your gigs or riding in limousines?

KOKO: Well, I'll tell you. It goes right back to what we just got talking about when you asked me, "How do I feel that I don't make the same kind of money that the rocks and the pops and all those folks make." It's the same thing with the limousines and this kind of stuff. I be picked up sometimes in a limousine. I fly sometimes. But to do this constantly or to do this all the time, no I don't do that all the time. Like I said before, I'm content with what I'm doing, and I'm content with the way I'm doing it. If I don't never fly, I just be out there in that van.

GUY: Which one of the many highlights in your career stands out?

KOKO: We did this tour up around New York, and we was going from this prison to that prison and that prison, and I have never in my life been locked up behind bars before in my life for nothing. I felt so stupid. And really, it's a funny feeling to be locked up even though I know I was going to get out because I was just there performing. But in order to go in there and entertain the inmates, they have to search you, pat you down. You have to register in. Then when you go in, you hear them doors slamming, kablam! [Koko adds a sound effect], with them big old keys about twelve inches long and

Interview with Koko Taylor

about as big as my feet. You're thinking, my God I can't even get out of here if I want. And if they decide not letting me out, I would have to stay here. This is the feeling that you get. You're saying to yourself: "I'm in jail for a couple of hours." You know, that was quite an experience.

GUY: It's not a good feeling being in jail.

KOKO: Yeah, it ain't no good feeling. Then sitting there looking at them inmates, most of them sitting around there looking happier than I am—just well contented like they at home. Well, I guess they is at home [Koko laughs].

GUY: How about headlining the 1988 Chicago Blues Festival? [Koko's first performance in six months since her hospitalization from a motor vehicle accident that she and her band suffered while on the road.]

KOKO: It was really super. It was out of sight. That was the first time I had ever headlined the Blues Festival. It was a real special night because that was the first real gig that I did since the accident. It was special—right here in Chicago where I live. You know and all the fans and the people that were so wonderful to me here with the benefit and everything. It made me feel real good to be at home and also to give back to them and show them how I appreciated what they had done for me. It was real good.

GUY: A low point?

KOKO: When my van broke down in Brooklyn, New York. When it broke down, it was after a gig. We couldn't get to a gas station where we could get a repair or somebody check it out. By happening on a Saturday night, the next day we still couldn't get a mechanic because that was on Sunday. We had to wait until Monday before getting a mechanic to fix our van. We missed the next gig, which was in Ithaca, New York. That was the first job that I have ever missed going to in my career in twenty years! That was a low blow. And we had stayed in New York all of this extra time with all of that expensive hotel, and the little money that I had made Saturday night was spent staying that extra two days trying to get our van fixed. That was one low blow.

GUY: What are your future plans?

KOKO: In the future, my plans is to continue to record, continue to tour, continue to spread a little joy all over the world with my Blues music—waking more people up to the Blues. There are a lot of people out there—you would be surprised—that ain't never heard the Blues and are not familiar with that kind of music at all.

GUY: You're often portrayed as a "regular" person. Is this an image you like to have?

KOKO: Oh yeah, sure, because that is what I am. I am just a regular person—down to earth and no bigger in mind than I've ever been. I've always felt that if you stay on the ground, then you don't have to do nothing but turn over. But if you get so high on a ladder that you forget where you come from, than you forget where you going. I'm just everyday people. I'm just regular people and that's that!

GUY: Are you a happy person?

KOKO: Well, I am a happy person. I try to live day by day to the fullest because tomorrow is not promised to nobody. So I just try to do my best every day as I go along and try to be happy. Most of the time I am happy. Sometime I get mad. When I get mad, I'm mad [Koko laughs]. They say I start rolling my eyes on the bandstand. So I guess it must be one of those rough days. The music ain't right or something. Most of the time, I'm just a happy-go-lucky person.

October 1988, Chicago

INTERVIEW WITH EDDIE BOYD
L. "Chicago Beau" Beauchamp

Mine is unhurried, disinterested joy
With no harm intended except
  to myself.
To take away from the hurt of
  others, indeed.
When and or if there became me
  myself to need.
Bah, for me these classic precepts
  have never crossed
Except for me they then became
  quickly uncrossed.
Universe? No! God? No! Man? No!
Only time, yes. She crossed me all
  the time.
—From Hart Leroy Bibbs's
  poem "Black Dilemma"

Didn't see no whiskey, but the
Blues done made me drunk.
—Johnny Young

Drinking certainly plays a major role in our society; however, I am curious about the role of alcohol, particularly in the lives of Blues-people. During the Chicago Blues Festival last May, I had the opportunity to interview my long-time friend, world-famous Blues pianist and songwriter Eddie Boyd. Eddie, who makes his home in Helsinki, Finland, has been playing professionally since the age of fourteen. At seventy years old, he has an unlimited supply of stories to tell. I asked Eddie to share with me some stories and views on Blues and booze.

There are a few Blues players today who have to be literally led to the stage and propped up to the microphone because they are so drunk. Others have suffered violent death and injury due to drunkenness. Eddie Boyd and Sonny Boy Williamson (John Lee) were the best of friends. Sonny Boy is considered by many to be the most influential of all harmonica players. Unfortunately, this genius and great spirit was cut down in his prime. Perhaps had he been sober it would not have happened; perhaps had his attackers not been in the clutches of inner-city desperation, Eddie would not be relating this sad story. Sonny Boy was murdered by thieves on June 1, 1948, on Chicago's South Side.

BEAU: Eddie, when I was growing up here in Chicago, most of us kids started drinking whiskey around the age of fourteen. How about you as a child back in Clarksdale, Mississippi?

EDDIE: My mother was a whiskey lover and so was my dad. So I guess I inherited liking to have a taste, but that never was no crutch for me playing because I never did trust myself if I would drink too much. You know, you think that when you drunk you pitchin' a bitch [playing] and raising hell, you know. Well, you are pitchin' a bitch, but not the kind you think you pitchin'.

BEAU: About what was the average age that people started drinking; people that wanted to get away from home and play music?

EDDIE: Well back in my time, it wasn't too many starting at the age I started.

BEAU: Which was how old?

EDDIE: I left home when I was fourteen years old. When I first started playing it was after I left Mississippi. I went to Memphis and started playing at different joints up and down Beale Street. Then I started to drink a little bit, but I never was the kind who would drink because I needed it to play. Everybody was around them honkytonks—them whores out on the floor dry grinding to catch a trick, they would drink, and I could sing and holler loud enough to hear me ten blocks away. I had some heel plates on my shoes, and it was me alone: no drums, no microphone, no amplification. So I would play. The one that could holler the loudest, he drew the biggest crowd. Them whores could get more tricks, and they be chipping me them nickels and dimes, and they'd pass me a shot of whiskey and sneak it up there in a glass. I don't know how they did it because those was prohibition days. All them joints was run by Italians, I don't know how they did it, but sometimes they would sell whiskey right over the bar. So I would take a little drink, but I wasn't one of them lush heads. If I had of been, it would show on me now.

BEAU: Sure it would. You seem unusually healthy and strong for such a fast start in life. Tell me though, Eddie, why do you think so many cats drink so very much?

EDDIE: Because they feel inferior, man, that's it! Because look, man, if you got stories to tell with the Blues, boy, you don't need nothing in the world but the opportunity to tell them. When you see people that is drunk all the time, I mean Blues singers, that's because they're not sure of themselves as artists. Now this is a fact: I know a few Blues artists that have switched to drugs. Now I'll tell you that is really against the grain of Blues.

BEAU: Yeah, drugs don't seem like a Blues thing. What about, you know, women. Cats drink so they can feel more comfortable with women and stuff like that. You think some guys drink so they can feel more comfortable with their girlfriends and things like that?

EDDIE: You mean when they're having sex and stuff like that?

BEAU: Yes.

EDDIE: Oh, yeah, yeah, plenty cats feels like that.

BEAU: Have you ever heard anybody play better when they were drunk?

EDDIE: Naw, shit naw. Well I seen some that I know'd could play good if they weren't drinking. But I never saw them when they wasn't drinking when they was playing. I know'd some was champions, man, much better piano players than me, and that sucker wasn't goin' be on that stage until he get half drunk.

I knew a guy in Memphis, they called him Dishrag 'cause he was always so raggedy, and that cat didn't read a note of music. Dishrag, he was a notoriety cat. He always walked with a greasy cap covering his crouch and bent over [demonstrates with an ashtray]. He was ruptured, and his pants would wear out there or either his ass was out and he'd go in like this, that the way he went in.

BEAU: Hiding his condition?

EDDIE: Yeah, with a cap, a greasy cap. But you talkin' 'bout piano playin', boy, I've haven't seen nobody yet man . . . I mean Count was my favorite man in the Jazz field, as Jazz, as standard Jazz, he was my favorite man. But Dishrag, he could play everything anybody could play and couldn't read a note of music. But Dishrag, you wasn't goin' to get Dishrag to the piano without drinkin', and he didn't need that to play. I never could understand that. He sat in with Duke Ellington's band, he walked up to Duke, that was the time they were using words like *gates, cats,* and *bossman,* and things of that sort, you know. He walked up like this, you know, this time his nuts was hanging out. He walked up to Duke and said, "Say, bossman, let me sit in one." When Duke looked at this guy, he thought it was a joke, and he said, uh, "All right, my man."

Duke had just recorded "Sophisticated Lady." Dish got down there, sit down with Duke's, I think it was about eighteen-piece orchestra then, and he played with Duke. Duke wrote all of that music himself; he played that what Duke wrote, and he played more than Duke did. But when he went in there he was drunk, but it didn't take the whiskey to make him play, but he would always be drunk.

BEAU: Always be drunk, huh?

EDDIE: Now when you see him not drunk, he was somewhere layin' on the bed.

BEAU: Recovering?

EDDIE: I mean daily, daily. I think he's dead now. I'm a poor hand to degrade somebody, so I know that a man like Dishrag was, I think he must have been born like that, he was a stone pervert, man. He used to play house parties for the aristocratic Blacks.

One time he played a house party, there was a pretty woman there. She was a school teacher, young woman about twenty-eight or thirty years old. Real pretty chick, and she was going to walk home. You don't know where this is, but Kentucky railroad, that's a shortcut in coming all the way where she was down McLemore Avenue. So she come through there, because such things as robbery and like that wasn't bad in Memphis, not in that part. You got to be down in the red-light district and any damn thing could happen to you, but this was out where the normal people lived. And Dishrag played a house party for these people. And that woman left, he heard her say she was going home. He sneaked out the house before he got his pay and he knew where she was going because he heard that. And he come out and ran and met her right by a warehouse. I know I could see that in my mind right 'bout now. He caught that woman, pulled his jacket off, and laid her on it, then tried to tie her to the railroad tracks. She hollered so loud and fought him so hard that in just a couple of minutes the police came before his drunk ass had done anything to her. He was too drunk to leave her alone even when the police was coming. They put that sucker in jail for ten years without parole. That's right!

BEAU: You think he's dead now?

EDDIE: I think he is, somebody told me that he was, I think so, because he was much older than me.

BEAU: What's his real name?

EDDIE: Um, I don't know what his real name is, I don't never know what's his real name. But everybody in the world knew his name as Dishrag. He was a bitch, man, he played with any, all the finest artists.

BEAU: If he was alive now, about how old you think he would be?

EDDIE: Shit he must be, I imagine 'bout ninety or a hundred now.

BEAU: He probably is dead. Eddie, tell me about some of the old times with you and Sonny Boy.

EDDIE: Me and Sonny Boy would get to go gambling, and me, I'd quit after I won a little, but Sonny Boy—he could win and stay lucky for four straight hours. You know when you play dice you bar 5, 9, and 4, but Sonny Boy didn't bar no points, he'd say "Make it." Boy, he would make it every time, he'd be raking in money with his eyes closed. He be done got so drunk he thought he was putting money in his pocket, but really he was dropping it on the floor on his right side. You see he was right-handed, so I stood on his right to keep all the hustlers from getting his money. He would gamble and gamble until he didn't have nothing left. He would get so drunk that he couldn't put the dice in the horn to shake them up. So I would take him to where we was staying and put him to bed so he could sleep it off. The next day when it was time for us to go home because the joint was closed on Sunday, Sonny Boy would wake up with a hangover. He could never get enough; he would drink till he was out. So anyway, I went and got him a bottle of whiskey to settle his nerves, 'cause I knew how he felt. I loved him. He was really the one that got me started here in Chicago. I put everything I had behind Sonny Boy.

So he would start looking through his pockets for his money, and say, "Goddamn, I done lost every cent." So I would let him sweat for a while, then I would pull out his money that he had let fall on the floor when he was too drunk to find his pockets. You know, Sonny Boy was so grateful that I had saved his money for him that he would split that money with me—that's the kind of cat that he was. That is what whiskey will do for you. The average person who drinks like Sonny Boy can't stop even though they know they should. There's something in that shit, man, they put in there to make you lust after it more and more till you pass out. That was him [Sonny Boy]. I tried so many times to get him to stop drinking, period. I kept on telling him about how many times he almost got into trouble by being so drunk.

I remember one time we was playing at the Club Georgia between Forty-fifth and Forty-sixth Street on State Street. Sonny Boy come staggering off the stage to go outside with his eyes almost closed, and he stepped right on this man's foot who was sitting at the bar. The guy said, "Get off my foot motherfucker." Sonny Boy said, "Take your foot and stick it in your pocket." You know man, that guy came out with one of them switchblades with a button on it so it will stay locked. So if you stab somebody and hit a bone it won't close up on your finger. Well, Sonny Boy couldn't see who he was talking to. That guy was getting ready to cut Sonny Boy when I started pleading for his life.

I keep my voice down real low because I didn't want that guy to think that I was trying to make him do anything. I said, "Man, please don't stab him, please don't stab him, he ain't worth going to the penitentiary for." I was trying to save Sonny Boy's life.

Later I told him that if he didn't stop drinking it was going to be the death of him. I said, "Man you goin' to fuck around drunk and get into a situation where ain't nobody goin' be able to save your ass." I told him he didn't need to be drinking like that because he was the star of the show and a big name known all over the country. Lord, I tried my best to get him to stop drinking. He had a complex about drinking and he knew it, but he would drink more to drown that thought. That's how he got killed. He knew he was making too much of an ass about himself.

One night he got drunk, and he was on his way home from Thirty-first Street, some cats saw him and picked up a piece of sidewalk and crushed the side of his head in. The side of his head was flat and blood and brains was running all down. I didn't see this when it happened, but a lot of other people, including his wife [Lacey Belle], told me what happened. He was so drunk he walked from Thirty-first Street to Thirty-third Street—that's over two blocks, with his brains just coming out all over his coat. He got on the doorbell, which he had done a thousand times, and he just laid on it. Now, Lacey Belle was slow getting to the door because she was sickly. They didn't have no buzzer to buzz you in with, they had a chain which unlatched the door. She pulled the chain to open the door downstairs, he fell in and said, "Lacey, they got me, baby," and wham! He hit the ground, and that's the last thing that he said.

That's how he went out, that's what alcohol will do for you. That's how he went out.

BEAU: Was he your best friend?

EDDIE: Yeah, him and Big Johnny Young, the both of them used to come over to my house after I separated from my first wife. I used to cook biscuits for them on Monday mornings after everyone went to work, Johnny was reminding me of that not so long ago. Man, I loved Sonny Boy like a brother.

June 1986, Chicago

INTERVIEW WITH FAMOUDOU DON MOYE

L. "Chicago Beau" Beauchamp

Great Black Music:
 Ancient to the Future
—Epigram of the Art
 Ensemble of Chicago

BEAU: It's been nearly twenty years since we first met. Let's do a catch-up for ourselves and for our readers. Ready?

MOYE: Ready.

BEAU: Your career is entering the third decade. You play with the Art Ensemble of Chicago, Lester Bowie's Brass Fantasy, the Leaders, the Great Black Music Orchestra, and as a soloist. You are on the move constantly playing around the globe. You are considered by many, including myself, to be one of the most progressive percussionists in the world. You have won the *Downbeat* poll six out of the last eight years. You are a force in world music—Black music; tell me something of the beginning of Don Moye, the musician.

MOYE: My father was a drummer. I have four uncles that were playing in territorial bands in New York State. Back in the '30s they were all playing saxophones. My grandmother was a member of the Daughters of the Eastern Star, which was a women's auxiliary, equivalent to the Benevolent Paternal Order of the Elks [Benevolent and Protective Order of Elks]. In her capacity of being a member, she was involved in the leadership somehow. They had concerts and everything back in the '30s, because they used to bring Duke Ellington in; this was in Rochester, New York. They brought in Duke Ellington and other big bands of the times, I don't remember which. But she would always talk about Duke Ellington. My father and his sisters and brothers also were raised around that kind of environment; and then everybody was a member of the Elks, which had a band, a big band, and then they had a marching band and drum majorettes and all of that. They also had a couple of jazz combos that worked out of that situation.

 So all this was prior to my being around. When I was coming up, real young, my grandmother used to cook; she was like a caterer and everything. She had her own restaurant for awhile. She did all the food service for the Elks Hall, which was right next door to her house. And upstairs, she lived over this place; I used to stay over there. Then there was this Jazz club nearby that brought in people like John Lytell, Grant Reed, Jack McDuff, Jimmy McGriff; and then

Famoudou Don Moye in his Chicago studio, 1989. Photo by Joan Hackett.

they had Rhythm and Blues acts coming through there, too. So I used to stay with my grandmother a lot of times and the cats would be playing and they'd eat there and I would meet the cats.

And then, as I was growing up, I was in a drum and bugle corps and singing in the church choirs . . . stuff like that. Plus, then my mother used to always take us out to see opera and stuff; she took us to a lot of different musical situations. I can remember going to see operas in the summer; they had these open-air concerts. We might see the opera one week, and then the next week we'd go see the Mormon Tabernacle Choir or something. And then the next week, Mahalia Jackson would be there. There was always something. She took us out to a big variety of musical things. And then sometimes she'd get tickets during the year to go see something. At the Eastman Theater we used to go see the different concerts and everything a couple of times a season or something like that.

BEAU: As a child listener, you were never underexposed to varied musical forms?

MOYE: Never. And at the same time, I kept going to my grandmother's house, and there were always musicians around there. And I was in the choir, and I would travel around with the drum and bugle corps. So it was quite a varied musical environment. And then records, we had all kind of records. My mother likes classical music a lot. And I had a cousin that played vibraphones, tenor sax, and drums. He had a lot of Jazz, Rhythm and Blues records, like a lot of Fats Domino and Ray Charles. And then we had all the popular music of the time, you know, James Brown, all that. So there was a pretty wide variety of music.

BEAU: So, as you were coming up, there was music all around, all the time!

MOYE: Yep, umm-hmm.

BEAU: When did you take the big plunge and decide that you wanted to do this for the rest of your life?

MOYE: Hmm. That kind of happened gradually. There never was a moment that all of a sudden, like wake up, "I'm gonna do this!" I was in school half the time going to college, doing gigs around and everything. And then a chance came up.

BEAU: Where were you at this time?

MOYE: Wayne State in Detroit. I went to Central State in Ohio for a couple years before that for a specific purpose; for being in an urban environment and for the musical exposure. Then I transferred away. I was playing around, subbing with different cats, when the drummer from one of the bands I was hanging with took a gig with a rock band. So I took his place, and soon we came up with a scheme to go to Europe. I thought this was an OK deal, but ultimately our parents influenced the decision.

So I just left school and went on the road here [in the United States] and, shortly, on to Europe. That was at the height of the Vietnam War, of protests in the mid-'60s and all that. A couple of the cats in the band, they used to kind of like dodge the draft a little bit. But, I mean, my situation was cool, I was always in control of the situation. In Europe things just kind of evolved. Eventually the band broke up—I maintained by doing lots of side gigs. I worked and lived in Morocco; Paris; Rome; Vienna, Austria; Copenhagen.

BEAU: I imagine you had many adventures in those places.

MOYE: Oh, yeah. You know, Beau, you've been there; it's never a conscious question of "What am I doing with my life?" Things kind of evolved naturally. It was never a moment that I had to sit down and say, "OK, what am I gonna do with my life?" and all that. It never was even an issue. It never has been. So I just kept doing what I was doing. There were times when—you know like—not so much like "What am I gonna do with my life, but what am I gonna do about my next meal?"

BEAU: What am I gonna do about this flop?

MOYE: Never really. We always had a place to stay. You know, I never had that much money, because any time I would get some money, I would spend my money on instruments, as opposed to, you know. . . .

BEAU: For you, are "survival" and "music" synonymous?

MOYE: They sure are.

BEAU: I understand you spent some time in North Africa. How was that?

MOYE: Oh, it was great. That was the glamour anyway, you know. I just dove into it. I was working with the Ganouahs in Morocco.

BEAU: Where are those people from?

MOYE: Well, they're all over, but they come from the south of Morocco. They would concentrate in the bigger cities for their performances. So I used to work with them all the time, you know, practice with them and learn their rhythms. They had interesting instruments. They had an instrument that looked like a snare drum, like a field snare. And they played rhythms on it. Then they had these metal castanets that the castanets in Spain are believed to be derived from, but these were metal, iron castanets. And they had music vaguely related to whirling dervishes, with similar rhythms and everything. Just kind of in that area of music, but with more African influences, more so than with Middle Eastern. And they had *daibukas* and many types of hand drums. But they used to do these dances that were related to the whirling dervishes, where they would twirl their heads at the same time while they were dancing and everything. They would play on and on and kind of go into a trancelike thing. The other dancers would just stand and twirl. These dancers were playing and twirling their heads and moving around.

BEAU: On my first visit to Senegal, I noticed a similarity in some of the musical styles—similar to Blues and Bebop. Was music in Black Africa a revelation to you?

MOYE: Well, it was up to a point. But see, I had already met up with a lot of African cats in the States and in Paris. And Detroit was a good experience for me, because I met a lot of musicians from Nigeria and Ghana and East Africa. When I was learning congas, they showed me a lot of the sounds and rhythms and everything. So I started working with different African groups, sometimes with as many as fifteen cats in a group. We would perform with dancers, chanters, and entire authentic ensembles.

Then I had a similar experience in Paris, because I was studying with a guy from the Continent named Titos. And there were other cats there from Mali, Ivory Coast, and Guinea. I also got into the language thing, Wolof and Molinkai being just a couple. I didn't learn a whole lot, but I got familiar with their structures and sounds. And music lives in the language. I'd say that by the time I got to Africa, it was more like updating my information.

BEAU: When did you first get to sub-Saharan Black Africa?

MOYE: The first time I went to Africa? I didn't even get to Africa till in the '80s. I went to Morocco in '68, but I didn't think of that as sub-Saharan Black Africa.

BEAU: So what about sub-Saharan Black Africa?

MOYE: Sub-Saharan Black Africa was like '82, '83, around in there. Then when I got there I was already more or less—there wasn't anything strange to it. It was just a matter of enhancement. But, see, the way I went to Africa, I went to Africa on an exchange basis. I didn't go there to study; I went there to make an exchange.

BEAU: Did you have similar experiences in other parts of the Black world?

MOYE: The same thing happened in Haiti, Guadeloupe, and Jamaica. Because I had already done my research prior to going there. In Guadeloupe, I knew all the musicians. Because when I was touring in France, there was a group called the Carribe Jazz Ensemble, and they were from Guadeloupe. And over the course of four or five years, they used to perform for us [Art Ensemble of Chicago]. I mean they were the opening band for us at a couple of festivals; Nice and Nancy. They'd been touring between Paris and Port-de-France. So I met them and became familiar with their music while in France. So when I got to Guadeloupe, we had great musical collaborations. And the same thing happened in Haiti. Because there were musicians there I had known here in the States, in New York, and in Paris, too. I had already ran the rhythms, so when I got there, the music was happening between me and them.

Interview with Famoudou Don Moye

I didn't have to find it [music], it was already happening.

BEAU: Throughout the Black diaspora, South America, North America, the Caribbean, and parts of Europe, it seems like Africa has influenced the music of the world more than any other kind of music.

MOYE: Yeah, it's the strongest force on the planet, musically. It has contributed the most. African music is expressed through Black Americans' creativity. Black American music is the only music that you can go anywhere in the world and hear it. I've heard Duke Ellington's music all over the world, in every country I've ever been in. I've heard some form of Black music as part of the street sounds that you hear in any place you go. And that's the only kind of music that I've ever had that experience with.

BEAU: How would you define Blues?

MOYE: Hmm, it's a true derivative of our African tradition of music—the rhythmic part, the vocalization, chord structures, and everything. Blues is the direct channel to the ancient music.

BEAU: Like field hollers?

MOYE: Yeah, it goes all the way back to griots. It's a direct link to the griots and our religious heritage. If it's got Blues to it, that's the unifying form.

BEAU: It's the undisputed link!

MOYE: That's right. As far as I'm concerned, I hear that in all the Black folk forms; I hear that same element. There's a unifying element that you don't hear in other music. Like Jazz is a derivative form and Rhythm and Blues is a derivative form. Blues is in the pure strain. Even if it's modern and extensive, it's remained closer to the original source. But, I mean, all of the music has expanded because of the wealth of information. We're living in a time of maximum exposure to all things. So of all of these derivative forms, Blues has remained closest to true form. You don't need nothing to make no Blues, just a Black soul.

BEAU: Historically, Blues artists have paid megadues. Unfortunately, there has been little unity between the artists, in so far as the business aspect of the music goes. But many Blues themes represent defiance—defiance of social norms and of religious ones among many. But rarely is there a defiance of either the White-controlled music business or the power of numbers against exploitation. In the music, you seldom detect dissent, which I think is vital to Blues-people; being in control of all aspects of their art. What are your thoughts on that?

MOYE: Well, defiance is just one level of it. Along with defiance, you have to have an organization behind it. There have been moments of defiance all throughout the history of the music, but the strength of the effort and the strength of the cooperation between the musicians and the unity is what always enables us to survive. Anytime that the musicians weren't as strong in their unity together, then it's like the control factor always went over to the *other* side.

BEAU: I know you and your people are dedicated to carrying the torch.

MOYE: Well, we're doing our part. We're using our organization; we've got people doing writing and other literary pursuits. We've got our video people, we're doing the recording thing and performing. Plus the business. We're not interested in expansion to a lot of people; we're just interested in increasing the impact of what we're doing.

BEAU: I think you all are going to have a serious impact on the world, a serious impact.

MOYE: I just finished a tour with Brass Fantasy. So in addition to performing, I'm a road manager with their band. That means that all deals go through me; I'm the man that gets the money and everything all the time. That's one less thing that Lester Bowie has to worry about. It's a different relationship. That's just one example of utilizing the network. Because I do the road managing for the Leaders and the Art Ensemble, too, so it was logical. But the advantage is I also play the music. So it's like, you know, expand the music at the same time, I'm doing the same thing I do all the time anyway in terms of the business. It works out well.

BEAU: Entrepreneurs!

MOYE: Yes.

BEAU: Bluesmen and twentieth-century griots?

MOYE: That's right, that's it. Urban Bushmen.

BEAU: Urban Bushmen. I hear you. Ancient to the future!

August 1988, Chicago

INTERVIEW WITH BIG DADDY KINSEY

Jacques Lacava

The following interview originally appeared in French in *Soul Bag Magazine*. Portions of it have been translated into English by Jacques Lacava and the editor. Big Daddy Kinsey's responses originally were in English.

LACAVA: Like I told you, we would like to do a major feature on you in *Soul Bag*. We would like to just run down your life story, run down your background, and then I'll ask you some more detailed questions. Can you tell me about the life of Big Daddy Kinsey?

KINSEY: Yes, well, I am Big Daddy Kinsey. I'm glad to be in your country, and I do have a story to tell. One day I plan on writing a book because we can't really tell it all in this interview.

As far as my association with music, I started way back about the age of six. My dad, as you know, is a Pentecostal minister, and the Pentecostal Church has, as far as I've known, always featured music. Guitars, tambourines, drums—whatever. Where we lived in the South was about fifty miles from Memphis. And every year they had, like, a national convocation. All those churches gathered in Memphis and had continuous services for twenty-five days. And my mother—every year she prepared food, and she would go and she'd take me with her. There was an older preacher there—they called him Guitar Smith. To me, he was a great spiritual guitar player. He used to sing a song all the time: "I Got Two Wings." And they'd have a broadcast come on every night at twelve o'clock sharp. I'd hit my mother's lap and sleep until that time, and when he hit the first note on that guitar I'd wake up, you know, for the broadcast. At that time I thought it was the greatest sound on guitar; as a matter of fact, the greatest sound I'd ever heard. So after the meeting was over, I'd go back home and get on my dad to get me a guitar. So he finally ordered me a guitar from Sears and Roebuck Company. I think it cost about $3.75.

Anyway, he finally got me the guitar. I'd held that sound in my head that I heard this preacher play back in Memphis, and when I got the guitar I kept messing with one string until I got it tuned where I could get that sound. I found out later that it was the key that Elmore James and all the guys played on slide guitar; a lot of people call it "Spanish."

So, anyway, I worked with that for a day or two. I had it down pat, and my dad and my mum they started bragging on me. They said, well he could play. So from then on, I started to play at the church services. I played everything that I heard, including Gospel. I mean, it just came natural to me. That went on for . . . well, I am ahead of myself.

But, anyway, I stuck with Gospel up until I was about maybe twelve or thirteen years old, and then I started easing out of the house. Muddy Waters, he was coming out of the rural communities, playing at Saturday night fish fries and what not. So close around to where I lived that I used to slip off and go and peep through the cracks to listen to him. Man, I guess when I first heard him play with that slide, I guess that went straight in my head, because that was my first experience with Blues.

Then I went back and picked up my guitar again. I got right on into that, and then another fellow in my community, they called him Herman Bishop, he heard about me and he heard about these young boys that could play Blues. So he met me at the neighborhood store—that was all we had in the community—and he walked up to me and said, "Hey, boy, what about playing with me on the weekend?" I said, "Yeah, yeah. You'll have to bring me a guitar, because my dad, he ain't gonna let me take mine."

So, the next Friday, I got dressed before I went to get the cows out in the pasture. I kept my dog with me. I let the cows out, and the dog cared for them home. We went to a place down in the Delta called Tupelo, Mississippi, James Cotton's hometown. We went down there and played Friday night, Saturday night, Sunday night, and I got home about three o'clock Monday morning. When I stepped out of his car, I stepped right into my dad's arms. He didn't know where I was. He was out looking for me. He told me, "I'm sure glad to see you, but I'm gonna give you the licking of your life," and he kept his promise!

And I rebelled. I just got pissed off, and I put the guitar away. I didn't play no more until after World War II, after I got back and got married and started raising a family. That's when I got back into it, because I wanted my kids to be musicians. I started working with a group back at home called the Soul Brothers. I blew harmonica with them and another guy, and Fred Robinson, the Great Baby Boy and Party Makers. I hooked up with them and did a few things.

By that time Ralph and Don were five or six years old. I bought Don a six-string guitar with plastic strings on it, and I taught him a few things, like the Jimmy Reed beat, and a few things by Mud [Muddy Waters] and some of my own things. By the time he was eight, he was playing everything: B. B. King and everything else. And Ralph, I knew all the time he was gonna be a drummer. He'd get a knife and fork and beat the bars out of the chairs around the house. So I told my wife, I see he's gonna be a drummer. So I get in my car and go to Jew Town in Chicago and I buy a thirty-five dollar Parade drum and snare for him. Then about six months later I went to a pawn shop, and they had a little Japanese-made Domino electric guitar there, and I bought that for Don and got them a little Kay amp, and from that point on we started doing shows.

I was working a day job at the time at U.S. Steel. Periodically, Unions would have a picnic in the spring, you know, for the workers. The president of the local, he had heard about me and my boys, and he says, "Kinsey, how about you and your boys playing for the picnic?" I said, "That would by my pleasure, Man." So this was our first professional job. We played that picnic, and I think they paid me seventy-five dollars. Don played through that little amp. We had little Melvin Simpson. You probably—I don't know if you have heard of Big Daddy Simpson, that was another recording group out of Gary. They did good, but Big Daddy got sick and they just. . . . But, anyway, Melvin Simpson, his son was playing with us. We had two guitars and a bass hooked to that little Kay. And Ralph, of course, was playing that snare, and I was singing and blowing harmonica. All hooked up to that real little amp. Man, that thing was jumping up and down on the floor.

But, that's how I started with the family; doing little jobs like that. I saved the money and then started working Ramada Inn circuits, Holiday Inns, and so on, and so forth. Now it is your ballgame. Now you ask some questions.

LACAVA: How did you build your first instrument?

KINSEY: Well, it was very simple really. You get an idea in your head when you are young. I wasn't able to buy a real guitar. But I wanted to make some kind of noise on strings. So I took the wire off my mother's broom; the wire around the broom to hold the straw. When the broom wore out, I just took the wire and got me two staples and stapled it upside the wall of the porch. And I got me two Garett snuff bottles to tight the strings with. Then I broke a bottleneck off from a bottle of Coke or something; I don't remember, it's been a long time ago. I used it for a slide. And that was it.

LACAVA: How did it happen that you played with your sons?

KINSEY: Well, from the time they were born—well—as a matter of fact, when I got married, I told my wife I wanted her to have me seven boys and, eh, she lied to me. She had six; we lost three. But, anyway, right away I could tell the boys was going to be musically inclined. From the time that they were two and three years old, I started burying in their mind what I know about music. I bought them instruments at a very early age. By the time Don was three or four, he was playing Jimmy Reed style and everybody's style that I know along with my own style. And Ralph saying how he wanted to be a drummer, so right away, I went and got him a Parade drum and snare.

From the very beginning, it was my intention for them to grow to be stars. Of course, at the time I didn't have the understanding that I have about music now. Same way when I was growing up. Muddy Waters and people like that were already stars, and I would have been satisfied at reaching their level at the time. Whenever you grow, you learn. So I saw later on, by the time my son was fifteen or sixteen years old, he had great potential. Oh, yeah, the sky is the limit, I mean, as far as my dream was concerned. I wanted them to go all the way.

LACAVA: Is there a difference between Blues and Gospel?

KINSEY: If you can play Gospel, you can play Blues. It's just the lyrics that are different. And me personally, the tunes that I write, I try to write tunes that say something. I mean, just getting the message across, and that's primarily all Gospel is. Now, Blues way back, way back during slavery time, Blues and Gospel was a way the people had of getting messages across to each other. It was their language for passing things on to the next farm or plantation, you know, without the master knowing what was happening. That's what it was all about when it started. So was Gospel. Actually it is really no different. Primarily, it's the same thing, and people are realizing it more and more every day. Matter of fact, most record companies now, they consider Black Gospel as Blues. Me, whenever I hire a piano player now, I try to get one directly out of the church, because that's where your best music comes from.

LACAVA: Do you still go to church?

KINSEY: I go to church as often as possible because it inspires me. When I hear Gospel music, it brings back a lot of pleasant memories and it inspires me to write. My dad is eighty years old, but he is still performing in his ministry. He still owns his church. That kind of bothers him a little bit; he is just wondering what's gonna happen in case he passes on. He would like for me or one of my boys to become involved in ministry [Kinsey lets out a chuckle], but, other than that, he finally accepted what we do.

LACAVA: Blues was often referred to as devil's music. Was it difficult for the son of a minister to play Blues?

KINSEY: When I was at home, they sent me out in the field to get water. The program *King Biscuit Flour*, from Helena, Arkansas, came on every day round about 11:00 or 11:30 in the morning. I would always make it my point to go get water round about that time. When you pump it, it's cold, but after a certain while it gets hot. And as I was staying listening to the program, when I got the water back it was real hot. And one day, Dad caught me, and I got another licking about that. But I kept on listening to Sonny Boy until I left there.

I had to go outside the house to play Blues. You wouldn't play Blues in the house or nowhere he could hear you. My mother was the same way. She was worse than my dad. But boys tend to overrule up the house sometimes, and when the old man speaks, you either cut it out or just leave home. That's what I eventually done. I left home and I went to Gary; started working in the mills.

Back in the early days, he'd be saying, "Devil is gonna get you playing those reels!" And when I got my kids involved in it, my whole family got down on me. But later on, they all came to admit that was the best thing I could have done.

Because during that time, that's when all this generation gap between older people and young people was coming up; gangs and all that stuff. So my boys, during all their growing up time, was with

Interview with Big Daddy Kinsey 19

me. They have never been in no kind of trouble. Because I know other kids their age, they went nuts. Most of them are doing time, back in the United States, got involved in gangs, drugs, and all that stuff. I mean, fellows that went to school with them.

My dad don't really like the music of today. But he did on this album, *Bad Situation*. I let him listen at the rough mixes; we did them in the basement on my four-track back home. He and my mother came by to the house, and I let them listen to that. He began patting his foot, and he said, "Son, that's a record." Well, that's what I had been waiting to hear over all these years. I'd been waiting to hear some kind of complimentary thing from him about the Blues.

LACAVA: I read about country suppers and jukehouses. Could you tell me what they were all about?

KINSEY: A country supper would be just like a bunch of people getting together, wanting to have some fun on the weekends. That was all they could do, I mean. They worked hard all the week, and on Saturday nights they want to party. The local bootlegger, we called him, was the guy that sold corn liquor and stuff like that. He would sell it a quarter a half-pint. They'd have fish fries. You would go to every creek to catch all the fish you wanted. Fish sandwiches sold for a quarter, fifty cents. There was a local guy around to make some kind of music. They'd have a guitar player. Then they take all the furniture out of the house and they would have a dancing house. It was lot of fun. Mud wouldn't lie when he said he played all night for a quarter, a half a pint, and a fish sandwich. And he did that. I remember it. I know he did it.

A jukehouse is a place where they run a after-hour joint. They have a jukebox in it to play records. They take a chance, violate the law, but most guys that owns those jukehouses, they was paying the sheriff off. They was gambling, drinking, and everything. Probably a little prostitution—everything. But back during that time you could buy the law if you had a few dollars. And then, if you stayed on the right plantation, you wouldn't have anything to worry about no way.

LACAVA: What was Muddy Waters doing at that time in Mississippi?

KINSEY: Mud had a good thing going in Mississippi. He had a jukehouse of his own. Oh, yeah, he sold his own liquor, had crap games; he really had it made. Well, his music is why he left. It was not because of too hard times. Because he was doing good as far as making money. But I guess he wanted to get at where he could record. Library of Congress recorded him before he left Mississippi, but it wasn't on the level that he wanted. He wanted to get known worldwide. Chess [Chess Records] did that for him. He often said that he made them millionaires and they made a name for him.

LACAVA: What was the relationship between Muddy Waters and the Chess brothers?

KINSEY: The Chess brothers took everything. But see, he didn't know about those things. Thanks to his manager, Scott Cameron, he got all that straightened out for him. The last nine or ten years of Mud's life, he made money, his business came together.

During the hit record years they stole from him, Chess would give him three or four thousand dollars in singles periodically, and they thought that was more money than he had ever seen in his life. They'd give him a new Cadillac every two years. They figured that's all we wanted out of life.

I got a late start because I wanted to learn something about the business of music, especially having my kids involved in it. I was approached by different companies back in the late '50s about a record; I knew something was wrong. Anytime you go in the country and you hear a man's record and he can't buy a packet of cigarettes! So I started buying books and learning about copyrights and all the mechanics of music. Then I started my own publishing company and my own production company before I started recording.

LACAVA: Where did you get your musical ideas from?

KINSEY: You got so many guitar players, it's hard to come up with something now that don't sound like somebody else somewhere done played it.

When I was working in the steel mills, getting my act together as far as a Bluesman, I was operating an overhead bridge crane. It's all electrically controlled; the heavier the load you put on there, on the motor, the different sounds you would get. Just like changing from one key to the other on your instrument. I would hum to the tune of the engine. I'd get my harp out, and sometimes the motor on the crane would be in the same key as the harmonica. I wrote songs that way. I was up in the cabin alone, eight hours a day. You created a lot of different sounds that way. My friend Jimmy Reed, he used to talk to me about his lifetime. He was a farm tractor driver, and he used to drive John Deere tractors all the time. But John Deere tractors had a different tone or a different sound from any other tractor; a pecking sound, peck-a-peck-a-peck-a-peck. . . . And Jimmy Reed used to make that sound with his guitar, and that's how he created his sound.

LACAVA: There is a sociological observation that the life of Blacks in the southern United States is rarely without racism. Was it tense between Blacks and Whites in your early days?

KINSEY: Oh, yeah! It was terrible back during that time. Of course, as long as you did what they called "staying in your place," it was OK, but it was a hard thing for me to swallow. That is one reason why my dad got me out of that, because I didn't never buy that stuff; I've always been kind of aggressive about that race thing. I mean—as a child—my dad and I used to be in the fields, and an old guy that oversaw the farm would come by and he'd be riding a horse, and my dad and I we'd be plowing, walking behind a mule. And he'd come up and try to start a conversation, and, well, it was not fun to me. We'd be out there in the hot sun, 120 degrees in the shade, and he'd be riding a horse. And there wasn't anything he said that was funny to me. Because after he'd leave, my dad would say, "Son, why aren't you laughing with Mr. Lockhart?" His name was Buddy Lockhart! [Kinsey laughs] I'd say, "Well, I didn't see anything funny." They come around and tell you jokes and things, and they expect you to laugh. I wouldn't have bought that.

I played at Ole Miss a year ago. They did a TV documentary on me, and this guy he asked me, "Big Daddy, just name me a few highlights in your career?" I told him, "Well, this is most certainly one of mine. I never dreamt that a White man would be walking behind me in the state of Mississippi asking me questions and giving me the red-carpet treatment like you've done." And there was a big laugh, but it was true. When I left there [years ago], in Oxford, Mississippi, they didn't allow Black men on the campus of Ole Miss back in the '40s. And that little circle there, where we actually played, Sears and Harris, when I was a kid I used to stand out there in that circle with overalls and bare feet and sell watermelons out of the back of a truck. That was as close as you could get to the mainstream of things.

December 1988, Paris
Big Daddy Kinsey,
March 18, 1927–April 3, 2001

THE BLUES REALITY OF MAXWELL STREET

David Whiteis

To those of us who love the true heart of the city of Chicago—its vitality, living history, and soul—the Maxwell Street Market shines like an irreplaceable jewel. The legendary open-air market, though perennially threatened with urban renewal, remains a living testament to the hardiness and irrepressible spirit of generations of people who have made Chicago one of the most diverse, vibrant, and exciting cities in the world.

In 1912, a city ordinance was finally passed officially designating the Maxwell Street area an open-air marketplace, but, as usual, the politicians were late in getting the news. The neighborhood around Thirteenth and Halsted on Chicago's Near West Side, which had been settled already by Russian and Jewish immigrants in the mid-1850s, had by then blossomed into a full-scale bazaar. Sweatshops and crowded tenements lined the streets; vendors, shop owners, and hustlers of every description hawked their wares seven days a week. Especially on Sunday mornings, the market attracted crowds of shoppers numbering into the thousands.

Early on, the community acquired a cosmopolitan, international flavor. Bohemians, Italians, Gypsies, Germans, and Greeks crowded into the vital little neighborhood in the early days of the twentieth century, adding the accents and flavors of half a dozen cultures to the already diverse mix of the community's street life. The pungent smell of everything from kosher meat and smoked fish to Mediterranean delicacies filled the air; more than 2,000 vendors and storekeepers stood in open doorways, dispensing merchandise from pushcarts and behind makeshift stands, competing for customers with gruff shouts, melodic chants, and song. A typical month saw more than a million dollars change hands on the street. Word was out all over the city that whatever you wanted to find, you could find it down on Maxwell Street. The atmosphere was pure Chicago: hard hustle tempered with the flamboyance and enthusiasm of a multicultural street fair.

Through the 1920s and 1930s, as the great Black migration from the South came into full swing, the community began to change yet again. A new wave of immigrants, bringing their own dreams and folkways as had the Europeans before them, began to make their home in the Maxwell Street community. Back home in the South, there had been farmers markets on the weekend; street musicians, traveling salesmen, and local craftspeople sold their wares on corners, at makeshift outdoor stands, and at church bazaars, their songs and spiels mingling in the air with the joyful, rhythmic cadences of itinerant preachers and Gospel singers. As these new residents settled in around the Maxwell Street neighborhood, the Sunday morning bazaar seemed little changed, except that the accents were now more likely to recall the Mississippi Delta than a European shtetl. Most significantly, however, there was new music in the air.

Music has always provided the backdrop for the bustling vitality of Maxwell Street. In the early part of the twentieth century, the mournful yet celebratory sounds of Klezmer music, the indigenous music of the European Jewish ghettos, could be heard amid the clatter and bustle of the open-air market. By the 1940s, newer traditions had taken hold; Blues musicians, songsters, and aging medicine show entertainers from the rural South lined the streets, sometimes running power lines into apartments and stores, but often still strumming and singing unamplified as they had back home, filling guitar cases and cigar boxes with change on Sunday mornings. This was the moment of conception, the essence of the cultural cross-fertilization between southern roots and the developing folkways of the urban North, that led to the monumental music now known as Chicago Blues.

No one knows exactly how many Chicago Blues musicians got their start on Maxwell Street, but certainly there have been hundreds. Some, like Muddy Waters, are reputed to have scuffled there during their early days, even if their pride always led them to deny it as they got older. Others, like Big Walter Horton, Homesick James, and Louis Myers, continued to play on the street even after attaining international acclaim. Every Sunday for nearly half a century, legions of other, less-famous musicians have filled the early morning air on Maxwell with the raucous, unvarnished sound of street-level Chicago Blues.

Some of the most significant moments in Chicago Blues history happened on Maxwell Street. It was here that harmonica genius Little Walter first stopped when he arrived in Chicago, strolling down Maxwell Street with his companion, guitarist Honeyboy Edwards. They fell in with veteran Big Bill Broonzy, who was famous as a kindly and supportive father figure to the young musicians who crowded around him and who showed Walter the ropes of the rough-and-tumble Chicago music scene and who helped pave the way for Walter's eventual partnership with Muddy Waters. That partnership would change irrevocably the face of American popular music.

In 1947, Little Walter recorded his first record. It was recorded on the Ora-Nelle label by Maxwell Street entrepreneur Bernard Abrahams, owner of Maxwell Radio Record Company. This was the first taste of the new postwar Chicago Blues, based on southern tradition but updated with a more propulsive feel, which would soon become dominant in Chicago and eventually lead to the rock-and-roll rebellion of the late 1950s. Music that would someday change the world was born in the churning, teeming crucible of life that was the Maxwell Street Market.

Since the glory days of the 1950s, both Maxwell Street and the Chicago Blues have endured some rough times. The music has been declared dead on numerous occasions, only to hold on and proclaim its durability through numerous revivals, "rediscoveries," and an apparently unquenchable spirit for survival. Time and neglect have taken their toll on the neighborhood, as well.

Several ill-conceived "urban renewal" projects have demolished most of the housing in the area. Now, during the week, the dust swirls silently across forlorn vacant lots, as shabbily dressed old men sit quietly on doorsteps or stand in alleys, sipping on wine and gazing across the desolation that has replaced what used to be one of the most vital, life-filled areas of the city.

But on Sunday morning everything changes. Before dawn, the vendors arrive by car, bus, and van to set up their stands and spread their wares. The transformation from desolate wasteland to once-a-week carnival is nothing short of miraculous. By 7:00 or 8:00 a.m., music blares from speakers and amplifiers on corners throughout the neighborhood. The streets, silent and empty only hours ago, are now alive with hustlers' spiels; the greasy smoke from Polish sausage, pork chops, and onions; the joyful racket of the Blues sung through cheap microphones and played on durable old instruments; and the visual farrago of random items of every description overflowing rickety old stands onto the streets and curbs and into the hands of eager buyers. Serious-faced shoppers mill around alongside tourists, musicians, local children out for a morning's adventure, and the unmistakable Maxwell Street conglomeration of dreamers, drifters, eccentrics, and characters who bring to this venerable old neighborhood the diversity and vitality so cherished by Maxwell Street regulars.

Years of tradition and heritage stalk the streets. An ancient woman, wrapped in a thick black overcoat on the hottest of days and peering out at the world through sparkling eyes set deeply in a wrinkled, shrunken face, tells of having been Bernard Abrams's babysitter during the days when he recorded the artists who would soon change musical history. A splintered old sign, sold for five dollars by an anonymous vendor, turns out to be the original 1815 Club on Roosevelt Road, the famous Blues club owned by Howlin' Wolf and Eddie Shaw before Wolf's death in the mid-1970s. The children of drummer Playboy Venson, harmonica player Carey Bell, and longtime Maxwell Street regular Pat Rushing drop by to chat, sit in with a band, and relive old memories.

Around, behind, and through it all, the music still lives. Pat Rushing, after a long and tempestuous career as a street musician on Maxwell Street, has finally retired to the more sedate life of a churchgoer, but his protégé Willie James has put together a raucous little band, known as Maxwell Blues, which carries on in the great tradition. Maxwell Blues sometimes features Pat Rushing's sons, Danny (drums) and Rico (bass), and they run through the usual lineup of standards by the likes of Muddy, Wolf, and Jimmy Reed, interspersed with a handful of originals and contemporary funk and Rhythm-and-Blues tunes, every Sunday morning in a vacant lot facing Newberry Street. (A shade tree that overhangs this area has been dubbed "The Blues Tree" by regulars.) Longtime Maxwell Street veterans like singers Little Al, B. B. Odom, and Little Bobby come by, along with elder statesman "Maxwell Street" Jimmy Davis. Davis, a former traveler with medicine shows down South who studied with John Lee Hooker before moving to Chicago in the '50s, is a living link in the venerable Maxwell Street tradition.

On a good day, as the music of Maxwell Street Blues rocks joyfully amid the Sunday morning cacophony, the beer and wine flow freely, and the life-dance of Maxwell Street explodes all around, one can almost forget the poverty and hard times that have marked the neighborhood since the beginning and that continue to weigh heavily on many of the regulars. There is nothing "romantic" about oppression, nothing heroic about suffering; but the lives and stories told on Maxwell Street are celebratory nonetheless, addressing both a resilience of spirit and a determination to prevail that have kept both the neighborhood and its people from being swept away by the often cruel tides of history that have swept against it.

Today, oblivion haunts Maxwell Street more ominously than ever. As redevelopment extends farther from downtown to the south and to the west, speculators are reputed to be chomping at the bit to buy up the vacant land and turn the area into an upscale neighborhood of dormitories, boutiques, condominiums, and fern bars. A group called Friends of the Market, comprising local merchants, landowners, and a few righteous-minded architects and artists from around the neighborhood, has taken upon itself the task of heading off gentrification and devising ways to preserve the spirit of the market while utilizing the acres of vacant land to the best interests of the city. Details are sketchy, and plans for the area remain uncertain, but it is obvious that the heritage and soul of the Maxwell Street neighborhood remain important to a good number of people.

Meanwhile, in the gritty spirit of survival that has char-

"Maxwell Street" Jimmy Davis performing on Maxwell Street, 1989. Photo by L. Beauchamp.

acterized the Maxwell Street area from the beginning, the market continues to thrive on Sunday mornings, amid all the rumors and threats of demolition and gentrification. A visitor with open ears and eyes, who has a sense of history and an intuitive feel for the street-level rhythms and cadences of city life, can experience more than half a century of Chicago history on that street every Sunday morning. Like Basin Street and Congo Square in New Orleans, like uptown Manhattan, like Beale Street in Memphis and old Hastings Street in Detroit, the Maxwell Street Market is one of the crucibles of American culture and life. Inside these sagging buildings and upon these cracked sidewalks, some of the most significant contributors to our national heritage have lived, sung, played music, celebrated, fought, and died. The ghosts of history mingle with living participants in one of the city's most venerable and vital traditions; together they make unforgettable music.

SOUTHERN SOUND
A Brooding under Blood

Eugene B. Redmond

**For Charles Rowell,
after summer, 1971
Baton Rouge, Louisiana**

Creole, collard greens
And hoodoo hymns against a
    gumbo sky—
    *'Soil song
    Spoil song'*
Dixie chant is Black road to
    steelhammermountain,
DeepSouth ritual is discreet strength,
Darklore is a harpdance in a
    lyricfield—
    *'Spoil song
    Soil song'*
Fatback, hogjowls and juju
And the mind is farmland/is
    swarmland
For this bee-busy commotion
And earthwind polychatter—

    *'Soil song
    Spoil song'*
Bloodland, blooddocks and
    bloodfruit
And a child, ripe:
And a mind, ripe with sting or strut
Like sugarblades of cane
Or Louisiana browngirls whose
    passions
Gestate in volcanos,
Hesitate under quiet cotton colors—
    *'Spoil song
    Soil song'*
Dixie Chorus is an African call/
Watutsi-tall, *greening with upsongs,*
Hoodoo hymns in a lyric field
Against a gumbo sky.

From *Songs from an Afro/Phone,*
by Eugene B. Redmond, 1972.

The question on the Blues streets was: "Will the *Blues Annual* be around after the first issue?" I never had any doubt, and neither did the new contributors, advertisers, and a key international magazine distributor, Ingram Periodicals. We introduced our readers to the work of Hart Leroy Bibbs, Quincy Troupe, and Kalamu Ya Salaam, among others, and continued with some contributors from issue number 1. Advertisers were eager to be a part of Chicago's new music magazine. The Italian retailer Benetton led the way by appearing on the back cover. This caused a sensation among Blues magazine publishers because international companies outside of the Blues business had rarely, if ever, had a presence in a Blues-oriented publication.

Many Blues artists wanted to showcase themselves: Sugar Blue, Big Wheeler, Billy Branch, Katherine Davis, and Sydney James Wingfield are among those who lent their support by taking out full-page ads.

The *Blues Annual* was rolling, and everyone involved felt really good about it.

INTERVIEW WITH PINETOP PERKINS

L. "Chicago Beau" Beauchamp

I have known Pinetop Perkins since 1970. We have hung out in London, Paris, Rome, Chicago, San Francisco. Pinetop spent eleven years as the piano player with Muddy Waters and is a founding member of the world-renowned Legendary Blues Band. This conversation finds me hanging out with Pinetop and his family in his South Side Chicago home, and we're drinking Old Grand-Dad bourbon whiskey.

BEAU: What's your hometown?
PINETOP: My hometown is Belzoni, Mississippi. B-e-l-z-o-n-i.
BEAU: When were you born; what month, day, and year?
PINETOP: 17 July 1913.
BEAU: Is Belzoni near Clarksdale?
PINETOP: Yeah, you go to Clarksdale then go east to Tutwiler, then take 49 W right on into Belzoni.
BEAU: Well, tell me, what was it like for Pinetop Perkins growing up. Were you "Pinetop" when you were a boy?
PINETOP: No, when I first started out, they called me "Little Willie," Little Willie Perkins.
BEAU: How did you get the name "Pinetop"?
PINETOP: Well, Pinetop Smith was my idol. I loved the way he played, and I listened to his records. And I recorded "Pinetop's Boogie Woogie" over again, and from then on they been calling me "Pinetop" ever since.
BEAU: "Pinetop's Boogie Woogie" . . . how old were you at that time?
PINETOP: Oh, I was young. I did it in 1951. I did it on Sun Records in Memphis.
BEAU: You've been Pinetop Perkins since 1951?
PINETOP: Yeah.
BEAU: Why did you leave Mississippi?
PINETOP: Well, I'll tell you, I left Mississippi 'cause I got tired of plowin' them mules down in there.
BEAU: Did you grow up on a farm?
PINETOP: Yeah, plowin' the mules out there is terrible; two legs trying to keep up with four all day long . . . that's terrible, man. I said, well, someday I got to do something else. OK, so then I started driving tractors in Mississippi. I drove a

Pinetop Perkins in Reykjavík, Iceland, during a 1992 tour. Photo by L. Beauchamp.

tractor around there for a pretty good while. That's what kept me out of the army; driving them on a government farm at Howard Oxen up in Clarksdale, Mississippi, during WWII. I was A1 [draft classification] and everything, man, but then that cat come in and call my name to come and get me off the bus. He said we were fixin' to go to Camp Sherwood.

BEAU: So you actually got drafted.

PINETOP: Well, I don't know how he got me off of it [the bus], but he told the people [at the draft board] that he had around about two hundred head of men on the place drivin' tractors. And it took it them all night [processing people] till about six of us were left. So the man said, "I can't be feeding you all corn and beans and stuff unless I can have me some tractor drivers." And my name was called—just random like. And I used to keep the boys laughing at me all the time, you know. I'd say, "Yeah man, I'll tell you one thing about it, I wouldn't mind goin' fightin' nowhere for somebody, but I ain't ever knew I had an uncle named Sam." I used to keep them laughing at that all the time. And then when he found out I was a mechanic, he put me in the shop rebuilding tractors and stuff like that, putting sleeves and stuff on them.

BEAU: You were actually in the army or outside of it?

PINETOP: No man, I was on the plantation.

BEAU: So you weren't in the army, you just did the army's work?

PINETOP: Yeah, on the government farm. I get a check right now, understand, because I was on the government farm. I love that. Uncle Sam take care of me.

BEAU: You found that uncle?!

PINETOP: Yeah, I found that Uncle Sam.

BEAU: Did this happen in the '40s?

PINETOP: No, the '30s.

BEAU: Did you personally see anything in Mississippi like lynching or anything like that?

PINETOP: No, I never saw anything, but I heard about it. Some of it was right near me. It's a cat down there they called Pullum . . . they laced him. What happened was they shot him and killed him. And there was Bird Doggit, he was a cat down there that loved colored people, and Pullum was one of his boys.

BEAU: Bird Doggit was a White man?

PINETOP: Yep. So Johnny-come-later, he got killed.

BEAU: So the White folks killed him because he liked Black people.

PINETOP: Yeah, 'cause he liked Black people.

BEAU: Where was this?

PINETOP: Right in Clarksdale. In a little ol' place out there they call Dublin, I believe. They drug him till all the meat come off his bones after he was dead, they say.

BEAU: Was it the Klan or somebody like that?

PINETOP: Yeah, it was some kind of Klan.

BEAU: Despite all the things we go through, there are many elements that keep Black people together: the church, music, and so on. We brought many traditions with us from Africa like hoodoo and root doctors. What has been your experience with these things?

PINETOP: I worked for a hoodoo doctor, but I never did believe in it. I worked for Dr. McBride out in Clarksdale. His head was white as snow, and everybody was coming to see him like they was at church. Now my mother was living then; she was cooking for him and I was working around the house.

BEAU: So the people referred to him as Dr. McBride?

PINETOP: Oh, yeah, and the people would come by the droves to see him.

BEAU: Would the people be cured when they left?

PINETOP: They seemed like it. There's another boy that used to be around here in Chicago years ago, they called him "King," but his name was Johnny Parker. Johnny used to work for another hoodoo doctor down around Elizabeth, Mississippi. And when he got ready to work on a woman, he'd say, "Bring that bitch-wolf on in here." That's what he'd say when they came in, but when they went out they seemed all right. I don't know what he do to them, but I never believed in it myself.

BEAU: When you were working for Dr. McBride, exactly what were you doing?

PINETOP: I was taking care of things around the house—a houseboy, like. Kept the yards and stuff clean. When people bring their mules and stuff in, I'd feed them. The man had a plantation. Dr. McBride.

BEAU: Did he have a sign out that said "Dr. McBride," or did people just know he was there.

PINETOP: Yeah, he had a sign up.

BEAU: Was he respected in the community?

PINETOP: Yeah, from all over they'd come to see that man.

BEAU: There is so much sensationalized bullshit going around about hoodoo. In fact, Johnny Shines told me it was bullshit that Robert Johnson made a pact with the devil in order to play better.

PINETOP: A whole lot of it was . . . but I never did know Robert Johnson; I never did get a chance to see him, but I heard his records. Just like learning from Pinetop Smith—I had musical talents . . . I could just pick out his tunes on piano. Everybody likes my style, which is different from his; people like the way I play boogie-woogie. So, my style I developed down in Mississippi from listening, much the way Robert developed his. There was a piano player down there called "Terrible Sludge"; he could play piano . . . man, oh, man, but he couldn't sing nothing. I learned some stuff from him, but he didn't learn it to me. I got it from picking out on the piano listening to him play, 'cause he didn't make records. There was another cat they called John Wesley, and I used to love hearing John Wesley play. He could play ballads and everything else.

I'd say, "Oh, look at this." This is sort of how Robert Johnson did; he could listen and learn real fast.

BEAU: So where did you go next from Mississippi?

PINETOP: Here's the way it was. Before I came to Chicago, I was on *King Biscuit Time* with Sonny Boy Williamson [Rice Miller], you know, about four years in Helena, Arkansas.

BEAU: Who was in the band?

PINETOP: Joe Willie Wilkins on guitar, James Peck Curtiss on drums, Sonny Boy [Rice Miller] on harmonica, and Huston Stackhouse on guitar, and me on piano. When I first went there, I was with Robert Nighthawk. We was on the Bright Star program advertising Bright Star flour. Then this interstate grocery man said to Sonny Boy, "That man playing the piano over there, I like the way he play; tell him to come on over here and I'll pay him to play on *King Biscuit Time*." I give Robert two weeks' notice, and I told him, "I hate to leave you, man, but I got to go over here where I can make some money." So I left and went over there [King Biscuit] after two weeks' time.

BEAU: Do you play another instrument besides piano?

PINETOP: You see my first instrument was guitar. I was playing guitar bad, man, till I got this muscle cut out of my arm in Helena. One of them bad women got a hold to me over in Helena.

BEAU: A woman stabbed you in Helena?

PINETOP: Yeah, look here . . . no more muscle (shows his forearm).

BEAU: What year did this happen?

PINETOP: Oh, that was way back there, around '44 or '45, around in there.

Interview with Pinetop Perkins

BEAU: How did this happen?

PINETOP: It was a freak accident. All right, me and the boys was drinking whiskey in the back of a place they call Dreamland Cafe. So we drinking whiskey. Then this lady came in there and went to the bathroom. You know how them come in the month like a hog bleeding or something. I shoved the door to, and her old used-to-be husband put about two or three barrels of ashes against that door so she couldn't get out. She was in that place, man . . . about an hour or an hour and a half; she couldn't get out. Now, I'm the last person she see shut that door, and when she come out and seen me, boy, she just laid on me; lit in on me with that knife.

BEAU: She thought you'd done it to her.

PINETOP: And I ain't done nothing. She was one of the High Brown Follies, them team dancers on the road show. She was in a dancing team on stage. That girl that cut me, they called her Mickey. That girl could dance that stuff, man. But I wasn't nothin' to her . . . but her used-to-be husband caused this freak accident. So, after she found out what had happened, her and her mother worked at paying my doctor bill. And everything I figured that I wanted, they had it out there to the hospital to me. But still I couldn't get this hand back together, so I couldn't play guitar no more. So right now, I can't play no guitar; I can pound down, but I can't squeeze. After awhile of squeezing it goes to paining. And you know you got to squeeze hard.

BEAU: What was the next stop after King Biscuit?

PINETOP: I come on into Memphis where B. B. King and them were.

BEAU: Beale Street.

PINETOP: "Beale Street Blues Boy King." That's why they call him B. B. King. All right. Me and him got together and started advertising Lucky Strike cigarettes. When B. B. come on there saying, "Be happy, go Lucky," we'd light up. And the peoples thought it was a whole band up there; wasn't nobody but me and B. B. I played there a while, then I come on into Chicago and got with Earl Hooker, a *bad* guitar player. Boy, that skunk could play. But now Earl started playing with me way back when I was in Mississippi—but he got sick and his mother came and got him and put him in the hospital. And when I come up here this time, I started with him again 'cause he said he was well. "Man, I'm well," he'd say. He wasn't well; no sooner did we start playing, we'd have to carry him back to the hospital.

BEAU: What did he have?

PINETOP: TB [tuberculosis] . . . and so he died. He was young, about forty-four. Him and Otis Span died around the same time, both of them in their forties.

BEAU: I remember Otis, I remember Otis very well.

PINETOP: Yeah, well, he was about forty-two, forty-three when he died.

BEAU: He had that goiter on his neck, you know—that growth coming out on it.

PINETOP: Yep. So people thought I took his place in Muddy Waters's band, but I didn't, you know. . . . Otis started a band himself.

BEAU: Along with his wife Lucille?

PINETOP: With Lucille, yeah. They started a band they self. They were doin' pretty good, but then Otis got sick and he had to go. So they put him in the hospital, and he died. Earl died a little before he did.

BEAU: Did you work with Howlin' Wolf at all?

PINETOP: No, he cussed me out 'cause I wouldn't play with him. "I play more than Muddy Waters" [Pinetop imitates Wolf]. I wanted to tell him that I didn't want to swap a devil for a witch, but I wouldn't say it, I wouldn't tell him that. "Well," I said, "I don't just jump from one man to another, and I'm doin' fairly good." I was workin' . . . and then Muddy carried me all over, all over the country, all over the seas, everywhere: Paris, Germany, Australia. Muddy had me places where I never would have went, you know. All over, Tokyo; I been all over there, man. Yessir, Australia, Sidney, Melbourne, Perth, all over the place.

BEAU: So would you say that being with Muddy was really a gratifying experience?

PINETOP: An *experience* in my life. But I wasn't makin' too much money, but I could get by. Them different places over there . . . we went all over the islands over there. We went to one place on an island somewhere over there, boy, and somebody put a smoke bomb up under the bandstand and shot it off. I told Muddy we better leave here, man. We left, too.

BEAU: Do you remember where it was?

PINETOP: Man, I don't remember what little island it was—a small island.

BEAU: Was it warm there?

PINETOP: Warm, nice and warm.

BEAU: Polynesia or somewhere?

PINETOP: I don't know where it was, it was out in the middle of the ocean. We had to get one of them old "putt-putt" planes to go over there, you know. Boy. You remember when a plane had dropped a motor off here in Chicago? Well, this was just after that had happened, after that engine fell off that plane. And I was sitting beside the window as we was goin' down [landing]. After awhile, goddamn, I see somethin' pass by the window. Shoop! I thought the motor done fall off the thing. Lookit there! Then the wheel went by the window. Shoom! What are they doin'? Well, I didn't know if it was the engine or what. Well, we got on in, and that's when they put the smoke bomb up under the stage there. But I forgot the island, man; I'm tellin' you, I was glad to forget it 'cause I was scared. I got back home; I was so scared, man, I'm tellin' you, they put me in the hospital for a week and a day; she'll tell you [gesturing to his wife]. My heart beatin' out of rhythm. The old doctor up at there at the counter told them, "He ain't got nothin', but maybe he scared; put him up in the room and let him rest some." Boy, that was terrible, man. My heart was beatin' all messed up—I was weak.

BEAU: I have fond memories of Big Bo who worked for Muddy, how about you?

PINETOP: Yeah, I know Bo.

BEAU: That cat could pull out a knife faster than anybody I've ever seen. What about you and Bo?

PINETOP: Me and Big Bo could have some fun together. Bo, he'd always keep you laughing about somethin' . . . and so one night me and Bo was comin' on home and so the other boys were over there in that blame truck. There was a van weaving on the other side, and Bo said, "Ba-ba-ba-ba, look at that there-there-there, he's asleep, man." He stuttered, you know. He went over there close to them and blowed the horn so they wouldn't be goin' to sleep. So Bo was alright. His name was Andrew Brown. He was somethin' else. That cat was a drivin' scoundrel; didn't know his name in boxcar letters, but he could drive.

BEAU: And he protected Muddy?

PINETOP: Yessir, yeah, that was Muddy's bodyguard—ain't nobody mess around with Muddy.

BEAU: I'll never forget one night me and my partner, Julio Finn [who Muddy called "Little Billy Boy" because he is a younger brother of Billy Boy Arnold] was in Boston. This was when Otis was still in the band. Some people in Boston gave Muddy a birthday cake. So Muddy said, "Little Billy Boy, go ahead on and cut the cake for me." So my man, he pulled a knife out to cut the cake. Then Bo came up there with his knife. Click. "Ta-ta-take that goddamn knife out of that cake, that's Muddy's cake. Don't you touch Muddy's cake." And Muddy said, "It's all right, I told him to go ahead and cut it." Bo said, "You sure?"

PINETOP: He better tell him that or you're goin' to get cut. Man, Bo took care of Muddy, man. There was the time that we had a devil of a wreck, man, when I just started with Muddy in '69. We had a hell of a car wreck comin' from Covington, Tennessee.

BEAU: Oh, yeah, I heard about that.

PINETOP: All right. If Bo hadn't drove that day, we all would have been killed. OK. This car run up beside the highway and cut across. When he cut across, we had done about sixty or seventy miles an hour apiece. People standing by said it look like two freight trains hittin'. Boooom! The light up on top of the car knocked a hole up in my head. My knees went all through the back, all up in that iron back there. Messed my knees all up; I couldn't walk for about three, four months. OK. Bo [who was driving behind Perkins's car] took the ditch over there on the side of us. If he hadn't a did that, man, me and Muddy, we'd be dead, too. All of us would have been dead, all jammed up into the car. A slick brand new station wagon, too. Just had bought it. Caprice. Pretty thing. They had to tow that thing off; demolished it. Lets you know what kind of road it was. Warren was driving the station wagon we was in; killed him dead. Last thing Warren said was, "Oh, look it there."

BEAU: What was Warren's last name?

PINETOP: I forget the last part of Warren's name, but anyway, when they found out he was dead, the peoples come got him; they carried him back to his hometown. I forget where his hometown was; it was in Mississippi someplace.

BEAU: He was driving y'all?

PINETOP: He was driving us. And Bo was driving a van behind us. Muddy was sitting beside me. Man, broke all the bones up in his hips. Oh, man, they had him up in traction for about two to three months. And then the boy they called Peewee Madison was in another hospital; cracked his ribs and stuff. Muddy and me was in the hospital together. All my knees was knocked out of shape, a hole in my head. I'm sittin' there lookin' at the man sew my legs back together and all of that stuff. There's a gash there right now, you can see it. The knees went through the ironwork in back.

BEAU: So you were sitting in the back seat?

PINETOP: Yeah, beside Muddy, right beside Muddy. Peewee was in the front with Warren.

BEAU: Don't you think that it was a damn shame that an artist of Muddy Waters's stature wasn't being flown from town to town or traveling in a comfortable and safe tour bus, like they do with the rock groups?

PINETOP: You know, that's what was supposed to have been done, but they didn't do it. All right. But at that particular time, after Muddy got hurt in that car, man, he got scared of automobiles.

BEAU: He said, "Hell with that shit," right?

PINETOP: Right. Then every time they wanted him in, he flew. Otis and them guys came in the truck, in the van and stuff. So one time the boys told me, well, "How come you don't fly with Muddy?" Well, that would be a good idea, but I was scared of planes at that time. I was afraid of planes, man. And when I went overseas and came back, my heart was beating all out of rhythm. So I went to the County [hospital], and the man told them, "Ain't nothin' wrong with the cat but he's scared to death." And if that cat hadn't shot off the bomb under the bandstand . . . I was never so scared. That's the way it was.

BEAU: So you don't mind flying now?

PINETOP: No, I'll fly, but I tell you, I don't like it. But I will fly because I'm scared of cars, too—not unless I'm drivin' myself.

BEAU: Did you get along with Muddy pretty good?

PINETOP: Oh yeah, I got along with Muddy like two brothers, man. Yeah, I got along with Muddy all right. But he didn't pay no good money though. He never did. He kept all that money in his pocket; had a pocket sticking out, man, looking like he had doorknobs in his pocket and we didn't have nothin'. You know what I mean?

BEAU: What was your average salary?

PINETOP: Oh, when I first started with Muddy, you know how much I was gettin'? I was gettin' $125 a week.

BEAU: That was in 1969?

PINETOP: Yeah, $125 a week; that's all we was gettin'. So me and Sonny Wimbley, he was playin' bass, we had made up our mind to quit 'cause we wasn't makin' any money. We'd get back home, and we didn't have any money to do nothin' with. So we got with Muddy and told him, "Hey man, you ain't payin' us enough money. We can't be out here on the road, everybody's got family, you know." "Duh-duh-duh-duh, I'll raise y'all's salary $10 more." Nothing. When we go overseas, three. . . .

BEAU: $300?

PINETOP: Man, it wasn't nothin'. That food over there is high.

BEAU: So at the end, how much were you makin'? What's the most you ever made with Muddy?

PINETOP: It wouldn't be no more than $300 a week. That's all. People thought we was raisin' Cain out there. We wasn't doin' not nothin', as Louis Meyers would say. We was out there makin' *that* man some money.

BEAU: So why do you think this happened?

PINETOP: I don't know what happened, but I know good and well we wasn't gettin' no money.

BEAU: And there were six cats in the band?

PINETOP: Yeah, bout six cats. All right. So last time I played with Muddy (you see, I quit him before he died) . . . the last time I played with Muddy, we had to go to Tokyo. I tells him *all* this time, made this cat mad with me, I'll tell you— I tells him I ain't goin' over for under a $1,000—all the boys heard me. No Tokyo. So he gave up. He tried to get somebody to go over there with him, but he couldn't get nobody. So, man, him and that Scott Cameron [Muddy's manager] were over there, man, they was so mad and mouths was stuck out so far you could have walked on those lips.

BEAU: Lips stuck way out?

PINETOP: Yeah, man. So we all got back here in Chicago. Scott thought Jerry Portnoy was the one that was doin' it [leading the revolt]. It wasn't; it was me. Then one day Scott Cameron said, "Hey, Pinetop, Muddy done fired Jerry, and all the other boys were goin' on with Jerry; you goin' to stick with Muddy?" And I said, "No, I'm with the boys," and I hung the phone up. That's the time I got the Legendary Blues Band: me, Jerry, Little Willie, Calvin [Fuzz] Jones, and we all got this other boy out of Boston playin' guitar with us. I forget that boy's name. But anyway he played nice guitar.

BEAU: White cat?

PINETOP: Yeah. And his wife got tired of his being on the road, and so she got him a job at the post office. OK. We got us Louis Meyers to play with us awhile. We couldn't get along with him. Boy, that cat's somethin' else. Every time he see us talkin', he'd say, "Y'all goin' on and on, on the round table on me." He didn't like Jerry Portnoy too well. "That Jerry teachin' y'all some stuff; he ain't no good," he'd say.

BEAU: Yeah, well as far as Louis is concerned, Little Walter was the only harp player in the world.

PINETOP: Yeah, Louis loved Little Walter. Walter used to play with us before he went with Muddy . . . with me and Sonny Boy right there in Helena. But you know, we didn't need two harmonica players. He played with us in Helena before he started makin' records. So Walter told us, "Well, guess y'all got the harmonica player here, Sonny Boy. Y'all don't need me; I'm goin' to Chicago and make me some money." Later, we made us enough money, and we went to Chicago, me and Sonny. After awhile, he [Little Walter] done gone off from Muddy and gone on his own. Next thing you know he come out with "Juke," and I said, "This boy Walter is gone now."

BEAU: Had he lived, there ain't no telling how far he would have gone musically.

PINETOP: Well, that boy, he had a gift with a harp—he could have played anything with anybody.

BEAU: So, all in all, working with Muddy was rewarding, but the money thing was the only thing that wasn't happening.

PINETOP: Yeah, the money is the only thing that wasn't happenin'.

BEAU: Do you think Muddy's manager had something to do with it?

PINETOP: Yeah, he had something to do with it. Well, look here, when Scott Cameron started with us, you know what he had . . . an old piece of Plymouth with the fenders falling off it. And man, then he was with us on our regular route about six or eight months—brand new car. Bought a home out here—mansion. He sold that home, and now he bought in California. This house that Muddy had out here, Scott got the big money out of that. That cat got over like a fat rat, man. When we used to be with Muddy, every Christmas we'd have a bonus comin'. Scott cut it out. Told Muddy to give him the bonus.

BEAU: Scott cut out the bonus?

PINETOP: Yeah. And every time we'd get what I call a little scab royalty off the records, Scott Cameron would send us one of Muddy's checks and say you get somethin' out of that check. Anyway he could see if there's a penny or dime or somethin' or another, he's goin' to get it. I told Big-Eyed Willie Smith that we gettin' messed over. OK, after we got the Legendary Blues Band, we swapped a devil with a witch. A guy up in Wisconsin.

BEAU: What happened with him?

PINETOP: Boy, that son of a gun, boy, lookit here, he'd gut you. He'd book the band for about $2,000 and pay the band $1,000; I found that out.

BEAU: So you pay your boys a lot better?

PINETOP: We all get the same thing, understand. All we had to do was take out the overhead, the gas, the tires, and somethin'. All of the previous; I had what you called a united band; we all got the same thing. See, they had never had somethin' like that happen to them before. I went over here to whatcha call it, Italy, you know what I mean—come back home with $5,500.

BEAU: How about your days with Little Milton; you quit him once didn't you?

PINETOP: I did. But I quit too late, but it don't ever be too late to do good, let me tell you.

BEAU: That's right.

PINETOP: I quit just about the right time. One day it was a parade. All right. OK, the boys was over across the street on the other side over there. And I couldn't make it over there where he was. OK, and so I couldn't break through that parade no kind of way. I was walkin' and that parade was long, man. I tried to get to him, but all I could do was this: wave at him. And I told him to go on ahead, 'cause I can't get through there. Do you know that Little Milton got mad at me and started to talk to me like I was a kid or somethin' when I did see him. I said, "Hey man, I'll tell you what you do. From now on, you get yourself a piano player." I ain't been with him since, 'cause you don't talk to me like that. I couldn't break through those people, in the parade. "When somebody work for me, they're supposed to do like I tell them." I said, "Wait a minute, man, you don't talk to me like that; I'm old enough to be your granddaddy." He was cussin' and goin' on. I said, "You don't do that to me, because I'll be lookin' all upside your head, I'm goin' to tell you. I ain't lyin'. Be ready to hit the floor." So I said, "Best thing for me to do is to quit." "No, you don't quit now, you got to play with us." "No, no I ain't playin' nothin', you get someone else." From then on I left, 'cause I knew what I wanted. Ain't nobody talk to me like I was a kid. Well, I'm trying to tell you, Milton was like that. And see, before it would get too far, I just told him what it was like and then left. I played with Milton about three weeks; that was it.

BEAU: He had an attitude?

PINETOP: Yeah, he had a bad attitude. Years ago, Oliver Sain fired him.

BEAU: We Blacks create a lot of music as a result of our out-of-Africa condition. From Samba down there in Brazil, to Reggae, Blues, Jazz, and so on.

PINETOP: Yeah, we Africa people.

BEAU: When you were coming up, man, did you play other styles?

PINETOP: Yeah, everything. Look, when I first started playin' piano, you know what keys I was playin' in? E-flat, B-flat, and A-flat; and now I can't play in that, because you start playin' with these boys, you know, in E and A and D and C and stuff like that. They pulled me out of those keys, and I swear I can't get it back like I want it.

BEAU: What do you think about cats like Ellington?

PINETOP: Um-hum, Lord almighty.

BEAU: Who's your all-time-favorite piano player?

PINETOP: Jazz? I'm goin' to tell you who he was, and you're goin' to say you like him, too. The Count.

BEAU: Count Basie.

PINETOP: The Count, my main man. Yessir. And when it come down to the sweet music, I liked that cat that would play the clarinet, now what was his name? That cat had a big band.

BEAU: Bennie Goodman?

PINETOP: Yeah, Bennie Goodman; big band, yeah, I liked that. And then there was Erskin Hawkins. But I really liked Joe Liggins. I just love that thing, "Honey Dripper." I got that record around here somewhere now.

BEAU: Now here's a question for you. This is an important question. I think anybody can love and appreciate anybody's anything. I can love the Chinese ballet . . . I can love Polish folk dance, but I can't be that. What do you think about White people who say that they can play Blues and feel it just like a Black person.

PINETOP: They can't do it. No way.

BEAU: They can respect it.

PINETOP: They can respect it, but they wasn't born in the Blues field—we was. Africa people was born in the Blues field; even if they can't sing it, they understand it. We's down in Mississippi gettin' cheated all kind of ways. You've got the Blues, even if you can't sing it, dig. That's what Blues is all about. It's a feelin', that's what it is. Blues is a feelin'.

BEAU: Pinetop, what do you think of the Chicago club scene?

PINETOP: If you want a nickel and a nail, it's good. They take a nickel and give you a nail. That's what the Chicago clubs is about. So that's the main reason I don't play around here too much. Yeah, once in awhile I might play a club. But it's like I was over here at the whatcha call it over here, I didn't get my price, but I just went on because he wanted to try to get a little thing goin'.

BEAU: Well, if you had to put together the perfect, great Blues band of old cats living and dead, who would you put together?

PINETOP: Little Walter on harp, Robert Junior Lockwood on guitar, Bob Stroger on bass, and turn around and get A. C. Reed on horn.

BEAU: That would be it for you?

PINETOP: Hey man, that's as nice as I can make it.

BEAU: Hey, thank you.

PINETOP: Glad to be with you, Beau.

December 16, 1989, Chicago

WELCOME HOME LUTHER

Jacques Lacava

There is a tendency to take for granted what happens next door and is accessible to us. This is what is happening to Blues and Chicago artists in their hometown. One of the most popular Bluesmen in Europe, Luther Allison, enjoying a very well deserved reputation because of his remarkable performances, spent his adolescence and was initiated into music in the Windy City. Allison is a charismatic character and an exhilarating musician. The warmth that exudes from his music is an expression of an explosive mixture of Blues and Soul and of a voice tinged with the fervor of Gospel. Allison's stage presence is legendary: bright, sensual, humorous, and provocative.

Why did he make his home in Paris after spending much of his time traveling between Chicago and Europe? One could write a long list of Jazz and Blues artists who had to go overseas to find recognition with a passionate audience. Luther has now become attached to France, where the French receive him well and celebrate him joyfully because he is one of the first great Blues guitar players to become an expatriate. He followed the path of a few piano players like the late great Memphis Slim.

The band Luther has pulled together is made up of members of many different origins, from American to . . . French! He even adopted a young prodigy, Little Sammy, a twelve-year-old boy from the suburbs of Paris. Luther's presence in the Paris area influenced the vocations of some aspiring musicians and promoted a growing number of French Blues bands.

Luther saw the clubs of Chicago's Black neighborhoods close one after another and felt Blues lose its popularity. Recently, he witnessed a renewed interest in the Blues, which is honored in the gigantic Chicago Blues Festival.

Growing up in Arkansas in the Deep South and living the life of a young Black brought up on a farm during hard times prepared Luther for the first stage of his itinerary: a common departure to the urban ghettos of Chicago. This led him to a life of an underdog proletarian but also gave him the opportunity to learn how to play Blues guitar in a melting pot of styles.

He attended school on the South Side and became friends with the son of Muddy Waters and met the patriarch. Musically, he was mostly influenced by the Texas sound of Freddie King and by Otis Rush. Allison participated in all the Sunday matinees and battles of the Blues at the local Blues bars with guitar in hand. His style developed in the core of the West Side sound, which caught the attention of Delmark, a local label. Luther did not turn a deaf ear to the Soul music of the 1960s, becoming an excellent interpreter. He also experimented with the possibilities of the electric guitar in an approach reminiscent of Hendrix, although Luther and Jimi went their own way and did not influence each other. By the end of the 1960s, Murphy Dunne organized a daylong celebration with the veterans of the Blues. Luther was part of the young-bloods package. He even participated in the original Chicago Blues Festival.

He stepped into an exceptional fate. He quickly assimilated the Blues of his time and started an American career paved with stepping stones and victories—like his contract with the Motown label. But the rewards of his talent mostly consisted of endless tours and days on the road without financial returns. He hired Chicagoans like Maurice John Vaughn, Steve Freund, and Professor Eddie Lusk to back him up; his shows were unlike other Motown bands: orchestrated. Because he is a Bluesman who improvises on the spot, his sidemen had to follow him as he ad-libbed on the guitar, the harp, or vocally with a sound as gravelly as a Baptist preacher's. Allison is an important artist who operated a kind of fusion between Blues, Rock, and Rhythm and Blues in the 1970s: All sorts of sounds burst from his guitar.

The music of Luther does not always accommodate the narrow scope of the recording studios: He is at his best onstage. Older than fifty, he still is one of the youthful Bluesmen of his generation, and his powers are at their peak. He made a strong return to the foreground with a live album recorded in Berlin, where his seismic guitar shook the Wall last spring. His fascinating dynamism and energy have been preserved recently on a digital recording taped live during a concert.

Allison has attempted repeatedly and unsuccessfully to make a living by crossing over into the Pop-Rock scene. Luther returned to his first love, the Blues, and broadened the spectrum of his repertory that honors many of the facets of Black music.

Luther recently invited his twenty-four-year-old son, Bernard, in whom he puts all his hopes, to join him in Paris. The prodigal son, who played a long time with Koko Taylor, also is a very gifted guitarist; a killer slinger, more of a virtuoso who assimilated the sounds of modern Rock. He will without a doubt become a European "guitar hero." Currently he backs up his father or plays in a power trio.

To a certain extent, Luther is the "keeper of the flame" of the Chicago West Side style and perpetuator of the musical legacy of his brother in arms Magic Sam, who died an early death. He is very attached to his roots and rejoices every time he comes back home. But he arrives with an original style in his bags, because he knows how to let his music evolve by gathering and mixing new elements. In Europe, he lost less time riding on the highways between gigs and made the effort to write his own songs, influenced by the world music of the African diaspora.

Luther Allison,
August 17, 1939–August 12, 1997

THE BEAN AND THE NEWK
Hart Leroy Bibbs

Perhaps it's the same old night-and-day story: youth against age, pupil against master. Until this day, no other reason can be advanced as to why The Newk done all what he did to The Bean (disrespected him like he was nobody hornsky).

In his own times, The Bean was a musician two generations ahead of himself. It was not possible to make a musical distinction between the two of them as to which of them was the better or worse. They both had wide souls that can be only from having paid plenty of dues. Haphazardly then, things can happen—like The Newk falling into life at the height of The Bean's times.

In the recording studio that day were plenty of impartial witnesses: the engineers and promoters and spectators in the most modern studio in New York (with good light and acoustics—already in itself a million-dollar ambiance).

The change came on like a lightning stroke, catching everybody unaware that the rules upon leaving were changed completely from the entrance regulations. The Crescendo! The Newk had hung up a sign that said "Out to Lunch." The Bean was locked out of the office for notes and bars; The Newk's playing meant exactly what the sign read. From earth onward into outer space, he bounced from one note to another, intertwining a sure knowledge that he couldn't miss one single jump or note.

It shook The Bean's confidence in himself even. He could hear that there wasn't going to be anything left for him to deal on—no notes, no harmonies, no riffs, no nothing. No, not even Blues.

It was something rare for a man of his experience. Music was The Bean's be-all and end-all, and this young upstart was bringing him some new finger-popping shit that he wasn't sure how he was going to deal with. But he could see the fit of the bind he was tied in; he decided to lay back and stroll awhile to bide his time. "Blow! Blow! Blow, Bean!" The Newk shouted.

It was evident then to The Bean that The Newk was dead serious. It was evident to him also that it wasn't no use of him thinking that youth would dash its brains out in falling upon the hard rocks of experience. It was like a light before it finally blows out, winking and blinking a preliminary warning. The Bean had heard a compliment at first, an inspired outburst; and along about the third blink, he began to understand a challenge. He transformed the challenge into a jazzy, slick riff: Blow, Bean, Blow; all your best must show!—the last chance before the knockout of unshaven grace notes.

Bravado entered; and The Bean lit out on a don't-do-me-no-favors chorus; all of taste tone and form. Suddenly, though, a chill seized him along the bone marrow of his spine: Burning flashes of Stepin Fetchit turning white to witness a ghost; Montan Moreland outrunning speeding cars; Herb Jefferies, the singing Black cowboy, chasing White lady Indians across Hollywood's plains.

The Bean knew he was dead dealing then, burning everything in sight and sound. But the persistent shadows of age followed him. Finally red-eyed anger accused The Newk of abusing out history. Reflection was called for. A sudden will to action now could only become a sort of patriotic suicide: There is only the hero or the loser. He didn't want The Newk to worship him as the hero, but he didn't want The Newk to finish him either. The past gave way to warm feelings of paternity—body and soul—realizing in the aftermath what he really wanted was for the young Newk not to be afraid to be a hero: Him or me was à la mode; the rock breaks the scissors that cut the paper; on ad infinitum etc.

Then, in three double steps (seven leagues apiece), The Newk bounded to the tops of his chops and sprayed red on the Cheops of Quetzalcoatl. His tongue tripping stumbled into his soul on fire. Holograms of angels and devils made musical feast. He played the guilt of the giants and the innocence of the elves. Torturing wisdom, a measure could only become coda to coda and thereon reach into rarer regions of music where the wind ceases to howl in conflict but whispers its urgency, being not impulsive to choose its directions. Just go-go-go. The Bean was trapped in a time rut of dying classicism. Allegro complications, pianissimo crescendos, ad libitum amoroso, but adagio mountains crumbled prettily again and again. Bach and Chopin and Ravel died in flurries of crippled expectations.

Then The Newk's heart bled—like the passion of St. Matthew—on the coda. He attacked the head of the tune from its middle so confidently, mysteriously that doubt never entered his mind.

Brilliantly brave with love (con anima, con expression, energetic with majesty and fire), a graceful force from motion to the spirit of motion tenderly as walking on air—capricious the cadence. Delicately determined to clear his throat of pride and torment, he bounds and glides. Silence is decision and the ironic is innocence, though he laments the sweet menace of passion. He weeps melodically along a violin's bounced strings, as a phrase of resolute strength ponders it playfully to rob sorrow of somberness. Notes segue into notes metronomically on chromatic sensibilities. Bird lives! Solemn, sonorous. Tatum and Monk cannot die.

A tranquility extends him into swift, light free tempo—like a prelude to an overture where a nasty solo fades blue. Back to pure heads untainted by stamps of security (gigs), unblended by assimil humiliations. Bean lives!

Something of a race's knowledge lies lodged parasitically in our bloodstreams because in the planet streets of Harlem there are no swimming holes nor creeks with muddy banks. Yet The Bean, slurring, slid in some mud. He made many wild streaks—naked terror—to find alternatives, if not resolutions. But red-light notes on blue chenille bedspreads came as hard as the pebbles on the creek's shores.

The Newk, peaceful, warmed by the first heat of morning sun, catapulted off a makeshift diving board (a plank—no more) and described relativity: pure suspension with a perfect gainer two-and-half somersault. The very pads of his saxophone soles fumed and screamed, loosened their glue strings and danced naked downhill to the old swimming hole (which in slang is called "harmonic peace" because it is still heated by early morning sun).

Because The Bean's belly wells up in water, he refused to swim at all; he fished off the bridge instead. He had fashioned a crawdad-net crisscrossed with the finest strings of restful-swing tone and technique—a simple tool, and beautiful as a primitive motif. He was all patience and sweet melodic tones hung on threads of golden goodness. Was he sweet! God, was he sweet! His cracklin'-cornbread sympathy, his collard-greens-and-hambone common sense, were all being attacked—if not downright disrespected.

The Newk then bucked to the left and winged to the right, impassioned all the way. It was a hard judgment on blank paper with no lines and no spaces. Sure enough, the melody was unheard; but it was already killing sweet.

It was an old trick bag The Bean used, a beautiful Kansas City sundown in the honeyed style of slow-colored masters.

The Newk began flapping and feeling, reeling and squealing and splashing colors everywhere. He came as close to levitation, as surrealistic as a horn (let alone one man playing one horn) can get. Suspension! Pure color chinning itself up on invisible bars. Arms out, perfect double-ring suspension. Iron biceps bulged in his jaws' armature. As if hesitation could only be a catastrophe, he waited or wanted not for ideas.

The Bean attempted to intrude on politeness to age and concert C, but the segue was wanting; the concert was canceled.

The Newk was in a fury. He jumped down The Bean's throat (with all four feet, as they say in the business of Jazz) with street graffiti. The Bean tried to plead a case of lilies-and-lace security.

No go—blow cause the naked Newked meaning of life could only be skull-and-crossbones poison pointing to a survival road. The Newk hopscotched along the path, waving a shroud for his flag. He jutted his chin out, tripled-tongued the reed, and pulled his lips back into a joker's grin. This caused chimes to boom in The Bean's near future. Astrarmony was the harmonic aside made when he forecast stormy weather in The Bean's next solo.

These were tactics that brought The Bean to his knees. Still he couldn't give up. Strategy called for a chopping-off-the-head situation: bluff or duff for a king as he was. While he forced tone and technique down on their knees with him, he screeched nervously; red notes ran all over the mountain lines, screeching into the yellow spaces.

Even more harmonic insolence and chromatic sumptuousness on a mystical foggy bridge. The Newk clucked like a hen, crowed like a cock, then soared like an eagle off a mountain peak way off somewhere (in Africa—Kilimanjaro!) dominated by a hermit.

Being vulnerable on all sides then, The Bean had never before lit such warm fires in circular-dimension pits of his stomach; nor had ever that mother's tongue embraced music language so ardently. His last trembling tremolo rumbled to such deep depths of horn-bottom that pots and pans, clocks, and barometers fell off the walls in The Newk's house. By this time, though, everything was upside down to The Bean.

All around his rim, The Newk was music dancing and teasing. The Newk was standing on his head, circular breathing high notes that shone in the pitch of blues. And shining bright that high noon, way up high and blue in the sky, was a Newk Astre.

Hart Leroy Bibbs,
February 6, 1930–August 31, 1994

A GUN IN THE HAND IS WORTH . . .
Kalamu Ya Salaam

it was a cliché
in a sad sort of way, the way
these weird, oppressive social
games are played

it happened in a community
center (so called)
a food stamp office
she was old, tired
had an injured hip, a
pillow, a cane,
and was number two
hundred and one
when the cut-off was
two even, brother man
on guard dumbly overdoing
his duty invited her
to stay out, she asked
to rest inside, he denied

then like a saturday poker game
with a newcomer taking all
the chips, it turned unnecessary
nigger ugly, "bitch, if-in
you wasn't so old
I'd go upside yo haid,
this here office is closed
i said,"

"son, what did you say?"

the repeat hissed snake like
crossed his teeth, calmly
her old hand went
inside her old bag
and came up with her
old gun and with her
old voice she slowly
repeated an old phrase:

"well play like i'm
sweet sixteen and
hit me . . . !"

THEY SAY THE HOOCHIECOOCHIE MAN DONE UP AN GONE

Quincy Troupe

For Troy, "Boss in the hot sauce"

you were the heart-healing glory back then when you sang
your fat-back collard green doodoo blood flames, choochooing
train whistles that broke double string guitars, washboarding
gin scrapings & funky-butt sapphire-stars—jeweled fingers hip on
hips—these mojos double-clutching were your calling cards, juju
pain framing your call & response muddy river hot sauce
add catfish & no-count stupid cracker bosses, mean up in your voice
speaking no nonsense, now they tell your white lightning hoodoo
done up an gone poopoo, done gone an stuck in your throat like a needle
or a chicken bone caught in the words of some sinning preacher, that's what
they tell me old hot sauce, that your deep secret sweet healing song done
gone now & catch there in the web of drink & dope, like dew do to moss
& is caught there now in a death choice of pure-de constipation, boy
they tell me now that silence is boss of your juke joint hoodoo
tell me now that your voodoo done sank pitiful as the river
running low, O blood deep once delta soothsayer whose songs echoed bones
running & weeping beneath the mississippi's unmarked graves, were the tomb-
stones that marked where those spirits laid down they heavy heads, so where
the magic done gone now out of your double-edged songs, your guitar choking
boss baritone of the rusty-razored voice of too much gin & whiskey
rotgut dues utterance of blue magic hoodoo buried deep in your hot sauce
so where the coochiecoochie sawblading lyrics done took themselves now
vowel-stretching voice of wolf-tickets & calls of moonbreaks
they tell me your two-timing songs knee-deep in chained history
done gone long silent now forever clued into your bloodshot eyes
looking like two blown out lightbulbs, they say your double-clutching
voice done gone the way of deaf-mutes, that's what they say blood
hoochiecoochie flame healer, that's what they all say

FUNKY-GRACE (FROM THE HERO SERIES)

Eugene B. Redmond

He took the lion-lunge,
Hey! Hey!
He took the tiger-step,
Hey! Hey!
He took the tomb-trail,
Hey! Hey!
He took the sacred-plunge.
Hey! Hey!

He made the ocean-leap
Hey! Hey!
He made the gong/gong-call!
Hey! Hey!
He made the death-mouth,
Hey! Hey!
He made the freedom-creep.
Hey! Hey!

He at the juicy—blues
Hey! Hey!
He ate the rat/roach flat!
Hey! Hey!
He ate the numb-stare,
Hey! Hey!
He ate the airborn-shoes!
Hey! Hey!

He caught the sassy-space!
Hey! Hey!
He caught the totem-call!
Hey! Hey!
He caught the kill-flame!
Hey! Hey!
He caught the Funky-Grace!
Hey! Hey!
He caught that Funky-Grace!
Hey! Hey!
He caught that Funky-Grace!
Hey! Hey!

FROM THE *ORIGINAL CHICAGO BLUES ANNUAL*
Issue Number 3

The year 1991 was a challenging and eventful year for my publishing company. Finally, we moved into a real office from a mail box; 2,500 square feet at Institute Place in Chicago's River North district. From there we published *Literati Internazionale* and *Original Chicago Blues Annual* (*OCBA*), coproduced a concert in Poland, and began producing a series of Blues records in collaboration with DIW Records in Tokyo.

OCBA number 3 is the first issue in which we translated some of the contributions into Italian and French in order to reach more people in lands where the Blues enjoys immense popularity and *OCBA* was establishing a solid fan base.

INTERVIEW WITH LESTER BOWIE
L. "Chicago Beau" Beauchamp

I met Lester Bowie and the Art Ensemble of Chicago in Paris in 1969. On many occasions we have enjoyed fine Havana cigars and talked about good times past and those that we hope are ahead for us. Finally, we have gotten around to taping a conversation that reflects some of Lester's history and his ideas on music and other matters.

BEAU: You're famous now. How did it begin?

LESTER: I ain't that famous; if I was I would have some kind of cash. I'm maybe a bit well known in some areas, but I ain't famous. My father was a high school band director. He played trumpet. All of his brothers were brass players; his father was a trombone player, so it just kind of came in the family. My brothers are all professional musicians and ever since I can remember we've all been playing music.

BEAU: Where did y'all come up at?

LESTER: I was born in Maryland, but I come up in St. Louis, Missouri.

BEAU: So most of your musical youth was in St. Louis?

LESTER: Yeah, all of it. I was in St. Louis from the time I was about two years old up until I left to join the military. I was born in '41, so in the mid-'50s was my real musical youth.

BEAU: How many were in your family?

LESTER: I got two brothers, Byron and Joe.

BEAU: No sisters?

LESTER: No sisters. No females in the crib; just my mommy, that was the only one. We couldn't stand girls—it was weird. You know sometimes cats don't like girls. We even named Joe before he was born. Wasn't gon' have no girl [big laugh]. Now, for somebody who didn't like girls, I got four daughters and a granddaughter.

BEAU: That's what you get.

LESTER: Yeah, that's what I'm saying.

BEAU: What section of St. Louis did you grow up in?

LESTER: Well, the Black section. When I came up we didn't see many White people. I was about fifteen before I knew any White people.

BEAU: In your youth, did your father take you around to clubs?

Lester Bowie boarding a tour bus in Den Hague, the Netherlands, during the 1993 Tradition of Chicago Blues Tour. Photo by L. Beauchamp.

LESTER: What happened was I had a band at fifteen. At fifteen I was a professional musician in the union.

BEAU: What styles were you playing?

LESTER: Dixieland, Boogie-Woogie, and R&B type stuff. Actually during that time I worked a few gigs with Chuck Berry; around '54 to '55. We worked a lot of shows people were having; high school dances, talent shows, that type of thing.

BEAU: Did you work over in East St. Louis, Illinois?

LESTER: No, not until later. This is the first period I was playing. We played mostly in a teenage kind of setting. Later, after I joined the military and came back, that's when I started playing with Oliver Sain, Little Milton, Albert King, and all those cats. I played in East St. Louis almost every night then. It was the hang.

BEAU: What branch of service were you in, what year did you come back?

LESTER: I was in the Air Force, and I came back around '61 or '62; it was in the early '60s.

BEAU: In the Air Force were you a part of the orchestra or band?

LESTER: No, I was in the police. See, when I came through, I auditioned for the band, and they said they didn't have any openings for a trumpeter in the band, but I could be in the bugle corps. I was given a choice of being in the bugle corps or the police. At that time I couldn't stand bugle corps; I thought that was beneath me because I had played in a concert band, solo coronet. So I wasn't gon' play no one-valve bugle; that was for simpletons. So I rather be with the police force and play with them guns and get to hit me a couple White boys upside the head. I used to be def on them White boys. So I spent that time in the police. During that time I was also involved with a band. I had a regular gig with a Blues band in town [Amarillo, Texas].

BEAU: What was the name of the band?

LESTER: I can't remember the name of that band, but the guy that ran the band, his name was Topps. Had the sweetest press-role I've ever heard, and he had a hell of a shuffle. He could shuffle his ass off and his role was pretty like Art Blakey's.

BEAU: So y'all was just playing stomp down Blues.

LESTER: Yeah, just stomp down Blues in Amarillo, Texas. I joined the service to travel and ended up spending all my time in Amarillo.

BEAU: After Amarillo, you went back to St. Louis?

LESTER: Yes, then I went to school. During the time I was in the service, that's when I decided to become a full-time musician. Because before I had been playing a long time, I had been a professional . . . doing union gigs. I was a pro from fifteen; that's when I first started paying union dues. Give the cat [union man] ten dollars every time he catch you. I decided to go ahead and play music while I was sitting up in jail in the service. I was in solitary confinement.

BEAU: What were you in there for?

LESTER: I was in there for whuppin' a White boy's ass. I had shot up the barracks shooting at this White boy. They had got me for attempted murder.

BEAU: It was as a policeman you did this?

LESTER: It was as a policeman. The service was some of the biggest fun I've ever had. It went the whole gamut: from police to prison. It was a great experience; it really got me focused. I learned how to get organized, which is real important out here. Some of what I learned in the military, like organization and discipline has become basic in dealing with the music. You have to understand that discipline is important. Everybody in the Art Ensemble is a veteran except Moye. And that's been basic in us being able to be together all this time. We've lived in barns and tents and out in fields just like in the army. If we hadn't been able to know how to bivouac, we never would have survived.

BEAU: A lot of Black folks around my age were repulsed at the idea of going into the military during Vietnam, fighting for White folks' wealth and ideology. I realize that during your military period there was much going on in terms of war, but your music and life are quite contrary to the images one has of a staunch patriot. Would you shed a little light on that for me?

LESTER: Well you see, that has nothing to do with training. You see the military is good just for the training. Plus, I had a ball. It was great. I wanted to get away from home. My choices were getting a job, go to college, or join the military. I ain't had to get no job yet. I ain't interested in having no job at all.

BEAU: I heard that.

LESTER: For me, the military was adventure, man; a motherfucker getting to go out on his own. I learned how to get that good pussy and out there fucking, drinking, and gambling and shit. I mean, I learned all the things in life that you be reading about but you don't get to do as a kid. All of a sudden I'm smoking cigarettes, weed, and stuff; plus I was the police, too. To me that was a whole lot more interesting than going to college. But I wouldn't been in there during Vietnam.

BEAU: You were so close to Mexico, did you play at all with Mexican musicians?

LESTER: No, didn't even take the horn down there. All we did down there was drink and fuck.

BEAU: How old were you when you got out of the military.

LESTER: Twenty-one. I was in there three years and seven months.

BEAU: So, with a lot of new experience under your belt, you headed back to St. Louis. Then what?

LESTER: Like I said before, being in the military taught me some discipline, 'cause before that I had no idea what I wanted to do. I learned about winning and losing, about a lot of things. So I got all that out of my system. I made my decision while I was in solitary confinement—I was already in jail—I got busted again while already in the jail, that's how I ended up in solitary confinement. Two weeks in what they call the black box. No light and just a slot where they slipped your food in. In this box is where I got my shit together, because I didn't have nothing to do but sit there and think.

BEAU: What was your total confinement time?

LESTER: It was around four or five months.

BEAU: So your initial beef was shooting at a White boy?

LESTER: It wasn't malicious or anything really, but this White boy from Tennessee took my seat in the TV room. So when I asked him about it, he came out of his southern bag: "Yeah I took your seat, so what," he says. Well, I ain't never been afraid of White folks. A lot of people [Blacks] got that fear built in, but I don't. So I grabbed him by the collar, pulled him down, pulled my gun, and fired off four or five shots right next to his head and said:

"Motherfucker if you ever think about saying some shit to me like this again, I'll blow your head off."

This cat was begging.

"Lester, please don't kill me."

So for that, they thought they was punishing me, but they was really helping me. It was another experience. I got to check out the appeal process, the lawyers, the jail time, and so on. Nice experience. And it was giving me resolve. I thought to myself, whatever I'm doing must not be that hip 'cause it's led to this black box, and I don't want to see no more of this box. Everything I thought I must have wanted to do was a mistake. So I decided to get serious and be a full-time pro in music. But I knew I didn't really play that well to be a pro. I wanted to be a Jazz musician, and I knew I didn't know enough songs or anything. So when I came out of the service I went to Lincoln University for a year in Jefferson City, Missouri. While I was there, I was also playing in a Blues band. I've played in Blues bands all my life. That's how I made my living. I'm a pro and wanted to work, and the Jazz gigs weren't paying nothing; I just did them for fun.

BEAU: You've got a real deep feeling and love from the Blues.

LESTER: Oh, yeah, I'm a Blues cat, actually. When I came back, I played with a cat called Jack Harris and the Invaders. We played the central Missouri Blues circuit.

BEAU: This is when you were at Lincoln?

LESTER: Yeah. Check this out. The head of the music department called me in one day about me playing with this Blues band. He says to me that as a student of Lincoln University's Music Department, he didn't feel that it was appropriate for me to be playing in a Blues band. I told him to kiss my motherfucking ass. I told him to get the fuck out my face 'cause I make my living playing this damn horn. And that I ain't no seventeen-year-old motherfucker just coming out of high school; don't tell me what the fuck I should be playing. He did get to me, and even at this time, I don't care too much for church people and scholarly types, people like that. There are some church people that I like personally, but what the Black church has stood for I don't agree with at all. These people, the educated people, the Black educators—these people shun the Blues. They call Blues "Devil's" music and bad. Well, the Blues is our deepest culture . . . these notes that the Blues singers is singing go back hundreds of years. And these are Black people that supposed to be educated, you dig, against the real Black music. To this day, I have mostly disdain for church people and the church philosophy and middle-class Blacks. I really don't like them kind of people at all. *Ebony* magazine type motherfuckers . . . you have to hold me back sometimes. I think these kind of people have done a lot to thwart the advancement of Blacks because they are anticultural. Anytime you take your own creation and say it ain't shit in lieu of some motherfucker that's playing Mozart or some shit. . . . The same cat at Lincoln once before wanted to expel me for practicing Coltrane. I was playing some diminished chords, you know. Then this cat fell up talking about that ain't your lesson.

BEAU: How long did you last at Lincoln?

LESTER: I was there for a year. But I was there for just one thing though. There was this great teacher there named Marshall, a trombone player. Ironically, he wasn't the head of the music department; he was the band director. He was a hell of an instrumentalist. The only reason I went was to take lessons from him, because I wanted to be a pro, so I knew I had to go into a period of intense playing. So I never went to classes, I never bought a book. I just went to my trumpet lesson and practiced twelve, fourteen hours a day. I did my gigs and that was it. I was really poor. Then I went to North Texas State for a year because they was supposed to be so hip in Jazz. A White-boy Jazz school. I learned how racist Jazz can be. These motherfuckers are down there studying Black music; you can degree in Black music down there, right, and Black people don't even like the stuff; and you got White folks in Texas offering the shit as a course you can get a degree in, and they got nerve enough to be racist down there—and they studying Black music. They see the benefits of it but still want to dog us. They don't want to give nothing up. So I went to school just to study and practice. I had no intention of ever finishing. I just wanted to get good enough to go on the road.

BEAU: So that was it, two colleges.

LESTER: That was it, good-bye. Then I started working with Albert King, Oliver Sain, and married my fist wife during that time.

BEAU: What was her name?

LESTER: Fontella Bass. She was singing with Oliver Sain at that time. '63, '64, around in there. Then I started working with Oliver.

BEAU: How many children did that marriage produce?

LESTER: Four. Two girls and two boys. And I got two more girls with Debbie, my current wife.

BEAU: After the hookup with Fontella and Oliver, how did y'all end up in Chicago.

LESTER: What happened was Fonnie [Fontella] started recording for Chess Records. Her and Bobby McClure had a record out called "Don't Mess Up a Good Thing." So she was working quite a bit around Chicago. Then after she made "Rescue Me" and that started moving pretty good, then we moved to Chicago. This was around '65.

BEAU: You wanted to be close to the studio?

LESTER: Yeah, and be close to the cash.

BEAU: Did you play on some of those Chess sessions with Fontella?

LESTER: Yeah. And after "Rescue Me," I became her musical director. That's when I really got a lot of experience leading bands. Now, by me being Fonnie's musical director, I got to be with a lot of different bands like Jackie Wilson's and Jerry Butler. If they wanted an extra horn, I'd just play. I had plenty of bread, so I wasn't worried about money.

BEAU: Was this a happy period for you?

LESTER: Oh, yeah, I've always been happy. I been happy all my life.

BEAU: You felt good about the music and the way you were growing—the transitions and changes.

LESTER: Yeah, shit, yeah, I was happy. I had a '51 classic Bentley, a motorcycle, a hip apartment in Chicago; I was plenty happy.

BEAU: When did you hook up with the AACM [Association for the Advancement of Creative Musicians] cats?

LESTER: Well, when I first came to Chicago I was doing a lot of sessions down at Chess. You know, jingles and other stuff. There were cats down there that later went on to become Earth, Wind & Fire. In fact, Maurice White was the studio drummer; a lot of cats were around in there then. But I was bored. So they had this cat to take me around. One day, he asked if I wanted to go to a AACM rehearsal; he said I wouldn't be bored. So Muhal Richard Abrams was having the rehearsal; man, I had never seen so many weird motherfuckers in my life . . . in one place. I said this is home here. As a musician, there's always a couple of dudes you hang with. But here was thirty or forty crazy motherfuckers all in one spot. I mean Roscoe Mitchell, Anthony Braxton, and Abrams; eccentric-type cats. So I made that rehearsal, and Muhal had me play a solo. Before I got home good, the phone was ringing. Cats calling up asking me to be in their band. Roscoe Mitchell, I hooked up with him. He had his own band, the Roscoe Mitchell Quartet. So this was fun, and it was a challenge. And I always wanted to be a Jazz musician. I was doing pretty good with what I was doing. So I didn't really need the bread; I could do what I wanted to do. You know, my old lady has a hit record out, and I was working. Shit, I was paying myself a salary. So when I got into the AACM, it was a real challenge. I always wanted to be more than just a studio musician. I wanted to be like Miles and Dizz and those cats . . . a professional Jazz musician.

BEAU: When was the transition made to the Art Ensemble of Chicago?

LESTER: Well, Roscoe already had a group that featured me. The Roscoe Mitchell Quartet featuring Lester Bowie. Then we decided to have equal contribution without featuring anybody's name. So we called ourselves the Art Ensemble. It wasn't until 1969 when we went to France that we became the Art Ensemble of Chicago. The French gave us that name, I guess, to differentiate us from other musicians. Then the name stuck.

BEAU: Was there any particular reason all of you decided to get up and go to France?

LESTER: Yes. We wanted to be professional musicians playing Jazz. Up until this point, I was a professional playing different types of gigs. One day over at Chess Records or with Fontella, the next day with the Art Ensemble or Jackie Wilson. We found that we had a unique style . . . a unique way of playing together, and we wanted to do that exclusively for our whole living. We felt the only way we could do that would be to pack up as a unit and start developing our concepts together, somewhere else. Since some people had expressed interest in us in France, and we had records out over there, and they were pretty popular, France was the natural choice. It turned out to be a good move. I sold all of my furniture and everything to help finance the

Interview with Lester Bowie 51

move. We moved over with money 'cause I had a lot of shit. We wasn't on no street corners; we had a beautiful crib in Saint-Leu-la-Forêt.

BEAU: Tell me about your arrival, the landing. That must have really been something.

LESTER: Oh, man. We came into France with a Volkswagen van full of instruments, and I had two kids with me at that time.

BEAU: Did you come on a ship?

LESTER: Yeah. Music life is a great time if you just go on and trust it. Yeah, we came on a ship. The captain found out we were musicians and gave us a place to practice. I mean, this trip was a gas. New York to Le Havre. This was the last sailing of the SS *United States*. And the staff was all Brothers; the kitchen, waiters, everybody. We hung with the crew, and we was probably the only Blacks on as passengers.

BEAU: Did you finance most of the trip?

LESTER: Yeah, but that then didn't bother me. It wasn't like taking a chance or anything. Anytime you take a band intact anywhere, you're going to work. You can take an intact band to the jungle or Siberia. They're gon' say, "Give them a gig." A Black band especially—anywhere in the world you can work. We were working within three days of hitting France. We were working three nights a week.

BEAU: How long did it take you to find a place to live?

LESTER: We stayed in a hotel about three days. Then we found a real estate agent, dropped a couple of thousand dollar bills on him, and boom, we was in business.

"Yes, monsieur, whatever you want." We got that big house in Saint-Leu.

BEAU: When I arrived in France at age twenty, I was wild-eyed and eager to swallow up as many new adventures and experiences as possible. I added a couple of new definitions to words like *wild, fun,* and *lush life*. How did y'all feel just being there?

LESTER: You always feel good finally doing what you want to do. We were finally playing the music that we like to play. We were having a ball; I mean, we having a ball—the cats were going crazy. Plus Paris was jumping then, too. The revolutionary thing was happening; political multiculturalism was happening. Then there's just the idea that we're over there making it. We supported our families, we had a nice house. We went over there with one truck and came back with four trucks. So without specific details of everything that happened . . . it was a great time. But we gradually got tired of it. We wanted to go home eventually.

BEAU: How long were you there?

LESTER: Two years.

BEAU: Through the vine, I heard y'all was having a rough time with the French at one time.

LESTER: Oh, yeah. One time the tax man confiscated all of our shit: trucks, instruments, everything. Then they had us in jail. But we got that rectified pretty quickly. Then we got kicked out of France once. Here's what happened:

There was a radio program about us on Radio Luxembourg. It was just about us. The show portrayed us as revolutionaries, damn-near Black Panthers; and by the way, they happen to live in Saint-Leu-la-Forêt. So the big boys in Saint-Leu were like, "What, they live here?" So the order to oust us came not from the police but from way up, some royalty. A lot of the land in France is still owned by royal families that have some clout. You know, dukes and duchesses. In reality, the other people come up under them: the mayors and police chiefs.

So this thing was like a movie. The next day after the broadcast, the police showed up at our door. Some inspector in a trench coat with a grimace on his face. He had two uniformed cats with him as backups. So our dogs had them stopped at the gate (that's from our military training). They told us if we didn't leave town, they would escort us to the border. Well were planning to hit the road the next day anyway, so their threat didn't make a difference.

BEAU: Hit the road like gypsies?

LESTER: Yeah, we were gypsies all that summer. We had all the equipment. Trucks, tents, stoves, heaters, everything. I had my family. We had police dogs. I tell you, we were ready. We stayed at campsites all over.

BEAU: Did y'all have some gigs lined up?

LESTER: Yeah, some, but we were out there on the road. Gypsies. You see there are so many things you can do collectively. I mean, we were living good out there. A couple of grand from a gig would go a long way. We lived in camps for the entire summer of 1970. We ended up in Sweden, then we moved on into hotels when it got too cold.

BEAU: So you must have had a good scouting thing happening?

LESTER: Oh, yeah. And the military training thing was key. Advance scouts would check out all kind of shit: gigs, food, people, etc. But like I said, if you got a band intact, you gon' get some gigs. How you gon' be a Black band, and ain't gon' get no gigs? Who in the world don't wanna hear no Black folks play no music? I don't understand why cats get scared to go on out there.

BEAU: Having lived and played in France, what are your impressions of the French people?

LESTER: Well, they're kind of doggish; not all of them, quite a few have personalities. I mean, most Europeans' background is one of wars and colonization of Africa. I mean really, they've dogged a lot of people. And they have this kind of presumed intelligence; they presume that they're really cultured. And they are in a certain sense, but in other ways they're really barbaric, crude. Most Western nations are like that. They didn't get to be big Western nations walking on roses or no shit like that. I mean, they became France by cutting off motherfuckers' heads.

BEAU: So after the gypsy adventures, were you stateside bound?

LESTER: Yeah, we headed back on a boat, an Italian boat. I believe it was the *Michelangelo*. With all the equipment and stuff, that was the only way we could travel. And I tell you, we had some great voyages on boats.

BEAU: Still, at the time of your return, the Art Ensemble did not have a name in the States. What was your game plan for developing your market and keeping the music together?

LESTER: Once we left Europe, we knew we could always work there. That's the way we set it up. We wanted to go back to the States because we wanted to be home. If we couldn't get no work, that didn't matter 'cause we would be home. But we knew we could work in Czechoslovakia or Warsaw or somewhere. We had set up a network. See, we approached this as world marketing for our music, not on just a local or national level, but worldwide. If you got your thing going internationally, you gon' work. You may have to go far, but you work. We have to go to Tokyo next week. We can't buy a gig in Chicago, but we have to go to Tokyo. So we set that up years ago. I just can't imagine living in those places, though. After awhile, it wears on you. Different country, different land. You have to talk slow to be understood. I mean, if you want to assimilate into their thing, like becoming French, that's another thing. To me it ain't no gas to be French. I like being an American Negro. I like that.

BEAU: You like being a blood.

LESTER: I *like* it.

BEAU: You've played a lot of music with countless groups and your own groups: Brass Fantasy, Roots to the Source, and others. Who would you like to be musically?

LESTER: I would like to be America's favorite trumpet player. Lester Bowie, a household word.

BEAU: You've had all kinds of times with money: lots of money, little money. What do you think of money?

LESTER: I like cash. It's not an end. It's like a tip, a little extra. Like I say, though, I have had fun. I can't remember a time when I was truly depressed. Money doesn't determine my success, although money is nice to have. I mean, I bought a Lexus, being me. I would never change who I am, though, to have some money. If I can't afford something I want, I'll just wait until I can.

BEAU: So you're not thrifty or conservative with money.

LESTER: No. I'm a spendthrift, actually. I waste a lot of money by normal standards. I could try to put the brakes on it, but I don't think of it as such. I spend a lot of money. I tip heavy, 'cause I know people that wait tables is working hard, too. Plus them heavy tips get you good service.

BEAU: Has your life been gratifying.

LESTER: Yeah, and that's the amazing thing. I'm a family man. You can manage all these things and still be a responsible citizen. The biggest and best thing I got going is my family.

BEAU: Want another cognac?

LESTER: Yeah.

BEAU: Would you make a final comment on the state of financial affairs of Blues and Jazz?

LESTER: I think some White performers ought to start paying royalties to Negroes. I think the motherfucking Rolling Stones ought to build a six-block recreational, cultural facility for Black folks on the West Side where they made their money from. I think all these White entertainers that have used Black music should pay some sort of royalties. The Rolling Stones need to go down to them joints with a basket of money and pass out a few million dollars. If they were really righteous, that's what I believe they would do. They've stolen a lot of music, but I don't want to just fault White people; I have to fault Black people, too. I mean, we just gave our shit away. I know what they've done . . . but we're stupid enough to let motherfuckers have the shit; in a sense you can't blame someone for using it.

BEAU: Lester, we have to continue this conversation soon. Thanks.

LESTER: Anytime, anywhere in the world . . . thank you.

September 1, 1990, Chicago
Lester Bowie,
October 11, 1941–November 8, 1999

INTERVIEW WITH BRUCE IGLAUER

L. "Chicago Beau" Beauchamp

As a tribute to Alligator Records' twentieth year and its founder, Bruce Iglauer, and as acknowledgment of the tenacity and dedication required to make any endeavor successful, I am pleased to have Bruce Iglauer share with our readers the Alligator story, his story, and his views on the music business.

BEAU: Bruce, it's nearly twenty years for you with Alligator?

BRUCE: Technically, in two weeks . . . no, three weeks. 1991 will be the twentieth year of Alligator. Well, the first release wasn't until August of '71, so, I don't know whether technically the first year starts in August or the first of the year. We're proclaiming 1991 our solid twentieth anniversary.

BEAU: Twenty years ago . . . or twenty years ago plus. What was going on in your life to make you decide that Alligator was something you wanted to do?

BRUCE: Well, I came to Chicago, actually, in the beginning of 1970 right after I finished college. And I came here because of the Blues. I was in college in Appleton, Wisconsin, but my family's from Cincinnati. I had been coming down on the weekends and hanging out at Jazz Record Mart, and Bob Koester was taking me out to hear Blues on the South Side and a little bit on the West Side. I became real fascinated with the scene, and when it turned out, courtesy of the draft lottery, that I wasn't going to be drafted and stopped worrying about that, I decided to pack up and come down here and be on the scene. I really didn't intend to start a label or even really to stay for any period of time, but I figured I'd go on and do graduate school.

BEAU: What was your major?

BRUCE: History of the theater. I really have no business background, I have no music background; in fact, I can't read music or play. I mean, *really* can't play an instrument. And, you know, I came down to Chicago, and Bob hired me as the single Delmark Records' employee. Delmark was run out of the basement in his store at that time. I was primarily the shipping clerk, but I also worked behind the counter in the store and, at that time, there was no Blues on the North Side and there were very few record companies doing much recording because Chess [Records] had been sold and was in the process of kind of being moved out of town and Vee-Jay Records was already bankrupt. It was a tough time for Blues on Black stations in town because it was sort of that period of time when there was sort of a move away from Blues, as it was kind of old-fashioned.

BEAU: We're talking what year now?

BRUCE: 1970. It was a little past the heyday. Everyone was gone. Mel Collins was doing a few things. And, uh, I mean there were little singles that would come out now and then, but it was really betwixt and between periods, so Delmark was, by the standards of the Blues scene, an active label . . . maybe releasing one or two records a year. So a lot of the musicians would come and hang out at Jazz Record Mart, partly to get noticed by the label and partly because fans came in and sometimes a gig would develop out of that. It was a bridge. It was a way that musicians could find a way to play outside of the ghetto club scene. And I was so fascinated by the scene that every time a musician would walk in, I was excited. Jimmy Dawkins was there a lot, Mighty Joe Young was there a great deal. Carey Bell was there. They were all either recording for, or about to be recording for, Delmark. But everyone would drop in. Big Joe Williams lived in the basement, sometimes for three, four, five months. He would come up from Mississippi and live there, just in the basement of the record store. I remember Little Brother Montgomery was there a lot, and Sunnyland Slim would come by. It was quite a little scene, and it was a tiny store.

BEAU: And what was the address of the store?

BRUCE: 7 West Grand. Two doors from where they are now at 11 West Grand. There was no back room, it was just the basement that was full of cockroaches and me, and the record store upstairs. It was kind of a dirty, grungy record store, but it was kind of a fabulous experience because I was a very naive guy and I was just thrown into this scene.

So I was working at Jazz Record Mart. I was hired to work part-time my first week. My first week was a sixty-hour week. And every night I was going out to the clubs. I had a little car that I had inherited from my mom, and I spent a lot of time at Theresa's. I was going to the clubs that Bob went to.

BEAU: Like Peppers?

BRUCE: Peppers on Forty-third, the Blue Flame on Oakwood. I used to go to Rose and Kelly's to see J. B. Hutto. I went to Walden's Corner a lot and the L & A on South Pulaski. And then little places like the Upstairs Lounge and the Sportsman's Lounge at Roosevelt and Central Park (they tried to kill me there). The One Step Beyond on South Kedzie, I remember that one well, because they *really* tried to kill me there. I almost took one step beyond. But I spent a lot of time at Theresa's, and Junior [Wells] took a liking to me, and he would arrange for me to avoid the fifty cent door charge, because I was making what I was making. I was making thirty dollars a week, that was my pay. I wasn't paid by the hour. But Bob bought me lunch.

BEAU: So I see you were really living nine inches to the Blues.

BRUCE: Yeah, well almost died. I was living in a one-room apartment in Uptown and having a wonderful time.

BEAU: How old were you at the time?

BRUCE: I'm 43 now, so I guess I would have been 23 then. I grew up, you know, in a comfortable middle-class household in the suburbs, and I was very protected. I went to a comfortable middle-class college, you know, with ivy and red brick and stuff, and I was very protected, and then I came to the South Side. It was a big education—and real fast.

BEAU: So was coming to Chicago and jumping into the Blues a real adventure for you?

BRUCE: It was an adventure, and I thought that all Blues musicians were gods that walked the earth. Now most of the White people that were hanging out on the scene knew each other, and most of us hung out at the Jazz Record Mart. Typically, with the exception of Theresa's and sometimes Pepper's, if I saw another White person in the club, I knew who it was. I mean, you didn't see strangers. And two or three of us would hang out and go out together, like Wesley Race, who is now the president of the Wichita Blues Society; Steve Tomachefsky, who worked at Delmark after I did; Jim O'Neal; Dick Sherman after he came back here. I think he was living in Seattle at the time.

It was all I had because, you know, I didn't have a TV. I had my stereo, records, little raggedy car, and I had the Blues scene; and that's all I did.

BEAU: So for you, and correct me if this is the wrong use of words, this kind of severance, let's say, and I don't know whether it was temporary, from your background and your culture was a severance in order to procure some kind of lasting and meaningful knowledge of another culture . . . in this case, this particular side of African American culture. This kind of severance, do you have any regrets about it . . . the way you lived, the conditions you lived in?

BRUCE: Oh, there were a couple of things. Well, first of all, it was an adventure and I was a hippy, if you like. I was just a real '60s college kid. I was involved in the antiwar movement, I was involved with the civil rights movement—nothing dramatic. I was always in the second line of people. I'd get hit by the eggs instead of the rocks. I mean, I wasn't an organizer, but I had that set of kind of late '60s kind of ideals. When I came to Chicago, I didn't really see that I was, like, slumming or anything; it was just kind of an adventure. But because I didn't see it as the way I was going to live forever, there wasn't a sense of any disappointment—it was exciting. It was exciting all the time. Every day was exciting. You know, when you come from a middle-class background, you know, if worse had come to worse, I could have run home to mommy. You know, realistically, it wasn't like living upstairs at Forty-eighth and Indiana and having nobody to fall back on. I always had my family to fall back on. So realistically, I didn't feel like I was having a terrible lifestyle; I felt like I was having a great lifestyle.

BEAU: So it was the price of an education of sorts?

BRUCE: Well, I didn't consider it a price. If I'd been making a good salary and driving a nice car, it wouldn't have been as much fun.

BEAU: If you come from a particular background and you want to interact with some other culture, nobody can fault you for the background you come from.

BRUCE: I've never tried to claim to be anything but White and middle class, you know. I was not trying to be, you know, what used to be referred to as a "White Negro." I wasn't trying to pass myself off as anything but a middle-class college kid from Cincinnati who was having a great time on the Blues scene.

BEAU: When did you decide that you may want to start recording people; what was your motivation?

BRUCE: Well, actually, when I went to work for Bob, after a few months I began dropping hints. I was his gofer at the studio, and I got to go to Junior Wells's sessions and Roosevelt Sykes's and Robert Jr. Lockwood's and Jimmy Dawkins's and a few others.

BEAU: So you didn't know anything about the music business. You were learning?

BRUCE: I was learning every moment. I was learning by what Bob did right and what Bob did wrong.

BEAU: And on the wrong tip?

BRUCE: Well, because, right after I came to work at Delmark, Bob's first child came. And he was already in his late thirties, he had never had a kid, and he stayed home a lot. So I ended up answering the Delmark phones and dealing with a lot of musicians. And besides hearing the nice things they had to say, I'd here the complaints. So I began to learn a lot of things from listening to musicians about how they perceived their careers and what they looked for from a record company. But actually, I had no intention of starting a label. I would have, at that point, been happy to have been at Delmark forever. I was just having a good time. But I really wanted to do something with myself. And originally, one of the reasons I had come to Delmark is I had promoted a Luther Allison concert at my college, and Luther and I got pretty friendly, and he was with Delmark. So that was part of my motivation, and I wanted to produce Luther. And a few months after I came there, Luther and Delmark and I all had a falling out where he severed his relationship with Delmark and put me right in the middle of it, and he created a lot of tension. I almost lost my job over it. And, frankly, Bob would have had a right to fire me, because I got confused on who I was really working for. I had a loyalty to Luther, and I should have had more of one to Bob since he was my boss. It all got involved with some papers Luther was supposed to sign. I was just the delivery boy, and Luther said he didn't want to sign them, and I said I better call Bob, and Luther said, "No, let's talk about it." And rather than extricating myself from the situation saying, "Bob, I've got a problem I can't solve," I let Luther drag the situation on until it was too late. When I came to work and didn't have his papers signed, Bob said, "What the hell's going on? Why didn't you call me?" and he was right, he should have fired me, but he was nice enough not to.

So, anyway, I became disenchanted. Luther Allison ceased to be a god who walked the earth for me and became a human being who was taking care of he rather than taking care of what I thought his priorities should be.

But meanwhile, I fell in love with Hound Dog Taylor and the Houserockers. I had met Hound Dog before I even came to Chicago. Eddy Shaw had a club on the West Side, on West Madison. I saw Hound Dog out there but not with his own band, and then I saw him again at Theresa's on a Blue Monday, but not with his own band, and it was always a disaster, nobody could follow him. He'd start a song and stop and laugh and tell some joke nobody could figure out; he would start another song and stop it, you know, and I thought, this guy's just a clown. He's funny and he's strange looking and he's obviously lovable, so people let him get up and screw around on the bandstand. But then he told me he had a gig down at Florence's on a Sunday after, and that was at Fifty-fourth Place and Shields, and I went down there and heard him with his own band and everything changed. They were so tight, and it was such an instinctive relationship where musicians work together. Just the three pieces, you know, no bass, just Hound Dog and Brewer Phillips on guitar and Ted Harvey on drums.

I kept going back and, you know, I'm a slide freak, I love slide guitar . . . always have. And it was so much fun, I really wanted to catch it on record, it was real important to me. It was my band. I felt like this was something that I had discovered, not in the sense that I had really discovered it, but nobody in the outside world, if you like, knew about this band. This was strictly a South Side situation or a West Side situation and, really, Hound Dog didn't play the upper level of clubs. He would play the places where the whole band got fifty bucks, or less. And he wouldn't play the clubs good enough to have liked a PA system; Florence's didn't have a stage or anything. They just moved a couple of tables and had these Sunday afternoon jams.

So I went to Bob Koester and I said, "You got to hear Hound Dog Taylor." Bob had never seen Hound Dog with his band, that was my understanding. And he kind of put me off; I mean, in a nice way, he told me he had other priorities. Of course, I wanted to produce it, too; that was part of my agenda, you know, I had my ego already involved, and I kept kind of badgering him about it and he kept putting me off.

Meanwhile there were a few of us, especially Wesley Race, who were as addicted to this band as I was. Wesley came to me one night while I was working behind the counter at the Jazz Record Mart. The store was open until nine at night and I was by myself. Wes and I were there just shooting the bull around, listening to records. And he said, "You know, I got a thousand dollars that I've saved up, and if somebody else would get involved, you know, I'd put up money for a record company." Like an idiot I said, well, I guess I could do it. And at the last minute . . . (I had inherited $2,500 from my grandfather that I had that I could do with as I pleased). At the last minute, Wes's father-in-law got ill, and they needed the money for some medical expenses, and so Wes had to pull out. But he was with me every step of the way in terms of what rehearsal we did, in the studio, and helping with liner notes, and, you know, he acted like he was my partner, but he couldn't put any money in, and so I was on my own.

And at that point, I didn't see, really, that I was going to have a career as a guy owning a record company and doing nothing else. I thought I'd keep working at Delmark and take care of this at night. I'll sell to these few little eclectic distributors who sell Blues records, the same ones that Delmark had, and I'll continue with my day job. And, part of the hidden agenda was, *I'll show Bob*. I'll make this a little bit of a success, and he'll see that he should have trusted me, and next time he will.

But it got away from me real fast. It became bigger and much more frightening to me than I had ever anticipated, and within eight or nine months after I put out that first record, Bob took me aside and said, "You've got to make a decision. You're coming in, and you're bringing your packages and doing your business, you know; it's like either you work for me or you work for you. But if you work for me, you gotta act like you work for me." And he had cut me a whole lot of slack in those months, and I said, well guess it's time. So in June of 1972, I went out on my own. I had only one record out, and I became self-employed . . . which I guess I've been ever since.

BEAU: So, uh, that's a good story. . . .
BRUCE: I've told that story before. In fact, you just got the short version.
BEAU: So, 2,500 bucks, energy and ingenuity and watching someone else do things that you didn't agree with and . . .
BRUCE: Well, some things I did agree

with. I mean I used a lot of the same distributors that Delmark had, and then I also knew that some of them weren't big enough and powerful enough. So I went out searching out stronger ones. And I also knew that there was this progressive rock radio that existed for a little window of time between 1969 and 1972 or '73, and they would play some Blues to rock-and-roll fans. And Bob wasn't reaching those people, so I targeted those people.

BEAU: Your direction varied greatly from Bob's?

BRUCE: Yes. I wanted to sell records to people very much like myself, and Bob was not in touch with, if you like, what we call the sixties generation, and I was. I knew that kind of radio, I knew the rock-and-roll press: *Rolling Stone, Cream,* a few things like that. And I also got involved real early in booking. Kind of because I had to and because my bands needed to work, and there wasn't anybody to represent them. I discovered very early that Hound Dog didn't know how to negotiate, he didn't know distances. Hound Dog was functionally illiterate, I mean, who knew a great deal—he had lived for fifty-five years—but he didn't know how far it was to Des Moines, Iowa, or how to figure out what to get paid there or how to book a motel room in advance. He didn't have a bank account to deal with the front money and deposits, and so I drifted into booking and management. It was really by default, but somebody needed to do it.

BEAU: That's how you created a situation out of a situation.

BRUCE: Well, you know, people look at Alligator now. We have a hundred Blues records and a few other things as well. And they think that there was like this big plan. And it really isn't true at all. I was kinda like making it up as I go along... a lot of it.

BEAU: You are in a sense synergized with another culture. What kind of responses do you get from White people?

BRUCE: Well, people ask me how I feel about being a White person and a Jew (though not a religious one) dealing primarily with Black musicians and whether this has caused a conflict for me. And how I feel about White people's appreciation of music. And frankly, it's never been a real big issue for me. I can feel this music, and I don't expect that I feel the music in the same way that I would feel it if I had lived in the South or if I were Black. I'm not dealing with the realities of being an African American, you know, which are not always such fun realities. Blues is an art form; if it communicates, it's got to communicate outside of its own culture, and that it does.

Communicate differently, perhaps, but communicate nonetheless. It's never really been any source of conflict for me, I've never spent a lot of time saying, you know, asking myself if I am some sort of hypocrite or something like that. Perhaps if I was getting rich and the musicians weren't, you know, I would feel that there were someway somebody could fault me. But the fact is that I'm living adequately, and I'm pleased to see that at least some of the artists that have recorded for me, as a result of it, or partly as a result of it, are living significantly better than they were living before. I'm very proud of the fact that Koko Taylor just moved into a lovely new house in Country Club Hills and paid for it.

BEAU: Paid cash for it?

BRUCE: They wouldn't give her a mortgage because of the rates. But Koko picked cotton; I think she finished the third grade. She's had a rough time. There's somebody working on a documentary of Koko, and she said, you know, she spent a lot of her life, as she put it, down on her knees but not praying, you know, scrubbing White folks' floors. And Koko, you know, talks about the work ethic. I work hard, but Koko Taylor works *real hard,* and, you know, she's earned every bit of that. And I'm very proud that I was able to be the bridge for her, and I'd like to be more of that. That makes me feel real good, to see that she's secure and her family's secure.

BEAU: Well, there are many stories of unsavory dealings with Jazz and Blues artists by record companies. Certainly all are not as well intentioned as you.

BRUCE: Well, I think that there have been people in the record business who have been taken advantage of. I think that there have been many, many more people who have lost their shirts in the record business. It's an easy business to lose money in. And a lot of artists, frankly, want to believe that their records did better than they actually did, and it hurts the ego to think that you put out your creative effort, put your whole life on a record, and not a whole lot of people buy it. Beyond that, there are a great number of people, in the old days and even now, that I think just don't understand and choose to do that. Just because someone's not well educated doesn't mean that they don't have good judgment. You know, it's easy enough to consult somebody about a contract, about a piece of business, and it's easy to say no. People have said no to me, I mean, I've approached artists who have said, "Sorry, I'm not interested." And I respect them for that, even though I think, in some cases, people make poor decisions about their careers; that's their decision, it's their life. And I look back at, like, Chess, and I wasn't around for Chess (they were just winding down when I got here). I don't know anything about their business except all the stories I have been told. But I do know that the royalty rate in Chess's contracts was the very same royalty rate that the White rock-and-roll people were getting at that time, 5 percent of 90 percent. Very low by today's standards, but very normal by the standards then.

BEAU: Five percent of 19 percent?

BRUCE: Of 90 percent. The 90 percent still shows up on contracts because it's based on breakage in 78s in transit. It's another little thing, you know, you negotiate. It sounds like a lousy royalty now, but it was the norm then—big artists got it, too. Beyond that, as to whether the accountings were straight, I have no way of knowing. But one of the things artists seem to tend to forget is, and I wasn't really intending to talk about this tonight, generally, if an artist is under contract with a label, all of the expenses of recording are recoupable against royalties. Which means that, if you hire sidemen, run up a big studio bill, and nothing comes of the session, either the producer decides it isn't good enough, the label decides it isn't good enough, or the performance just isn't good enough, or somebody doesn't show up, or somebody shows up drunk—or the music doesn't come together for whatever reason—those costs are charged against the artist's royalty account. So, for example, you look at the books they have of these Chess sessions, and you see a Little Walter session where eight sides are cut but nothing was released; well, I don't know why nothing was released, but I do know that that session was charged against Little, that that session was charged against Little Walter's royalty account, and that's proper because the artists get advances against those royalties, so all the risk ultimately does fall on the labels. I'm not 100 percent sure all those old record men really ripped those artists good and proper, I'm sure they were smart businessmen who played the game the way everyone was playing it then. But as to whether Chess treated their artists worse than CBS, I really don't know. I know it's easy to accuse.

BEAU: I've never heard a negative comment about Alligator's dealings.

BRUCE: As far as our reputation, I stand on my royalty statements. And, you know, I've got stacks and stacks of checks, I'm just in the process of finishing paying out over $200,000 in royalties for this six-month period, some of them to publishers and some to artists. I'm late, and I still owe yet another $62,000, and that's where I'm trying to scrape up the money. I still owe artists and publishers money and I'm embarrassed that I owe them, but I'm very proud of the fact that, as far as I can tell, every penny is in place and everybody's getting what they earn. And I've even raised some of those old royalty rates without being asked to, because I felt, I guess I felt guilty. Hound Dog's original royalty rate was 5 percent of 90 percent. That's what everyone was paying in 1970. Hound Dog's records ought to earn that and more because I decided that it wasn't fair, not because Hound Dog's ghost or anybody else came.

But, you know, I try to run a pretty clean business. It's probably been one of the reasons the company's remained small. For example, Chess found ways to scrape up enough money to hand money to DJs under the table and over the table. I don't do that. Maybe if I did that, I'd get more airplay, but I'd have to find the money somewhere, and I'd have to find it in cash. I do my business with checks, so everything is traceable. I don't know where I'd scrape up thousands of dollars in cash, except selling records for cash, which means the sales wouldn't be recorded anywhere and the artists wouldn't get royalties. So I don't do that kind of thing, but, you know, I didn't get into this business thinking I'm gonna get into the record business to make a lot of money. I got into this business because I'm a fan and because I heard musicians that ought to be recorded. I didn't get into this business to go broke, but I didn't go into it thinking how I can make the largest sum of money for myself. As you can see, this is my home, it costs me $21,000 fifteen years ago. It was a wreck. I don't have a family; I don't have any dependents except a cat. I live in promotional T-shirts and jeans. I don't need a lot of money, and if I had more money, I wouldn't change my lifestyle. I mean, there are a couple of things I'd like to do, but not much. But what I really wanted to do was make records. And I am making records. Living out my dream. It's not like I'm climbing on a cross or something. Sure. I'd like it if I could pay my bills more easily, but I'm usually the happiest guy in the world because I had a dream and I got to live it. Like a little kid that dreams of being a cowboy, and the next thing you know he's on a horse and there's some cows. I had a dream of running a Blues record company. . . . I got to live it. How many people get to live their dream out?

BEAU: Not many. Not many dare to dream, as a matter of fact.

BRUCE: Well, it was a much smaller dream than that.

BEAU: What do you say now when, for the bulk of your twenty years, you and a few others from various parts of the country, and Europe, have been pretty much the spine of Blues recording? And now there's a big surge in popularity, and all of the sudden, bigger companies are buying out smaller Blues labels and signing artists they never thought of a couple of years ago.

BRUCE: Well, every few years it seems as though the major labels (the ones that own their own distributing companies and therefore can reap more profit per unit, or as I call it, records, they call it units) get interested in some form of roots music, be it in Blues or in the sort of progressive Country thing that was happening for a while or a World Beat or Reggae. And they come in and they pick artists who are amongst the most popular in the field and they try to develop them, and every once in a while they succeed, as they did (at least for a moment) with Robert Cray. But mostly what happens is the sounds of the music get co-opted by mainstream rock and rollers and the people who created the music or are part of the tradition go back to whatever their respective community is and go back to playing within that community. I look at what happened to Reggae, where one or two people have roots from Jamaica and everybody else ended up basically playing for peanuts. And it became a cult theme. The same thing has happened with a lot of the Country artists who they thought would cross over to the mainstream and really haven't. And I'm very pleased for Robert Cray, he's a friend of mine, he's a really good guy, he worked really hard, paid a lot more dues than most people did. I'm very pleased with the success that John Lee Hooker's had, although I would be even more pleased if John Lee had had that success without every rock-and-roll star in the world sitting in on that record. It would be nice if people appreciated John Lee Hooker for what he is. But he runs with fast company, and, you know, they're trying to make the same record over again or make another one.

BEAU: With who?

BRUCE: I'm not sure who all. I haven't seen the list of guests. But I know that they're doing the same thing with bringing in a lot of guests. And I'm not sure they can repeat the formula, because I wish people would buy a John Lee Hooker record because it was a John Lee Hooker record. And I look at B.B., who, I'm told by a fairly good authority, MCA would drop as an artist because his sales are very disappointing. But it would be such a bad PR move that if they cut loose the king of the Blues. But the fact is, B.B. isn't selling records by their standards. I would love to have his "nonsales"; those numbers would appeal to me. But those companies are set up to sell hundreds of thousands of units, and if they don't sell hundreds of thousands of units, they drop artists.

Now my stable has been raided a little bit by this new subsidiary of Charisma, which is a subsidiary of Virgin, which is distributed by Warner Brothers, called Point Blank, and they signed Kinsey Report and Albert Collins. Both of whom, let me emphasize, both of whom they signed, nobody jumped contract, OK. I had a two-record deal with the Kinseys, and they made their two records, and did a real good job with it. And with Albert we never had more than record-to-record deals. I never sat down and put a multiple-record deal on paper; we had an understanding, I thought. But, legally speaking, he had every right to do what he did. My best guess is, and by the time we see this publication we'll know, that this company won't succeed. And I think they won't succeed with Albert Collins because mainstream rock-and-roll radio is not going to play records by middle-aged Black Blues guitar players. No matter how much they may sound like what's on the rock-and-roll stations, they still are middle-aged and Black, and how many middle-aged Black artists get played on rock and roll in any field of music? *Zip!*

The Kinseys certainly have a better chance. They're younger, they're good-looking; they're a band rather than one guy and some sidemen. But the record hasn't happened in England. And they've got Larry McCray under contract from Detroit, who is really an unknown artist here. I haven't even heard of him, but they say he's quite talented. I know the numbers they need to see, the numbers of sales they need to see in order to consider this a profitable venture, and I think they're going to have a hard time seeing it. And I suspect that all those artists will be back with independently distributed labels within a year. But the artists need to find out. And they need to be satisfied that they had a shot, and it did happen. If it does happen, bless their hearts, I'll sell a bunch of their old records.

BEAU: So you're right there where you're supposed to be—dream and all intact.

BRUCE: Yeah, I'm still living out my dream.

BEAU: Thanks for your time; this has been an extremely informative interview. Thanks again.

BRUCE: My pleasure.

December 11, 1990, Chicago

A FEW WORDS FROM A CHICAGO BLUES MAMA

Deitra Farr

Deitra Farr in Playa del Carmen, Mexico, during the 1994 Straight Ahead/*OCBA* Blues Cruise. Photo by L. Beauchamp.

There are more than eighteen women singing the Blues in Chicago today. Our voices sell watches (Zora Young for Timex); newspapers, dog food, and pizza (Valerie Wellington for the Chicago Tribune, Pizza Hut, and Kibbles & Bits); detergent (Barbara LeShore for Cheer); and cars (Gloria Hardiman for Nissan). They've even got my face on a bank advertisement (Mid-Town Bank).

However, the Blues field in Chicago and elsewhere remains male-dominated, and Blueswomen don't get the respect they desire and deserve. While Blueswomen are a hot commodity with the advertising industry, we are still viewed as something separate and apart from Bluesmen.

I find the greatest problem for the Blueswoman is being taken seriously. Blueswomen are usually hired as *special guests* to spice up the Bluesmen's shows or lumped together on Ladies Sing the Blues shows. Few Blueswomen front their own bands for various reasons. It is difficult for a man to hold a Blues band together, so it is extremely difficult for a woman to do so.

Like in other fields, many men resent being led by a woman. Many club owners are uncomfortable doing business with a woman as well. It requires a special toughness and sheer will for a woman to fight and make her way in the Blues field.

When a woman does put a band together, many people find it hard to believe that she is in charge. I've had many experiences with audience disbelief. During my shows, audience members wanting business cards or information usually ask one of the men in the band for it. They seem very surprised when the guys tell them to "talk to the boss lady." I'm often asked if I'm married to or dating anybody in the band.

I have chosen to deal with the headaches of being a band leader so I can be totally heard. Being in control of the bandstand is very important to me. I still have nightmares about singing for other people and then being drowned out by the band and having my songs ruined. Many Blueswomen have nodes on their vocal cords from singing with other people's bands.

Much has been written about the early Blueswomen, such as Ma Rainey and Bessie Smith, but little is known about the lives of modern Blueswomen. With the growing popularity of "Queen of the Blues" Koko Taylor, that appears to be changing. Recently PBS-TV did an hour-long tribute to Koko Taylor. I've often wondered about the lives of Blueswomen Big Mama Thornton and Big Maybelle, but they are usually not mentioned or mentioned only in the history books.

It is possible we know so little about Blueswomen because they tend to have short careers. Some like Alberta Hunter retire to live a "normal life," only to return in later years. I believe motherhood is one of the main reasons Blueswomen give up their careers. To make a decent living playing the Blues, it usually requires lots of touring. It can be very difficult or impossible to leave your children behind. Before I became a mother, singer Gloria Hardiman asked me to possibly do a few road gigs for her. She didn't want to leave her small children. She later decided to "leave them in the hands of the Lord" and go on the road.

I had trouble even before my child was born. While in Atlanta, Georgia, preparing for my Friday-night gig, I started to hemorrhage. An ambulance took me to the hospital, where I was told I was threatening miscarriage. The doctor told me not to perform and to have complete bed rest. Well, the club owner hit the roof. He had "important" people there to hear me sing. He didn't seem to care if I lost my baby singing the Blues for his *important people.*

I've often wondered what a Blueswoman can do to become more successful. The Ladies Sing the Blues shows magnify some of the problems we have. I've witnessed women on these shows almost come to blows over a song. There are a million Blues songs, but it never fails for at least two women to lay claim to the same song. What usually happens is they both end up doing the song, to the audience's dismay. This happens because some Blueswomen don't take their careers seriously enough. They sing the songs they hear other women doing, so you end up with a lot of women with the same repertoire. As Blues artists, we've got to become more serious and creative if we want to be taken seriously by others.

I feel that "Queen of the Blues" Koko Taylor has been an excellent role model. She has been most supportive toward other women in Blues. Most of us can recall her telling us to hang in there. She has hung in there a long time, and she deserves all the attention and financial benefits she is finally receiving. It is a lot easier, however, to hang in there when you've got a support system. Most Blueswomen aren't so fortunate. Koko was lucky to have her husband, the late Pops Taylor, in her corner for so long. Few women in any industry have been lucky enough to have a husband so interested in their careers. I have fond memories of seeing Pops right there with Koko, trying to make her job easier.

My experience as a Blues singer lies mostly in Chicago, but recently I went on tour in Italy. I was treated very differently there. People there respected me as a legitimate

Blues artist, and they were very interested in what I had to say. After that experience, I could understand why Blueswomen Angela Brown and Jean Carroll moved to Europe. Recently, the Blues field has been receiving more national attention, but I don't feel Blueswomen have received enough of that attention. Last year, I personally chastised a TV host for devoting his entire show to Blues yet not including one woman. With the exception of Koko Taylor, it does seem that White women who sing the Blues, such as Bonnie Raitt and JoAnna Conners, have benefited the most from this latest Blues explosion.

I feel sad knowing that in Chicago most Blueswomen remain undocumented, unrecorded, and unemployed. I feel the Blues audiences are being cheated because they aren't getting enough of what Blueswomen have to offer. Ironically, it was a woman, Mamie Smith, who recorded the first Blues record.

While it is difficult for Blueswomen to be successful, our numbers continue to increase. In Chicago, with its reputation as "home of the Blues," many Blueswomen from elsewhere come here. One woman arrived in Chicago from Kansas City because some musicians had told her she could make it big here, but to her surprise it wasn't so easy to compete. Before long, she was singing "Kansas City, here I come."

She didn't even say good-bye.

THE BLUES AESTHETIC
Kalamu Ya Salaam

maybe the easiest way to define the blues (and by extension, the blues aesthetic) is to define what it ain't.

the blues ain't slave music-didn't no slaves sing the blues (cf. *Looking Up at Down: The Emergence of Blues Culture*, by William Barlow, Temple University Press, 1989, for a good general history on the blues as a music form). we didn't become blue until after reconstruction, after "freedom day" and the dashing of all hopes of receiving/attaining 40 acres & 1 mule.

in essence the blues aesthetic is the cultural manifestation of former slaves expelled from the land, promised a new land, and ultimately, and callously, turned into an easily exploitable surplus unskilled and semiskilled, migratory, landless, politically unenfranchised labor pool. even when we left the plantations under what we thought was our steam, it was really an expulsion from the slave agrarian/plantation society into the emerging urban/industrial society. our so-called great migration should be seen specifically for what it was: mass urbanization.

this social process, this dispossession of the formerly possessed, set the stage for the two basic blues (music) forms: i.e., country and urban. in this case the labels accurately say it all. on the plantation our enslaved ancestors sang work songs, field hollers, chants, remembered and retained (often in a transformed state) african songs, colored variations of eurocentric music, but not no blues. first, on the southern roads moving from work camp to work camp, farm to town, town to city, and then, in the slaughterhouses and firestorm ovens (mills & foundries), etc. of the cities (both down- and up-south) is when and where we got the blues.

the blues is not african—samuel charters dedicated many years trying to chase down the african roots of the blues, the savannah heat laughed at him. bits and pieces of pre-blues forms floating in the night were carried to his ear on the wind, but he never found the song, not to mention the singer. although certain african elements (including scales and instrumental/vocal techniques) are undeniable, west africa simply did not have the social basis to give rise to a blues vision. west african colonialism, although far from culturally benign, wasn't even a sound check compared to the magic act of how africans became negroes in the u.s.a. melting pot. some of us, out of a real ignorance of what went down, underestimate the transformational force of slavery -> civil war -> reconstruction -> jim crow, but we ignore this unique historical development at the cost of rendering all our theories about black folk, blues aesthetic, etc. null and totally void.

no other people, except african americans created the blues, not even other africans enslaved other places in the western hemisphere. other african peoples in the western hemisphere went from agrarian slavery to some strained (and, of course, de facto fraudulent) form of urban industrial integration that generally lacked the obsessive racial segregation shown out in 99 percent of america—the "strange" (in american terms) racial reality and climate of black-creole-white/english & french new orleans vis-à-vis the rest of white-black/english-speaking america offers a homegrown comparison of caribbean and america racial mores and demonstrates our thesis about the difference between african americans in the u.s.a. and african americans elsewhere in the western hemisphere.

some day we will speak on the puritanism of the north combining with the racialism of the south and the effect of this combination on blues people, but, at this juncture, we simply note that any objective reading of comparative history will document the u.s.a. invented apartheid under the rubric of national democracy with social segregation. just in case you are wondering why there is a link between twentieth-century black south african culture and african american blues culture, the similarities are more than surface, but that, too, is another point for another time—however, less you miss the critical point, apartheid is nothing but the logical progression of racially based economic exploitation (u.s.a. "slavery -> sharecropping and segregation" / south africa "colonialism -> apartheid") facilitated, in both cases, by the rapid change of an agrarian-based society into an industrial/urban society.

while i am fully aware there are other factors, those factors supplement but do not substitute for the economic/political basis, not because economics/politics always takes the lead, but rather because the basic shape of america was enforced by those who put economics/politics in the lead, for those "conquerors," racial genocide and racism seemed sensible, logical, and a mandate from god, who after all had blessed these "christians" with the wisdom and strength to conqueror the savage red & black pagans.

within that context, it is obvious that what we are dealing with is not even just a music form/aesthetic, although it is mainly in the music that the blues aesthetic has most often been recognized by non-blues people, perhaps simply because of the comparative uniqueness of this music that is impossible to confuse or misclassify, especially when heard in juxtaposition to any eurocentric music. however, the mere thought that "the blues" is mainly music is ipso facto a grossly eurocentric misconception based partially on an inability to perceive african americans as having a self-defined total culture that includes abstract aesthetic considerations and mundane manifestations in everyday life as well as classical manifestations in archetypal artistic creations.

recognized or not, the fact is: blues people manifest a blues sensibility. after two or three generations, that manifestation gets culturally codified into an aesthetic that shows out in everything done, not just in the music, even though non-african american observers of african american culture have a hard time recognizing anything but the music. african american culture in general, and blues culture in particular, is literally a mystery to most americans, comprehended on roughly the same level as ancient egyptian sacred architecture and dogonian cosmic worldviews (both of which, need i add, are far more hip than the average, or exceptional, for that matter, american university in both physical representation and philosophical essence).

if i were to describe the blues aesthetic in culturally consistent terms, i would wittily use a metaphor such as, say, the blues is running a downtown, no trump, boston when life has dealt you nothing but low cards (and we all know bid whist is a game of chance, daring, improvisation, and skill all rolled into one, unlike bridge where bidding skill and strategy minimize the chance distribution of the cards).

our people's aesthetic, post-reconstruction and pre–civil rights, was concentrated on dealing with the hand life dealt us, which was generally disappointing and usually negatively disproportionate in its distribution of winners. i am saying that anything that individuals do, if it reflects their peoplehood, then it is best understood not simply as an individual act but rather usually reflects and is projected from the day-to-day living conditions of that people, culture, our public school education not to the contrary, is not the story of how "great individuals" created specific aesthetics (& artifacts) and/or ideologies (& social systems)—also, please note, we people of color prefer aesthetics to ideology, life is more interesting and fulfilling that way, thank you.

i further maintain that the end of a mass espousal of the blues aesthetic as the basic framework of the african american working class is marked by the wholesale acceptance of integration as a desirable goal by the african american working class and the concurrent destruction of our working-class economy—in other words, after reconstruction we developed a goods-and-services infrastructure that lasted until we abandoned concentrating on being/developing ourselves for the (dis)illusion of being/developing ourselves into others (an other that was often antithetical to the blues self).

but as with any good dialectic, in the process of moving toward/becoming like them, the contact with the other in turn drew the others to move toward/become like us. in fact, the very elements in the eurocentric community who were attracted to blues people were those elements that often represented the "repressed" currents of europe, those currents that were often branded as "primitive" and/or "permissive." it is no accident that most of the social background of whites who are heavy into the blues mainly includes jews, appalachian dispossessed drifters, second/third-generation eastern european descendants, and whites who philosophically gravitated toward non-christian currents of european thought. but, again, all of that is an aside from the focus herein under consideration.

unlike, slavery, segregation did not rule out the development of a black-controlled indigenous economy peopled in the main by black professionals and artisans and that provided the base support for african american society as a whole and was also glued together by our people's general desire for self-improvement that, of course, had a political vector. hence marcus garvey's unia—a blues organization if you will—really more blues (although it called itself "Negro") than african, notwithstanding the fact that it was quickly dubbed a "back to africa" movement, which, check it, is a natural categorization. wasn't no integrationists going to be even thinking (either figuratively, aesthetically, or literally) about going back to africa. witness: non-blues-based harlem renaissance poets *literally* psychologically recrossed the atlantic but turned north instead of south and took boat rides to europe (often paris, where the jazz age was in vogue, and the cubists had discovered africa, so these negro wannabe poets are running to study real culture from artists who are themselves busy studying africa and being attracted to sophisticated and/or authentic africans—talk about contradictions within contradictions).

fortunately, pathology is a different discipline from aesthetics, and we need not concentrate on deviance at this moment. there are a number of central elements of the blues aesthetic and a number of key manifestations. listed below is a condensed and simplified codification of the blues aesthetic.

the chief manifestations are:

1. *stylization of process,* i.e., whatever blues people did, it was done with a style that emphasized the collective tastes and at the same time demonstrated the individual variation on the collective statement, which is, of course, based in call/response but might more accurately be

identified as theme/variation, which if you know the history of the music, marked the movement from agrarian -> communal forms, to urban -> collective. for those who are wondering, the basic difference is that the communal form required the audience, in the collective form the artists became their own audience, and the audience moved from communal participant to observer of the collective, from proactive participant to quasi-passive observer, from ritual to entertainment. of course, none of this is absolute, but there was a shift that can be stylistically traced through the music if one cares to do so.

2. the *deliberate use of exaggeration* to call attention to key qualities (qualities to be upheld or dismissed; i.e., the "hip" or the "triflin'"; the ordinary is, of course, beneath contempt), with "wit" being one of the most salient projects of exaggeration, since humor is essentially nothing but an exaggeration of reality in order to make a point (you ever wondered why some people miss a joke that is really obvious? the reason is, if you don't know the reality you can't appreciate the joke precisely because the joke is a comment on the reality).

3. *brutal honesty* clothed in metaphoric grace, which included at its core a profound recognition of the economic inequality and political racism of america and, at the same time, a profound appreciation of the fact that every strength got a "weakness" and that it is better to recognize (and sometimes even ridicule) rather than cover up weaknesses.

4. *acceptance of the contradictory nature of life.* life was both sweet and sour, and while generally you had a pot of the latter, most everybody was guaranteed at least a spoonful of the former (here one must be careful not to confuse dualism with dialectics; life is not about good versus evil but about good and evil eating off the same plate).

5. an *optimistic faith in the ultimate triumph of justice* in the form of karma (what is wrong will be righted, what is last will be first, balance will be brought back into the world). this faith was often co-opted by christianity but is essential even to the most "downtrodden" of the blues songs.

6. *celebration of the sensual and erotic elements of life,* as in "shake it but don't break it!"

the chief cultural manifestations are: (1) country & city blues, (2) jazz, (3) african american fashion, (4) the orality tradition, (5) popular black dance, and (6) african american cuisine.

a brief aside: some say that music was "the strongest" rather than simply "the most well-known" manifestation of the blues aesthetic—to the degree that that assertion is true, it is because music was the least concrete, the most ephemeral, and therefore the least subject to inspection by outside forces, and thus the least subject to oppression. you see then that slavery would not allow a blues culture to manifest itself; that is why the blues aesthetic is post-reconstruction, and similarly, once a decision was made by the masses to try "integrating" into the american cultural mainstream, the blues aesthetic ceased to be the dominant mode of cultural expression precisely because it was not only not like the mainstream, it was often anti-mainstream in the clash of values and indexes of beauty.

while there are certainly other elements and manifestations, this brief overview will serve to keep our eyes on the prize and to help us understand why the blues seems to have fallen on hard times; i.e., why and when did blues people stop liking the blues? this viewpoint also implicitly suggests the value of a blues aesthetic in a postindustrial age—but the key question is where are the masses of our people headed? that's not an easy question to answer because right now we are in a period of rapid transition, fissure, and dispersal; i.e., we don't even live together as a people (the forces of integration are centrifugal by nature).

the integrationists, led by the ultracorrupt negro politicians (most of whom attain status without substance, and even when they do have some stroke they generally end up in a masturbatory posture) and the ultraimpotent athlete/entertainer (in the show business of sports and entertainment, we are nothing but the "show," often well paid for a brief period but always expendable for the next two-, three-, four-year sports/music icon). these two most visible categories of nationally recognized, high-profile black leaders have run their version of the american dream road show into the ground. at the same time, the political activists, the nationalists and leftists (two sides of the same coin sometimes), are ideologically bankrupt and devoid of major influence in inner-city america (which is not to say that there is no political struggle going on, but which is to say that all of it is either very local and lacking a national profile or else has no real currency among the masses). blues people are in search of a direction. that is why there is so much confusion manifesting itself as criminality and anarchy in the community—there is no community.

if we ever had the blues (in a simplistic, but not altogether inaccurate, sense), we gots it now, and now more than ever we need culture to give some direction and, hence, some hope to what appears to be a rather hopeless situation.

there is more, but you can't swallow but one mouthful at a time.

I, THE BLUES

L. "Chicago Beau" Beauchamp

I am every bright moment that
    Sonny Boy played.
I am the sparkle in every eye that
    ever saw him.
I am those who loved him but
    didn't know him;
and those that he loved.
I am the trapped ghost of black
    on black
death dilemma.
I am murder needlessly,
I am the Blues of ex-slavery.

I am nepethean indoctrination
from the seat of Christianity.
I am Islam in chains
in the holding pens of Gorée.
Yet, I am misery transformed;
in Sunday's tabernacles I am
the proclaimer of Apocalypse coming.
I am religion forsaken to keep my
children with me.
I am the Blues and hope of the
    sanctuary.

I am street life;
land of whoremasters and chili
    pimps.
I am Baby Bell, the whores' mystic,
who cut out his own soul
and served it on a platter of hot
    buttocks
to gawking, self-aggrandizing,
    aspirants
of whorecraft.

I am a 38-caliber self-inflicted death
sentence for partaking in pristine
    demons
turned inside out.
I am love for sale sold out,
I am Blues of the night.

I am idiolectic metaphors
written by illiterate hands;
master of lyrics with rhythm
as my mistress.
I am Gussie Williams shouting,
"You never shoot your pistol off
in my back yard.
Try me out and you will see.
You can have your coffee mornings,
that'll be all right,
but I've got to have hot sausages,
each and every night."

Yes, I am Muddy Waters, Ida Cox,
    Bessie Smith,
Howlin' Wolf and Maceo.
I am enough legends to fill the
    Great Wall
I am the unbridled intensity of
Black people's creativity.

I am the millions of African progeny
on whom the sun will never set.
I am the peace of Uhuru
and curator of my culture so widely
dispersed. I am the art of life,
I am Blues, I am Negritude.

FROM THE *ORIGINAL CHICAGO BLUES ANNUAL*

Issue Number 4

OCBA went through a transition with issue number 4. It went from a matte paper presentation to a glossy enamel paper stock that changed the entire look and feel of the magazine. We opened a satellite office in Milan, Italy, and Famoudou Don Moye accepted the position of vice president of international affairs.

There were stellar contributions from photographer Barbara Barefield and poet Julie Parson. We paid tribute to Katherine Dunham, matriarch of African American dance, and I had a "straight from the gut" conversation with Blues elder Junior Wells.

We coproduced the first annual Sardegna Blues Festival in Sardinia, and I secured the sponsorship of Italy's national airline, Alitalia.

In many ways, issue number 4 was how I had originally visualized *OCBA*.

INTERVIEW WITH JUNIOR WELLS
L. "Chicago Beau" Beauchamp

Junior Wells is a man of conviction, insight, and concern for his culture. He has traveled the world spreading the good news of the Blues for three decades. He is one of Black music's greatest songwriters and performers. Let us listen to the "Up in Here" wisdom and experiences of Junior Wells.

BEAU: Junior . . .

JUNIOR: Yeah, baby.

BEAU: Junior, I know you're probably still feeling sadness and pain about the recent accident your band was in, where one person got killed.

JUNIOR: Yeah.

BEAU: What are your feelings about the road, travel conditions, and what your cats went through?

JUNIOR: You know, always—you're feeling for those guys whenever you're out on a tour, you know. I mean, because you always tell people in the first place, when to leave, so they can take their time. So I told them that evening, and before in the morning, that they should leave. That morning I told George, I said, "Now, you all leave here."

BEAU: You told who?

JUNIOR: George Baze. I told him, I said, "Now you all get out of here about nine o'clock. If you leave here around nine o'clock like you're supposed to and take your time," I said, "Everything's going to be all right." I said, "Now, you leave." So they got out of the Checkerboard down there, waiting around. And they start waiting on the bass player. He called up; he way out south someplace and all this, this, and . . . this. And they didn't leave until late, you know. And I didn't want them to get in the desert at night. I'd rather for them to go on so when they hit the desert, you're in daylight. And they hit the desert at night, you know. And when they hit the desert at night, you know, it's no lights out there.

BEAU: No, it's pitch black.

JUNIOR: And all on the side of that highway, they've got all that gravel over there. So George had let the drummer drive, Willie Hayes. And they was going down the highway. So my bass player said Willie was driving fast and he hit the gravel. And when he hit the gravel, Locket, the one that got killed, said,

Junior Wells performing at the Chicago Blues Festival, 1989. Photo by James Fraher.

"Handle it?" Willie said, "Handling." So when he said that, the front tire went out and the back tire on the passenger side, both tires blowed out. When they blew out, it broke the tire rods. It got faster, you know. And Willie hit the brakes like that, did this here [swirling motion], went this way, straight up in the air, you know. Just went to turning over and over.

BEAU: All the equipment went flying around?

JUNIOR: Yeah. And then it's like, it threw Little Joe from way back in the back. I got that big maxi [maxivan]. And he was way back in the back. It just took him and sent him all the way through there, right up through the front window. And Ed, he was sitting behind Willie in the seat behind him. It threw him out through that side window. George, it just pinned him down. And the roof wanted to turn over, like it turned and just pushed on his head, broke the collar bone, fractured the other one, and broke some of these ribs [points to his lower rib cage] on him.

And Locket, they couldn't find him. So everybody was out looking for him. And they didn't know where he was at. So they went looking around the van. All they could see was his feet sticking out, from up under the van. The van turned upside down on him, And it hurt me so bad because I thought about just the idea that the van was on top of him, you know. And then I found out later that the doctor said no, said the van on top of him, it didn't kill him. He says it didn't. Something hit him in his head, and that's what killed him. He says he was already dead when the van got on top of him.

And this happened: A guy was passing by, one of them truck drivers. And he saw it pass by him. He was headed back, you know, towards, like, coming back East. And he saw this and he called up on the thing [CB radio], he said, "Man," he said, "I saw a plane, a small plane going down over here in the desert." And they said, "No, there's no plane over there." And he got about thirty miles down the road. And he turned around, came back. And when he came back, he was saving them. And he called up and got ambulances and things out there to take care of them and stuff like, you know. You know Joe, he had seven or eight ribs broke. One of my horn players, he didn't get a scratch.

BEAU: Real lucky.

JUNIOR: Yeah.

BEAU: What was Locket's first name?

JUNIOR: James.

BEAU: Tenor saxophone?

JUNIOR: Yeah. He played tenor, baritone, alto, bass, all that mess.

BEAU: Thanks for talking about the accident. I know it's painful. I put those questions first because I wanted to get the pain out the way. I know it's hard to talk about that kind of tragedy. Thanks.

JUNIOR: Oh, well, you know . . . you're welcome.

BEAU: But anyway, going on with your rich life of culture and music. Where do you come from?

JUNIOR: I come from West Memphis, Arkansas.

BEAU: What year were you born?

JUNIOR: 1934.

BEAU: And did you do any playing around Memphis?

JUNIOR: Um, no. I played after I came to Chicago. I came to Chicago in 1941.

BEAU: You were quite young when you came here?

JUNIOR: I was just a kid when I came to Chicago. My mama moved up here. She started working up here at the Illinois Central Railroad. She sent back and got me. She sent back and got one of us at a time. Me (I was the only boy). And I had three sisters who she sent and got one at a time. She got us all up here. And I was messing around with the harmonica; I didn't really do much with it. And I used to go back down on vacation, and that's when I met Rice Miller [Sonny Boy Williamson II]. And I heard Joe Willie Wilkins and all of them play. And Willie Love and I used to go around and listen to them, and I asked Rice would he teach me how to do some things on the harmonica. So he said, "Let me see your harp." And I had one of them old American Ace harps. And he throwed it on the ground and stomped on it. He said, "Don't never bring no mess like that in front of me. If you want a harmonica, you buy a harmonica, you know. You buy you a harp. Don't come in here with that mess." Harps wasn't but about fifteen cents at the drugstore, you know. They had a Rexall drugstore up there on the highway, and I went up there and got me one.

BEAU: In West Memphis?

JUNIOR: Yeah. And he told me he was gonna show me how if I got a fifth of whiskey for him. And I said, "OK." And he said, "Buy me a drink."

BEAU: When was this, how old were you?

JUNIOR: That was—I was ten years old; 1945. I said, "What did you say?" And he said, "I said, buy me a drink." And I said, "OK, I'll buy you a half-pint." And he said, "You don't buy me no half pint. What do I look like to you? You buy me a fifth." So I went and got him a fifth of whiskey. And at that time they didn't care whether you was a man or not, down there you bought whiskey wherever you wanted.

BEAU: You walk in and buy whiskey?

JUNIOR: They didn't care who they sold it to, you know. So I buy it for him, and he showed me a couple of licks on the harp. And I didn't get it. He said, "You ain't never gonna learn how to play no harmonica, you dumb sum' bitch. You ain't never gonna learn how to play no harmonica," he said, "'cause you're too dumb." He said, "You see that bottle of whiskey there? You bought it for me, didn't you?" I said, "Yes." And he pulled his knife out and licked it, and he said, "If you touch it, I'll cut your damn little throat." He said, "Now get out of my face."

It hurt me, like I mean, just like all this in here stomach got up in here. I said, "If I was a man, you wouldn't do that to me." That hurt me so bad, you know. And years later, after I saw him, after he come to Chicago and stuff, like when I saw him and I was playing harp, he looked at me and he said, "Junior." I said, "Yeah?" He said, "You want a drink?" I said, "No." He said, "You don't want a drink because of the way I treated you before." And I said, "That's part of it." I said, "But you wouldn't do that now." He said, "I'm not going to do that to you now." He said, "But if I hadn't did what I did to you then, you wouldn't be blowing the harmonica." He said, "You was determined that you would do it because I told you you were dumb." He said, "You knew that, didn't you?" I said, "I sure did." After he said what he said to me, my anger went away from me. And what he was saying to me was the truth, because I was determined. I was playing hooky from school and everything else while I was playing that harp. Mama used to come running out through the hallways [vestibules] 'cause I was running to different hallways trying to blow that harp. And people calling mama and telling her, "Come over here, 'cause we can't sleep. Junior over here playing the harp." And mama come and slap me all upside the head, "Get out of here and go home." And all of that stuff.

BEAU: Did you go to grammar school here in Chicago?

JUNIOR: Yes.

BEAU: Where did you go?

JUNIOR: I went to Drake.

BEAU: Go to high school here, too?

JUNIOR: I didn't go to high school until I got into things with the State Department. And I was doing such a good job for the State Department over around through Africa and Singapore and all over.

BEAU: Oh, you mean playing the Blues for the State Department.

JUNIOR: Yeah.

BEAU: You were a Blues ambassador.

JUNIOR: Yeah. You know, culture presentations. I was doing such a good job that Hubert Humphrey came to Abidjan [Côte d'Ivoire] to see me. He was living there at the Intercontinental. I mean in Africa, I mean it's hotter than hell, and they had a ice-skating rink in there and all that. So he invited me up to his suite. So he talked to Dick Waterman, my manager, about me, you know.

BEAU: What year was that?

JUNIOR: That was in '67. I was in Africa in '67 and '68. And I came out and I went back in '68 to Asia and all around through there. Vietnam and every place. I was in Australia.

Interview with Junior Wells

BEAU: So did you visit with Humphrey?

JUNIOR: Yes, I went up to his suite and talked to him. And he said, "Junior."

BEAU: Let me get this clear. It's Junior, Dick, and Hubert at the Intercontinental.

JUNIOR: Oh, yeah, they had it in the *Ebony* magazine where I was with Hubert Humphrey in Abidjan and all.

BEAU: So then?

JUNIOR: He sure knew how to make his guest comfortable in that suite. Anyway, he said, "Junior, I was very pleased with the reports and things of what you've done in a whole lot of places here in Africa. What we did in thirty years, you done done them in days." You know, most times you get in a place maybe one day or two days. And he said, "You done more than we do." And he said, "I think it's a great thing, and I'm very proud that we got a young man like you, you know. A smart young man with a nice education and everything." I said, "Well no, I don't think I'm highly educated. I only went through the seventh grade of school." He said, "What?" I said, "Yeah." He said, "You lying to me?" I said, "No, I'm not." He said, "Well, are you interested in going to school?" I said, "Yeah, but I just never had the money to do it good." He said, "Well, if you want to go to school, we'll send you." I said, "Yeah." I said, "You know, but it's going to cost me a lot of money." He said, "You working for the State Department." He said, "You don't have to pay no money, and you can go to school, too." So I did, you know. And he was right.

BEAU: Was he a pretty regular person?

JUNIOR: Yeah, he had a lot of Africans around. Beautiful girls and everybody. And he's sitting there with his shirt off and Bermuda shorts on. And he said, "Well, you know, Junior, I hope you don't get offended, you know, because I got these Black girls in here and stuff like that." He said, "I like Black people." I said, "Hey, I'm not prejudiced at all, and this is Africa, so I would expect Black people to be in here and everywhere." Then we came to be real great friends. He sent me to school and stuff like that. So I got that part straightened out.

And then after I left there and came home, I was only home for about two weeks. And the State Department called me up and asked me, "Junior, are you ready to go back out again?" And I said, "Yeah." I said, "Where we going?" And he said, "Well, this time we're going around through Asia, Southeast Asia and all that kind of stuff." And I said, "OK. How long are we going to be gone?" He said, "Sixteen weeks."

BEAU: That's a long time, sixteen weeks. Vietnam. During the war then, or just after the war?

JUNIOR: No, it was still going on. When I was up around Da Nang and I got to Saigon, and I went to Da Nang and all up around there. And they had a cease-fire thing, you know. They still had all those big guns going off.

BEAU: Must of have scared the shit out of you.

JUNIOR: It did.

BEAU: Good money, I guess?

JUNIOR: Oh, man, the money was great. The money was really great.

Then the third time he wanted me to do a thing, he asked Dick. And Dick said, "I'll tell you what. You're going to have to talk to Junior about it, because Junior's the type of person that's kind of a proud man for his race. I can't speak for that man." Hubert Humphrey called and said, "Junior, I want to ask you something. I know you not going to do it because your manager said that you was a very proud man in your race. So you might not want to do this." I said, "What is it?" He said, "I must be wasting your time, you probably ain't going to do it." He said, "Would you be willing to go to South Africa?" I said, "You mean to tell me you want me to go to South Africa? And I can live in their Luxury Hotels like the Intercontinental and things like that, because I'm working for the State Department. But I got to go out there and play for the Black people, and they got to come through the back door because the onliest people allowed to come in there are the people that works there? And you think I'm going to go out there?" He said, "Well, I really appreciate what you're saying, Junior, I'm glad you said what you said." I said, "That's me."

BEAU: That's beautiful.

JUNIOR: You know, that one I couldn't do. Not live in a hotel when they living out there in those little shacks and all that kind of stuff. And I'm over there representing myself and the Black race. I can stay in there, but they can't. I couldn't do that. He said, "Well, I really appreciate that, the way you said that and the way you doing your thing. Nobody should ever look down on you because you got the right idea. You're not just out there where you're making a dollar, you're out there also to stand up for what's right toward your race and yourself, too." And I said, "I appreciate your knowing that about me. I'm not trying to hurt anybody's feelings, but I'm just telling you what I won't do."

Then after that, when Humphrey ran for the thing and he didn't get in—they come up with the Republicans, it was all over with them. The Republicans, they didn't hire no Blues artists. They hired people like Sammy Davis Jr. or Bob Hope. Sammy Davis, he was on everything. Or else they hired Jazz artists and stuff like that, but that's not what the people really wanted to hear. You know what I mean, because the Blues is a feeling. And they was really, really appreciating it. And it made me feel so good to see . . . to look at people so Black and the colors that they had on. You know, they would be walking down the side of the road and all that green grass, the beautiful flowers, the colors that they had on, you know what I mean? Mister, it was something to see . . . Technicolor. And I saw people, I looked at them and looked at myself and then I said, "That one there could pass for my brother, look just like me." You know what I'm saying?

BEAU: That's what I discovered when I was in West Africa.

JUNIOR: I had to go the bathroom. I said "Where's the toilet?" Somebody said, "Right over there." So I went to the toilet. I'm in there standing, taking a leak. And a woman, she walked in. I know I saw this little thing over there with them foot things like; I thought maybe it was a shower. And she came in there and pulled up her dress and squatted down to piss, and I pissed all on my hand. I was too scared to turn around. I said, "Oh, man, they done let me come into these women's bathroom." And I went back and I said, "Man, why you let me go in the women's bathroom?" And he said, "No, that's everybody's bathroom." I said, "What?" He said, "Yeah. They don't think about nothing like that, man. People, they don't give a damn about shit like that. They don't have anything to hide, nothing."

My African experience was the greatest in my whole life.

BEAU: That's the most beautiful thing I've heard a Bluesman say in my whole life, what you just said.

JUNIOR: That's the truth.

BEAU: Since the hoodoo man went to Africa, the home of hoodoo, and the origin of our musical, mystical, and physical expression, how did you feel being there?

JUNIOR: It's an entirely different thing that you get there than you get in the United States from your own Black people. There, I feel like I'm back home because I was really, truly appreciated. Nobody wanted to fight you, stick you up, and all that stuff; that wasn't there. When I got off the airplane in Monrovia [Liberia], first thing they did, you know, was welcome me home. And they treated me so nice, I just had to go in the room and cry. I just looked at everything, and then I remembered the things I had saw and the things that went on right back here in the States. And how our own people wouldn't even try to get together with each other like they doing things right now. Theys doing one thing right now: killing each other.

And if they really look at the truth of it, they [Whites] want you to do this. And what do you see at the jailhouse? The Black man, he's in there. They want him in there. He dominates everything. And if he want to, he can dominate anything he want to dominate. The Black man, he's just as powerful. But instead of him trying to use this particular thing in the right way, he's letting the man bring in the drugs, put them in his reach, for him to sell it and kill up each other about it and things like that and so forth. And it's just as different in Africa as night and day towards people in their own culture. You know what I mean? It's such appreciation. Right now you could be playing in a club right now, and the African people, they gonna come up to you. But you can see Black kids walking on the streets now, every day, whatever. And you can be up in there, and if they say it's a dollar to come in, you know they say, "I ain't paying no dollar to come in, man. I don't have that much."

They had Tyrone Davis playing down there at Checkerboard one night. And there was some little girl, she out there. And all the peoples, you know, it's hot and a lot of people standing outside waiting for the show to start. So everybody's just standing around, stuff like that. So this little Black chick, she come up there, run up to the door, "Is Tyrone in there?" The guy say, "Yeah, he's in there." "Where his limousine?" she said. "I don't know. I saw him come up here in an El Dorado." "An El Dorado? Well, where's his bus at?" He said, "I don't know, but there's Junior." She said, "Who's Junior. Are you Junior? I know you 'cause my mama knew you. My mama know you. She used to come around here when you play. What's wrong with Tyrone, he ain't got his stuff?" I said, "Well, he came up here in what he wanted to come up here in." "Well, how much is it to get in there?" I said, "It's $12 in advance and $15 at the door." "$15! I wouldn't pay $15 to see my mammy play." A lot of people turned around and looked at her. I just turned around and went inside, and the White people followed me on inside. That hurt me to my soul. She was out there with her hair looking like screws on her head. Boy, that hurt me, I can't say. I just went on inside. That hurt me.

BEAU: Do you consider yourself to be fortunate?

JUNIOR: To have been able to get out and travel and learned things like I have, I've been places that the average person will never go. I've been anyplace I can name, except Red China and Russia, doing things for the State Department, you know. And that makes me feel like I'm a very fortunate person. For they say I'm an old Blues player, you know. And I'm proud of it. And I just wish that we could get our younger Blacks, not just the young ones, some of the old ones, too, together and let them understand that the onliest way that we ever gonna be anybody or do anything right . . . we got to do it. First, we gotta get our own house in order. And when we get our own house in order, we can get the rest of the things we want to get. But all we getting now is death, and the rest of them going to the penitentiary and all that stuff. Hey, this man that just beat the people out of all this money in this big bank. Do you see how much money this man messed up? I was down in Texas, in Dallas, this man done got all this money stuff there. And they said he might get the maximum of ten years.

BEAU: Which means he'll be out in three and a half.

JUNIOR: Yeah. I'm in Dallas, and it come on the news that evening. And I'm getting clothes out, getting ready to play, and it come on the news. There's a Black dude in a 7–Eleven store taking a package of Kool cigarettes, dollar and a half. They gave him life. Life. There's another Black dude and another White dude, the White dude stole the car. And him and the Black dude is partners, so they went over to the Black dude's house and picked him up. "Want to drive it?" So he drove the car. The police stopped him. The White dude told the police that the boy didn't steal the car. He said, "I stole it." The White boy got seven years; the Black dude got thirty years.

BEAU: The Black male can't get no justice.

JUNIOR: I'm telling you.

BEAU: So, was "Up in Here" written for the Blackstone Rangers, or did they just pick up the expression.

JUNIOR: It was a thing, popular thing to say. And I was in Europe when it came out; I had already made it. Me and Tyrone [Davis] recorded it the same day. Tyrone got mad because mine was a hit and his wasn't. So Dick Waterman sent me a wire to Europe, told me he was going to meet me in New York. And he told me my record was number one and had been number one for over two months. And when I saw him over there, I saw him at the airport in New York, he said, "Now, you don't have to go back down there to Pepper's [Blues Lounge]. You can leave that part alone." I said, "Why you say that?" He said, "I don't want you to ruin your image." I said, "Well, look Dick, I like you 'cause you've done a lot for me." I said, "But I can't do that. If that means that I'm going to ruin my image, then I'm going to ruin it. 'Cause as soon as I get to Chicago, I'm going down there." And I didn't let the hit records stop me from working. I didn't let it let me not play for a couple of months, nothing like that. They can't pay my price, but I do it anyway. I know they can't pay my price. They say, "Well, Junior, my place is small; I'll give you $350 a night." I said, "Man, OK, I'll do it." You know, it ain't gonna hurt me to do that, won't hurt me at all.

BEAU: No, it's our community.

JUNIOR: It means something to me. I don't want them to think that I'm walking around with my head up in the air like I smell some shit, 'cause I smell some shit; it's my own shit. It ain't nobody else's, you know. And I never had that little thing inside of me that because you got a hit record, you supposed to change. It don't change me.

BEAU: Do you think that there are any obligations on the part of these cats, these White musicians who made so much money on the Blues? I mean, an obligation to maybe establish a cultural center in the Black community or do some kind of good, you know? Some expression of their appreciation for having gained so much, even though we gave and give away a lot.

JUNIOR: Well, I mean, you had to give away a lot. You know, Ed Sullivan didn't have no Blues on the show. When the Rolling Stones recorded for Chess, they did Howlin' Wolf's stuff and Muddy Waters's stuff. When you looked up, they was on the *Ed Sullivan Show*. Mick Jagger jumping around and trying to act like Wolf. And I looked at all them kind of things, and I said, "Now, Ed Sullivan never had Blues on his show." But here's some kids come from England, and they're doing Muddy Waters's tunes, Wolf's tunes, and they on the *Ed*

Sullivan Show. That hurt. That hurt, do you know what I mean? Because I feel like that how come you couldn't had the real thing up there? Now you have a person that really witnesses to where he got a thing from; that's Bill Wyman. He witnesses where he got things from, you know, says exactly where it comes from. You know, they say it. And I respect that. I'm not prejudiced any kind of way at all. I'm not prejudiced. But I feel like why don't you let the Black man have his chance and his day, too? You taking his music. That's what makes me so mad today about the young Blacks. They don't want to be bothered with the Blues. But the White boys imitating the Blues, getting richer and richer.

BEAU: They don't want to be bothered on the business end.

JUNIOR: No. And it's our culture, and they're making millions and millions of dollars off of it. And these dummies walking down the street don't want to hear it. They don't want to do this. They come up with the rap, and they think this is a new thing. It's new to the White man. And the White man is making money on that as soon as you got it started. So the Black guys got it started, starting to get the White boy over there to do the same identical thing. So the White boy making more money than the Black boy.

BEAU: No, you never know. But here's something man, I want you to think about this. This is a real sore spot for me. I believe, and I've been all over, about as much as you, seen different things, and as far as I can tell, we're the only race of people, really, that have heroes—people that have a lot of visibility. Basketball players, stars all kind. But most of our heroes with all that money never address the cultural issues, and most of them act like they're living under a gag order when it comes to political outspokenness. They'll talk about gym shoes and some goofy-named cereal before they'll ever utter a word about anything positive for our young people regarding our culture and dignity. But White people, they'll talk about saving the whale, being kinder to hoofed animals, and build great opera houses and monuments to their culture. They'll talk about anything that's on their mind. But as soon as we get some money, we get the damn mink coat down to our ankles, a Mercedes, a Jheri curl, and some gold chains. I'm talking about Michael Jordan, most of them. They don't have nothing to say about the culture. If Michael Jordan said, "I think Blues is what's happening; love your heritage and take care of it," Black kids would give it some serious thought.

JUNIOR: Black kids like to stick with their heroes, but these cats don't stick up for each other.

BEAU: So what are your thoughts on the subject?

JUNIOR: Well, I don't knock no man for what he wants to be, but I will say one thing. I sure in hell wish that we would wake up and smell the coffee. Speak up for our people just like the White person does for his. You got to speak up for your people. Anything the Black man do, they get a White boy to do it, because they want him to. You start it, they get the White boy to do it, too. He imitates what you doing, and he makes the money. The Black man makes the money, too. But they turn it around right back to the Whites. And he puts it back into his race.

BEAU: Give it right back to the White people.

JUNIOR: But the Black, he don't try to put nothing back into his race. It's racist to do a thing against ourselves. We don't speak up like the White man does.

BEAU: Junior, do you have a word for the Black youth.

JUNIOR: I would like for the Black youth to understand about their own culture. Live up to it and respect it, just like the White man does his culture. And stop letting the White man take your culture and getting rich off it. We have to stop disrespecting our individual self because we could be respecting our culture and helping our race out, the way they help theirs. I'm telling the Black man to get off his ass and do what's supposed to be did. What you said about Jordan, all of them, they don't say nothing about the Blues. They don't spread nothing. They got some money, and they don't give a shit . . . and that's wrong.

BEAU: Thanks for your time,

JUNIOR: You got it.

April 10, 1992,
Buddy Guy's Legends, Chicago

Junior Wells,
December 9, 1934–January 15, 1998

Interview with Junior Wells 79

J. B. HUTTO AND LIL' ED WILLIAMS
Blues Legacy through Blood and Spirit
David Witter

Sometimes the culture of past generations is passed down not through yellowing photographs and dusty leather volumes, but through bits and pieces that settle in the soul. These fragments, a drumbeat that echoes the rhythm of an ax chopping wood, a slide guitar that sounds like a rooster's crow, and a voice that cries out through the black night air, were first heard by J. B. Hutto at his birthplace near Augusta, Georgia. Yet Hutto absorbed these sounds and took them to Chicago, where they merged with the Blues-pitched cries and riffs of Elmore James, Hound Dog Taylor, and Muddy Waters. Hutto also made sure that his nephew, Bluesman Ed Williams, would share in this legacy, learning from Hutto the most important thing a man can leave his kin: the power of the Blues.

"When I was eight years old and my brother Pookie was six, we stayed at 1706 West Lake Street, with a big back yard, thirteen cats, and nine dogs," Williams said, speaking from a garden apartment in Chicago's Garfield Park neighborhood. "The first time I saw him play, he and the old Hawks, the ones that played on the Delmark album, came into our backyard, set up, and started playing right in the yard. It was wonderful because we had all of these buildings around, especially the big project buildings, and everybody came out to listen. After that he would come over almost every weekend he was in town, and me and Pookie was watching him, and Uncle J. B. would see us and show us stuff, but he didn't think we were interested. But I remember one particular day he left his amp and guitar, and I was playing, and Pookie was playing the guitar that our mother brought us for his birthday. When Uncle J. B. came over and heard us trying to play, he must have said to himself, 'My, these boys really are interested.'"

This was an important sign from his nephews, and even though he spent much of his time touring Europe with the Hawks, Hutto also began to spend more time with his younger relations. During weekends, a special bond began to develop between Hutto and Williams, who instead of joining in with Williams's mother in scolding the young boys became their "watchful angel," yelling things like, "Leave those young boys alone. They are trying to learn this music."

Over the years, the bond became stronger as Ed and Pookie gradually grew from young boys into young men. It was at this stage that Hutto began to slowly press the boys toward manhood and even a life in the Blues. But like any proud guardian, Hutto watched over them and stuck with them when things got bad.

"I was about nineteen or twenty and Pookie was sixteen and J. B. walked into this bar we were playing at. We didn't know he was coming in, and we saw him. It was a place called Boss Joe's, and we were working our asses off, walking the floor like he did, but nobody was clapping. But J. B. got up and yelled, 'You know you all are sittin' up there like you's dead. Why don't you get up and give these boys a nice round of applause; they workin' hard for you.' Afterward, he took us aside and said, 'You know, you boys just might make it.'"

It was soon after that when Williams, who was becoming known as "Little Ed," also began to take on some of his uncle's musical tricks. These included the "open D" slide tuning; the thumping two-beat drums; the terse, shouting singing style of Hutto, Waters, and others; and the ragged, yet soulful, Maxwell Street sound. Onstage, the similarities between generations were even more pronounced. Like Hutto, Lil' Ed was known for performances that featured pigeon-toed duck walks and sliding on his knees across the club's floor, hopping from table to table, and jumping on top of and walking along the bar, slapping hands with the enthusiastic crowd. For many, these athletic feats would be enough, yet just as his uncle had done for decades, Williams did this while he sang and played the guitar.

Even with this tricks, Williams still felt something was missing. A short time later, he left his home and began living on his own. After he got a job at the Red Carpet

Lil' Ed Williams at home. Photo by Dave Witter.

Car Wash, spending ten-hour days attaching chains to car axels, often soaked from the water of the car wash on subfreezing days, a transformation occurred.

"As I growed up and came to start working, dealing with women, living in a one-room apartment, trying to pay the bills, I had a lot of heartbreaks. It was then that I began to know what he [Hutto] played. Especially when I started playing the real slow songs. I could feel what he was playing and what he was saying; I could feel him living his own life, the times he got drunk and sat down and cried. It was so close. It was like me up there singing his songs. But Uncle J. B. was different," Williams continued. "He wasn't B. B. King, he wasn't John Lee Hooker; it was him, and when he played the slide guitar it was electric, and people just went crazy. It was then that I began to understand what the Blues was all about."

This understanding led to more gigs and led to Williams signing with Alligator Records. Since then, he has put out over a dozen albums, toured the nation and the world repeatedly, and become one of the new ambassadors of the Blues, introducing the raw, electric sounds of Hutto, Hound Dog Taylor, and Elmore James to a new and largely unknowing generation of fans. But as Williams and his brother Pookie continue to take the Chicago Blues into the next century, he is saddened by the fact that the man who had the biggest influence on his career never saw stardom.

"Uncle J. B. played almost to the last limit. I think he collapsed one night onstage in Boston and went straight to the hospital. We went to see him at the County [Cook County Hospital], and at the point we could see that it was coming on the time when it would be over for him. Then they sent him home because he was at the point when he wasn't going to be around long. He had cancer," Williams continued, "and he had the sugar on top of that. When he died, it was a real hard moment in my life. At that point, when I saw him lying on his bed like that, I began to wonder whether I still wanted to be a musician. It was scary, because nowadays basically all the great musicians take it to the end. You don't see a guy working at his desk or waiting on a table to the last day, but people like Uncle J. B. and Johnny Littlejohn . . . now that man had some major heart attacks, and the last time I saw him he was so weak he could barely stand up. But he got himself up onto the stage at B.L.U.E.S. [a Chicago Blues club], picked up his guitar, and played, then slumped down in his chair from exhaustion when he was done. People like him and Uncle J. B. played till the end. It wasn't like he needed the money. He had his house and what he wanted out of life. But he just kept going because he had it in his soul. When I saw him suffering, it hurt me," Williams pleaded, "it hurt me more than anything in my life. He was so sick he couldn't understand what was going on, and I think about that still. I can see him lying in that bed, and a lot of times when I am onstage I feel him with me. In certain songs I sing, at some points I feel him over me. And that is what makes me want to push on . . . to go and never stop. People say do you really be hurt, or are you just making these faces; but I can feel it, and it hurts me. A lot of times when I get on stage and feel like I don't know what to play or sing, I hear him saying, 'Don't stop now, Ed, don't stop now. You just keep going.'"

THE BLUE BAYOU
Julio Finn

To John Ehle

*If you're going to de bayou
—you'd better take a mojo-offerin
with you.*
—Hoodoo Slim

INVOCATION

Praise be unto the Loas
—as 'twas in the days of old!

Praise be unto the Ancestors
—may their true story be told!

We seek permission for this child to enter
—by your grace—the land of the Hoodoo Man!

Aye, without the Gate he waits
—black gesso for your divine hands!

Forty-odd miles north of New Orleans, the bayous take on a particularly forbidding aspect, the foliage becoming so dense that the great swamp is always dark. The sun seems to deny it its light—indeed, such is the gloom of this saturnine swampland that it is enrapt in the mantle of an indescribable loneliness, as of having never suffered human presence. The eerie stillness of its waters, the blinding shadows, the haunted silence—all add up to the terrifying ghastliness of a wild and bewitched wasteland. Nothing here is as it is elsewhere: colors, bathed in the preternatural light, take on hallucinatory hues; the myriad constellations of plants exhale veritable mists of benumbing fragrances. It is the canvas of some demonic artist, a living mural depicting a deadly reality: *the bayous live by incessantly dying.* And it is this perfect defect that magnetizes lonesome travelers, drawing them into it. For once seen by human eyes, the bayous cannot but become a lesson, at once a tableau of the mysteries of life and the key to those mysteries. Once truly experienced, they become a mirror of the soul, its dramas and rites of initiation.

The lords of these almost uninhabited domains are the hoodoo men, the root doctors, men and women so inextricably enmeshed in the lore of the country their ancestors were stolen from that they are unequipped for the way of life of the towns. Theirs is the primitive way of teleology and homeopathy, the worship and pacification of the divine spirits, as practiced in age-old African tradition. To these holy herbalists the bayous are both temple and medicine chest; natural sanctuaries where they can live out their lives according to the dictates of their faith. Here there are no preachers to tell them to believe in the White God, no policemen to harass them for being charlatans. In this lost corner the hoodoos are free to cultivate that harmony which is a balance between interior and exterior forces. Their existence is at once preposterously simple and incredibly complicated: Nothing is either impossible or taken for granted. The bush doctors' worldview is a maze of interdependencies, of symbols and metaphors, signs and interpretations, rewards and sacrifices. They are at once hierophant and acolyte and are rulers of nature only so long as they are rulers of themselves. They are the evangelists of a persecuted religion in a hostile land; apostles of outlawed rites smuggled into the New World. Because of their special connection with gods, people came to them for their miraculous powers, for *wangas* and *mojos*, magic charms that would ensure good fortune and protect them from evil: fix-it powder, get-rich lotion, black-cat bone, unbeatable gambler's *wanga*, lover's cure-all—and scores of other never-fail talismans. While willing to profit from these rustic sages' divinely inspired knowledge, the people mistrusted them and usually gave the swamps they lived in a wide berth. Thus, ignorance and legend had made certain bayous no-man's-land. Publicly, people might put hoodoo down as "hooey," but no one was willing to put the rumors of unholy ceremonies to the test. And so to common belief the bayous remained the abodes of malignant spirits and conjurors or voodoo mambos and fetishers.

Some time early on in the twentieth century, a man with a guitar slung across his back entered the hamlet of La Rouge at dusk. The people treated him with what would in any other place be described as xenophobia but is known in these outlands as minding one's own business. Besides, he had all the suspicious hallmarks of the drifter, which among these cautious folks amounted to a license for immorality. But it was the guitar that put him beyond the pale and relegated him to the level of a hobo. A Bluesman! Everyone knew what that meant: He was singer of the devil's music, songs unfit for Christian ears! Unable to attain lodging for the night, the hobo lay down under a tree, his sleep watched over by two of the more vigilant members of the community. Next morning, he crossed the creek and branched off into the swamp, for what ungodly reason the people of La Rouge could scarcely guess—not unless he was going to seek out Papa Gil, the hoodoo man. It had been a long time since anyone had done that, way back when that feller had come up from New Orleans seeking the spirit of Queen Marie Laveau and had had to be carried out of there half out of his mind. Since then, no one had penetrated the Papa's swamp, that sullage of infamous memory. As for Papa Gil himself, the things related about him were uniformly frightening. He was said to be the oldest person in the bayous—at least 120 years old; he stalked the bogs in a huge black cape and hat and was attended by cats and bats; he sacrificed to the Lord of Darkness by the light of the full moon; and, among other unwholesome gifts, he had the power to transport himself hundreds of miles in a split second. Hence his incredible control over his territory, over which he watched with a jealous eye.

The deeper the hobo penetrated into the marsh, the more cautious he became; every step took him deeper into that daytime night, full of unknowns. He walked like a man with a mission—steadily but stealthily. Whatever it was he wanted, he wanted it badly, for even the sense of escapeless peril didn't make him turn back. He was afraid of the novelty of his situation, of plunging into a world in which he himself was his sole succor in event of disaster. According to legend, all kinds of creatures—earthly and unearthly—lurked in the swamps, and this one in particular had the reputation of being peopled by duppies and hobgoblins. Contending against these fears, the heat, and unpredictable, slimy road under his feet, he trudged on, kindling his courage with the thought of achieving his quest.

A gentle movement in the air told him that the sun

was cooling down, and, sure enough, when he arrived at the next clearing, the sky was diaphanous blue, as serene as crystal. The foliage, reflected helter-skelter on the water, stretched away to the horizon like a verdurous sea. Imperceptibly, his fear changed to awe and, like a man bewitched, he strode forward into the unfolding black blossom of the night.

Once arrived within sight of the abode of the hoodoo doctor, he sat down, more to clear his thoughts than to rest his body. Instinctively, his guitar found its way into his hands, and at once his fingers released clusters of soft, blue notes into the evening air. Unconsciously, he gave himself up to beguiling fantasies, in the train of which came memories of his recent past: the gang that congregated around the bandstand at Jake's, Loudella whispering thrills into his ear, the dancers caught up in their fiery tribute to rhythm. Then the whole of the Black Bottom, the Black people's part of town, rose before him—vibrant and searing in its struggle for life. He saw his grandmother—one among countless other grandmothers—going to work as a house cleaner in the White neighborhood. He saw his father and mother—lost in the infinity of other fathers and mothers—working in the fields, sweating their lives away for wages too low to sustain that thankless existence. He saw the juke joints under the spell of the gods of booze, frustration, and frenzy—and understood that, even in this, there was a kind of logic . . . and the notes began to fly from his guitar like sparks, like thoughts so sanguine that they could be expressed with safety only in an isolated place.

The hoodoo man's shanty seemed undecided as to whether it should stand or collapse. Through the open door the traveler could see that it resembled nothing so much as a botanical warehouse—gourds, satchels, and plants made up the bulk of its furnishings. Then, before he could announce himself, he heard someone stir and, slowly, like an image taking shape on a developing photographic print, a silhouette formed in the doorway. An old man, clad not so much in clothes as in beads and bracelets, stood there. His face struck the hobo as something wondrous and rare, and his eyes seemed to reflect the fire of stars. His face expressing the fear and awe he felt, the hobo attempted to speak but couldn't, attempted to raise his hand but couldn't do that either. The silence that bonded them was a hieroglyph of the void that separated them.

Sitting at the crossroads in the middle of the night, the man with the guitar replayed in his mind what had transpired between himself and the hoodoo man. Having finally found his tongue, he explained that he had sought him out because he wanted to make a pact with the devil, so that he would have power over music. Having heard that he, Papa Gil, was the greatest of the hoodoos, he had come to him, in the hope that he would use his magic to assist him in attaining his end. To all this the old man had listened with inscrutable indifference. After a pause, he had condescended to ask the supplicant only one question, almost baffling in its simplicity.

"How did you get here?"

Whatever store he put by its answer, he must have been satisfied, for he went into his shack and returned with a charm that he gave to the man. "Take that," he told him, "down to the crossroads, and offer it to the devil—I can guarantee the result." Then, having directed him to the nearest conjunction of the roads, he unceremoniously retired.

And now the man was squatting there, his guitar on his lap, waiting for the devil to appear. Though trembling with fear, he never doubted his ability to see the thing through—even though the price to be paid was his soul, he was ready to sacrifice it in order to become a Faust of the Blues. Indeed, his love of the music was such that he felt his soul a small thing to lose if the quality of his music could redeem his life. Now, let the devil come and put him to the test!

Dreamlike, enrapt in the mysterious aura of the bayous, with each instant seemingly a moment of truth, he sat and waited, expecting the devil to rise out the drifting mists and take shape. Several times he could have sworn that he heard footsteps, and once even a voice—as if someone was calling his name. But the hoodoo man had warned him about leaving the place where he had

The Blue Bayou

offered the charm, and so he stuck to his post. Anyway, if it was the devil calling, he knew where he could find him. Then, as dawn broke, he was forced to admit that he had wasted his time, that the sacred hour had passed.

Possessed with rage, he stood before the old man's hut, shouting abuse—"Old fake, damned imposter, shyster, hoodoo hooligan!" He had a good mind to give the rapscallion a lesson with his fists, to see that living ghoul on to that nether heaven beloved of his ilk. Then, with pitying sarcasm, he came out with what he had known all along—namely, that all that talk about hoodoo was simply a lot of bunk, old wives' tales used as mumbo jumbo to frighten children.

"I told you true," the hoodoo man retorted, "when I said that I could guarantee the result of your useless and vain sacrifice, and things have turned out just as I predicted. You came here overloaded with ignorance—about yourself, me, and the power you sought—yes, puffed up and seeking supernatural strength. Fool, you know neither that which you seek nor whom you seek it from. You called the Lord of the Crossroads the 'devil'—and after that blasphemy you expect him to fulfill your silly wishes! And I'll bet you don't even know why you think of him as the devil. It's because you believe in the White man's god—well, then, ask him to grant you your wish! It's clear to see that you've put your hopes of salvation in the Whites . . . when I asked you how you'd got here, you told me that you'd walked! Idiot! Don't you know you were brought here on a slave ship? Don't you know that you were auctioned like cattle, then fattened like a pig so as to fetch a high price? Haven't you the sense to see that the White man used his god to gain a hold over your will? No, you have seen nothing, realized nothing—and thus you will suffer under the White man's yoke till your dying day!"

The diatribe hit its recipient like an illumination. So irresistible were these truths that he could only retreat before them. The implications were dire: He was the offspring of slaves who, for some unfathomable reason, had sought to forget that fact. But how could he when, as was now clear, it was the determining factor in his destiny! Even his music was the product of it, and to forget slavery was to destroy his music's relevance. Black people, Blues music: The two were interchangeable, blood relations, affiliated by suffering. The corollary was that to be Black was to be Blue; the music was the Black people's shadow. The old man's wisdom had revealed this to him, and he was determined to tap the source of the wisdom.

"First," the hoodoo man admonished him, "you must be initiated into African worship, the worship of the ancestors. We slaves were brought from Africa, so our true gods are those of that place. We hoodoo men are practitioners of African science and African rituals—we believe in our ancestors. With their help you can become a man of power; without them, you are nothing—know, then, that the *loas,* the gods of your people, are eternal spirits who dwell within you—you must learn to recognize them and to heed their commands. And woe to him who ignores them! For they are jealous spirits and demand worship. You must put aside the White man's Jesus, under whom you are reduced to a pawn. Without the least knowledge of these things, you wanted to make a pact at the crossroads—know, son, that to acquire the power of a *loa* one must first become possessed, and you must be trained to handle possession. Had the Master of the Crossroads possessed you that night, you would have spent the rest of your life as a lunatic wandering through the bayous! I can see from your face that the idea of being possessed scares you, but you need have no worry about that. Contrary to what people think, to be possessed by a *loa* is a sign of merit, for they will only 'mount' those who are worthy. This is part of your birthright. So give up these unmanly fears—in order to receive the power of the *loas* you must prove yourself a man of power. To succeed at the crossroads you must have knowledge as well as faith."

Matter-of-factly, the hoodoo man also spoke to him about music. According to him, music was also a form of power, a rhythmic way of praising the ancestors and binding the people. He remembered the great voodoo meetings held on the bayous during the reign of Marie Laveau, the Hoodoo Queen of New Orleans, when hundreds of the faithful had congregated to praise the ancestors with dance, song, and music; nights seemingly without end, when the Arada drummers had lured Damballah and Erzulie into their midst; when Baron Samedi had appeared, brandishing his great sword; when Papa Legba, the Keeper of the Gate and Master of the Crossroads, had personally escorted the queen through the swamps. In those happy times the bayous rang with the jubilation of a thousand voices, and the thunder was drowned by the booming syncopation of a hundred drums.

It was nearly midnight when he reached the place where the two narrow roads met. The bayous, pungent with smells, were a cacophony of spooky sounds. He had been consumed by fear, but now he was determined to go through with it, excited by the idea of leading a more authentic existence. Henceforth, he would be different from other men, gloriously damned! The Bluest man in the Delta! With the moon as his witness, he began to follow the old man's instructions. First he saluted the Four Quarters and then sprinkled the voodoo dust on the ground in the form of a circle. Next he put the John the Conqueroo *wanga* around his neck and squatted at the meeting of the crossroads, with his guitar on his lap. Then, closing his eyes, he invoked Legba, using the secret words the hoodoo man had revealed to him. And slowly, the words began to take effect—he felt his mind loosening, being freed from its normal trammels. He became aware of the world in a way in which he had never experienced it before: The whole bayou seemed to be adhering to some omnipotent, universal force—its foliage, its creatures, its waters—all seemed to be calling his name. Branches reached out to touch him; the ground rose and fell under him; the air became a cornucopia of voices—caressing, promising, mocking, cursing voices; cries, wails, howls. Now there could no longer be any doubt; he was being possessed! Antibon Legba was coming to him, coming to "open the gate"! Then came the faces—frightful contortions, abominable combinations of human and animal features whirling bodiless through the air. Simultaneously, he desired to escape, was fleeing, was pinned to the earth; he had never come here, he had fled, he would be there forever. He was beyond time, with time, Time itself. A slave ship, vaster than the whole of the bayous, came toward him, coasting on a sea of tears. One great, insufferable lament arose from within its bows and then went echoing through eternity. Tens of millions of black women came to him, holding out to him their babes, whom they had saved from slavery by taking their lives. Of a sudden, distant rumbles were heard approaching from the Four Quarters, and he prepared himself for the coming of the great god himself. But as he was looking into the distance, he suddenly became aware that the *loa* had snuck up on him from within—Legba the Trickster! A hurricane of drums swept through him—and he realized that he himself was both the drummer and the drum. His hands and feet were whirling in every direction, using the air for a tom-tom. Then the beat broke out within him, knocking him about in the air, bouncing him along the ground. A multitude of hands hammered away inside him. Papa Legba celebrated his coming with a divine tattoo until, finally, satiated with joy, he laid his devotee down, Rhythm reborn in the form of Man.

BEBOP BLUES
James Otis Williams

I Bebop
Cause I paid 400 years
blues dues. Cause Atlantic crossing
memories cloud my Afro-sippi mind
like wide awake nitemares, cause
hurt burns napalm hot in my guts,
like slave master whip lashes, cutting
heartbreak into the unbending backs
of my ancestors. And Charlie Parker's
horn spoke true. "Parker's mood,
Now's The Time."
Swing Lo
Sweet chariot on lynch ropes,
let me ride the freedom Coltrane
Whistle/horn blowing like my
mind, long gone. Salty giant teardrops
roll down the slopes of black faces as
   my erupting
eyes feed Mississippi's streams/
   running
rivers swelling deep and red
with the blood I cried over you
freedom.

My blues birthed like beautiful
black babies in down south
cottonfields next to lonesome hiways
with no names, just numbers
51, 82, 49, 61. My song reads like
torn up love letters, scraps and
pieces of my broken heart, scattered
like tumbleweed drifting down
dusty alleys of towns of my youth
   where
the blues used to live.

Tchula, Mound Bayou, Greenwood,
Clarksdale, Grenada.
Said, "I'm leavin' this town baby,
your cryin' won't make me stay."

Charlie Patton lived like a delta heart
   beat
in son House, in Robert Johnson,
in Muddy Waters, in the Howling
   Wolf,
in me. And Buddy Bolden told
Jellyroll, told Satchmo, told Fletcher
Henderson, told Duke Ellington.
   Coleman Hawkins
was the King, Lester Young
was the president, Bill Basie was
the count and Billie Holiday, the
   Lady Day
felt the spirit. Charlie Parker
   heard the
call with Dizzie Gillespie,
   Thelonius Monk
and Charlie Christian. In walked
   Bud Powell
and John Coltrane had love supreme.
Wings over Jordan sang the word,
   Fairfield
Four, Blue Bird singers. Dixie
   Humming Birds
Robert Dorsey, Sam Cooke and the
soul stirrers sang the word.

Yes, I Bebop, I Be Blues,
I Believe.

BLUES BAR POEM
Julie Parson Nesbitt

Can you put this much blues, bourbon and clit
into a poem?
Can it make the room sway
                         hands beat
                                 hair swing
and jerk in time can it make hips rock
on a warm sea?
                women unwind?
Can it grind up slow in a long
                         wail?
Can it glint and gaze lights sit tight pound
in your stomach all night can it yell
and moan in a neon pulse
make you got to move jump dance or go down now
I love poems

Poems pull me into sleep.
Rip sleep to rise
drunk and sour in the ragged
city edges of the morning
light a poem's
fire.
But it's not cool sheets
                     slow fire
Doesn't make your blood spin
                         and linger
in a smoky lie
it's not a finger through new silk
                         skin
can't rock the table, burn your eyes
make soft flesh swell in the blood beat of the hot bar
a poem's just not
              an electric
                     guitar.

A PHOTO SALUTE TO BLUES GREATS

Barbara Barefield

Photographer Barbara Barefield has been a presence on the Detroit Black music scene since the early 1970s. Her photographs capturing the depth and energy of music people have been reproduced in publications and publicity across the globe. I am honored to have her participation in this collection.

Left to right: Koko Taylor and Sippie Wallace, backstage at Avery Fisher Hall, New York City, 1980. Photo by Barbara Barefield.

(top) **Alberta Hunter at the Music Hall, Detroit, Michigan, spring 1984. Photo by Barbara Barefield.**

(bottom) **Aretha Franklin, Detroit, Michigan, 1977. Photo by Barbara Barefield.**

(top) **Cab Calloway at the Paradise Theatre/Orchestra Hall, Detroit, Michigan, 1978. Photo by Barbara Barefield.**

(bottom left) **Lena Horne, Detroit, Michigan, 1980. Photo by Barbara Barefield.**

(bottom right) **Linda Hopkins at Avery Fisher Hall, New York City, July 1980. Photo by Barbara Barefield.**

(top) **Lucille Spann at the Ann Arbor Blues and Jazz Festival, Ann Arbor, Michigan, summer 1973. Photo by Barbara Barefield.**

(bottom) **Nell Carter at Avery Fisher Hall, New York City, July 1980. Photo by Barbara Barefield.**

(top) **Big Mama Thornton at Avery Fisher Hall, New York City, July 1980. Photo by Barbara Barefield.**

(bottom) **Miles Davis at the Masonic Temple Theatre, Detroit, Michigan, August 1981. Photo by Barbara Barefield.**

FROM THE *ORIGINAL* CHICAGO BLUES ANNUAL

Issue Number 5

Issue number 5 continued the celebration of ancestors, elders, music, rites, and rituals of the African diaspora. This and each of the following issues would contain this Yoruba Santeria greeting on one of the opening pages:

Iba ara ago o
Moyuba,
Omo de ko ni
Iba ara ago o
Moyuba.
Fe Eleggua Echu Iona

Greetings O people
I bow to you
I have come today
Greetings O people
I bow to you
Eleggua Eshu
Move out of the way

An interview with Billy Boy Arnold; an insightful analysis of the Blues scene by David Whiteis; and a tapestry of Black Chicago cultural rituals of the 1950s, '60s, and '70s, told to me by radio DJ Herb Kent are the crux of this issue. We celebrated Big Bill Broonzy and praised and celebrated recent ancestors Valerie Wellington, Albert King, Marian Anderson, Dizzy Gillespie, Sylvester Boines, Theresa Needham, Bruce Kaplan, Wayne Bennett, Johnny Christian, and Professor Eddie Lusk.

We reached out to Spanish-speaking people by translating some articles into the second most spoken language in the world.

"Long live the revolution for peace through culture, art, music!"

INTERVIEW WITH BILLY BOY ARNOLD

L. "Chicago Beau" Beauchamp

In 1964, Julio Finn and I went by his brother Billy Boy's house to get harmonica lessons. First, his wife served us tasty tuna fish sandwiches and pop. Then Billy said:

"Y'all got your harps."

"We got one harp between us, a C-harp."

"Let me hear you blow something."

We couldn't blow nothing. Julio tried, I tried.

"I'm gon' tell y'all the same thing," Sonny Boy told me. "You got to learn how to choke it. Then you got to practice every day." Then he played a few bars of "I Wish You Would." We tried to play the main beat but failed miserably. Then he played the "Hoochie Coochie Man" intro. He said, "The next time I see y'all, I want you to be playing 'Hoochie Coochie Man,' 'cause from there you can build up a lot of different riffs. But listen to records and practice."

That's how I got started, and that's how my friendship with Billy Boy began.

BEAU: When did it all begin?

BILLY BOY: It began for me, as early as I can remember, about three or four years old. I know I wasn't going to school, so I know I wasn't five years old. And I used to hear Blues records my aunt would play.

BEAU: In Chicago?

BILLY BOY: Yeah, I never lived nowhere else. So I used to hear my aunt play records, and I used to sing the lyrics.

BEAU: Your mother had records, your mother and your aunt and them?

BILLY BOY: Well see, we all lived together; my mother, her three sisters, my grandfather, and all us kids lived together.

They would play the current Blues records, the current hits. And I used to hear the records and remember the lyrics, those that I liked. I made the guitar sound with my mouth, I sang the verse, and then I made the guitar sound, you know, 'cause I didn't have an instrument. Anyway, I really liked Blues. I was aware that I liked it,

Billy Boy Arnold at Chicago Beau's studio, Chicago, 1993. Photo by L. Beauchamp.

but I wasn't aware that it would become part of my life or anything. I just really liked the Blues.

BEAU: Who was on some of those records that they were playing around the house back then?

BILLY BOY: Well, one record that really impressed me was Sonny Boy Williamson's record "Coal and Ice Man's Blues."

BEAU: So you met Sonny Boy?

BILLY BOY: Right.

BEAU: How did that happen?

BILLY BOY: Well see, how I got involved with Sonny Boy . . . I hadn't heard any records for four or five years. My mother and her sisters moved apart. And my aunt with the record player and records wasn't living there anymore. So I didn't hear any records for about four or five years. And then my grandfather gave my mother a record player and sent me records from his jukebox. He had a restaurant and hotel in Ohio. And he sent her the current records from the jukebox. And out of these records he'd send Jazz, Blues, and stuff, and one was by Sonny Boy Williamson.

And I didn't relate him to the early records I had heard when I was three and four years old, but I had just heard the sound of the harmonica and I was fascinated with the sound that it made. Actually, I was really digging T-Bone Walker. T-Bone Walker was my idol at the time. I didn't have a guitar, so I would just take a broom and strum it. You know, it's hard for us kids to get hold of a guitar, especially a poor kid. And anyway, I heard this harmonica and I thought, how does that guy do that on the harmonica? And, you know, that just sort of fascinated me. So I went to Sears Roebuck and bought a harp. Except I didn't even know how to play the Blues.

And then I heard some more records. I went to the record shop and got some more records, and that just escalated, you know . . . wild! Still I just wondered how can a guy do that. I didn't want to do it professionally, I just wanted to learn how to do it. And then my father mentioned that Sonny Boy came into the Club Georgia.

BEAU: Where was that located?

BILLY BOY: Forty-fifth and State. When he said he came into the Club Georgia I was surprised. I thought that recording artists were mostly like movie stars, where you never saw them close at hand—when I heard that, I was just kind of excited to hear that. And the more I listened to this guy's record, the more fascinated I got with this guy's style, the way he played. And then I was working in my uncle's butcher shop, and I saw a guy with a guitar, so I asked him for Sonny Boy's house number, and he gave me Sonny Boy's house number, and I went by Sonny Boy's house.

BEAU: And where was Sonny Boy living at the time?

BILLY BOY: He was living at 3226 South Giles.

BEAU: How'd that first meeting go?

BILLY BOY: Well, I got my cousin, Archie, and his friend and said, "Come on, we're going to the show. Before we go to the show, come on over by Sonny Boy's house." They said cool.

We was out at Ninety-fifth Street. And so we took the streetcar to Thirty-third and walked over to Giles by Sonny Boy's. We saw the show at Sixty-third and Halsted. We went by and rung the bell. We didn't know what the guy looked like or nothing—never seen him. This guy came, very dark, black skin color, a well-dressed man . . . came to the door. And he said, "Yes, can I help you?" I said, "We want to see Sonny Boy." And he said, "This is Sonny Boy." And I said, "We want to hear you play your harmonica." He said, "Come on up, I'm proud to have you." We went upstairs and he had Johnny Jones and his wife there. And he said, "They came to see Sonny Boy." And then he started talking with me. I told him I wanted to play the harmonica. I told him I could play just like him with his records. So he put the record on and hooked up his amplifier and microphone and all that. And I said, "How do you get that wah-wah sound?" And he says, "Choke it." So I said, "Well, show me how you do that," you know. So he started choking it. He started to sing everything we'd ask him to sing, you know. He started showing me how to choke it. And I was trying, but I couldn't get it. No, I couldn't get it. So he said, "Do it like this: Put your tongue between one and two, suck in." And he took about a half-hour showing me. And then he tells Johnny Jones, "He's gonna be better than me." Johnny Jones could play, too. Johnny Jones was as good as he was, Sonny Boy said. Anyway, that was the first meeting, you know. And he told us to come back, you know, and we came back. I met with him on two occasions. The third time I came by, he had got murdered.

BEAU: So the second time you met, had you improved?

BILLY BOY: Well, I hadn't really got it, no. I hadn't improved because it was only a week later, you know. Back then, me being a kid, it was hard for me to grasp it, you know.

When I went by the next time, he thought I had come to trade comics. He traded comics with kids in the neighborhood. Well, we didn't have no comics. I said, "Don't you remember you showed me how to play?" He said, "Oh, yeah, it's my little friend." He started showing me how to play the harmonica again. And he started telling us different things about his life. He was a real happy, optimistic guy. Happy-go-lucky.

BEAU: Was his wife home at this time?

BILLY BOY: Yeah, his wife was at home.

BEAU: Was she a nice lady?

BILLY BOY: Very beautiful. She was only twenty-three years old.

BEAU: That was Lacey, L-a-c-e-y?

BILLY BOY: L-a-c-e-y B-e-l-l-e.

BEAU: Lacey Belle.

BILLY BOY: She was very attractive, pretty brown skin. Pretty, beautiful brown skin. Real slim build, like a model. She had a very pretty face. We were sitting there talking, and she was looking out the window. And I remember looking at her and going . . .

BEAU: She was a beautiful woman, huh?

BILLY BOY: Yeah. I always had a eye for a pretty woman. Yeah, well, she was only twenty-three. He was thirty-four when he died; she was twenty-three. He married her when she was fifteen. She told me that.

BEAU: Where was he from?

BILLY BOY: Jackson, Tennessee. They were both from Jackson, Tennessee.

BEAU: You had to have been very hurt when you went over there and found out that he had been killed, that he was dead.

BILLY BOY: We rung the bell, and the lady on the first floor said, "Who you looking for?" I said, "Sonny Boy." She said, "Haven't you heard? He got killed; they killed him."

BEAU: Damn. At least you had spent quality inspirational time with him. And you were around ten or twelve or somewhere around there?

BILLY BOY: I was twelve.

BEAU: So what was the next step for you to follow up?

BILLY BOY: I just kept listening and trying. And then I started when I was fifteen; I started meeting some of the other guys. I met Muddy Waters when I was fifteen. And I met Bo Diddley when I was fifteen years old. I met Bo Diddley and I started playing, you know, around with him and his little group of kids. It was just two guitars and a washtub bass.

BEAU: What did y'all call yourselves?

BILLY BOY: At that time we were called Ellis McDaniel and the Hipsters. I started playing around with him. And we just played on the streets, you know, we was just kids. Bo was about twenty-three.

BEAU: He was older than you-all.

BILLY BOY: Yeah, he was older than me and Jody Williams, the guitar player. We was about fourteen or fifteen.

BEAU: What kind of guy was Bo?

BILLY BOY: Bo Diddley was very clean living. He was a very popular guy around the neighborhood. He could walk down the street and everybody would yell, "Hey, Ellis!" He was well known with all the kids.

BEAU: So you all hooked up with Bo. Did you travel on the road with Bo when his career took off?

BILLY BOY: Yeah, what we did, we had a demo we took to several record companies. We went to United and States Records. Leonard Allen was president. That was two labels within the same company. They rehearsed us for a week. Then a guy named Smitty who was vice president told us that if we really wanted to record, we should go up to Allen and tell him we really want a record and we don't want no money. We just laughed and never came back.

BEAU: How did Bo Diddley get his name?

BILLY BOY: Now see, the name Bo Diddley, the whole thing with Bo Diddley was just like a fluke.

BEAU: Who thought it up?

BILLY BOY: I did.

BEAU: How did it happen, the fluke?

BILLY BOY: Well, when I was playing with Bo Diddley when we was in the street, the bass player, Roosevelt, say, "Ellis, hey Ellis, there go Bo Diddley." Talking about some guy. It tickled me; it was the funniest thing I'd ever heard in my life. I just cracked up! So the whole, the whole story of Bo Diddley was born in the studio, during rehearsal. We was trying to get the song together. In fact, some of the lyrics of the song, a couple of the verses, I wrote right there on the spot.

BEAU: The "Bo Diddley" song?

BILLY BOY: Yeah.

BEAU: How's that song go?

BILLY BOY: "Papa gonna buy his baby a diamond ring." So we made that up in the studio. We was doing a thing called "Hey, Noxema."

BEAU: "Hey, Noxema"?

BILLY BOY: "Hey Noxema," with the same Bo Diddley beat.

BEAU: Noxema, like the skin cream?

BILLY BOY: Yeah. Bo Diddley used to sing "Dirty Motherforya," while we used to say, "Hey, Noxema." We used that same type of beat.

And so, naturally, Leonard wasn't interested in that. He was interested in "Dirty Motherforya," he was interested in the hambone beat. That's what it actually was. Bo Diddley had a acoustic guitar with a pickup on it and a tremolo. And you'd get a tremolo sound, you'd get that African, West Indian type of sound. And so we was trying to think of something else besides "Hey, Noxema." And I said, "What about Bo Diddley?" And so Leonard wanted to know what did that meant. He thought it might have been some kind of derogatory term for Black people. I said, "No, it means a some kind of a comical guy, you know."

BEAU: Bo Diddley.

BILLY BOY: Comical. And we didn't have no idea that the title of the song would be "Bo Diddley." Well, after we made the lyrics up, we was singing "Bo Diddley." So that was a possibility. But he had no idea that, as an artist, he was going to be called Bo Diddley until the record came out. In fact, the record was out all across the country before we knew it. It was playin' all across the States. And when Leonard showed us the 78, it had "Bo Diddley" by Bo Diddley.

BEAU: You ever get any money for that?

BILLY BOY: Well, I didn't get credit.

BEAU: Co-writer?

BILLY BOY: I didn't get credit, because at the time, you know, we were just passing ideas and wasn't thinking, you know. And when it turned to that, you know, I should have said, "Well, hey, I want a piece of that."

But that's a part of being fifteen and being young cats, you know.

BEAU: Yeah, sure.

BILLY BOY: Well, they made this record of "Bo Diddley" and "I'm a Man." We cut four sides, and at the same time, I cut two sides in the same session, which just came out on the MCA box. Some of the songs that I did, I did with Bo Diddley at that session. They have never been released before.

So Leonard let me do something at the end of the session. So we went there with the idea of both of us recording. And Leonard, as you know, was interested in Bo. And so at the end of the session, he let me do two tunes that are coming out in this box set.

BEAU: Which ones?

BILLY BOY: "I'm Sweet on You Baby" and "You Got to Let Me Love You." But anyway, the record came out in February, and it hit real big. It was hitting so big that they sent a White lady to Chicago to cover it. And then Willie Dixon and the drummer and the bass player went down to record it with her, but they didn't want Bo Diddley and his band to come down and cause a conflict from his records. Same guitar, you know. Bo Diddley's guitar style was the important thing.

About two weeks later, the record was hitting so hard, Leonard sent us on tour to go to New Orleans along with Howlin' Wolf. So Howlin' left his band behind, and he brought his guitar player, Jody Williams. We all drove down, and Wolf flew. Jody was the original guitarist with Bo; now he had become an advanced guitar player.

So we went to New Orleans. When we got down around Memphis, this White lady's version of "Bo Diddley" was on all airways, just tearing it up. When we got to New Orleans, Bo Diddley's record was very hot; it was sizzling. Both sides: "I'm a Man" and "Bo Diddley." We were walking down Rampart Street, and you could hear . . . they had the doors open. You had "Bo Diddley" on this side and "I'm a Man" on the other side. And it was just blasting all over, red hot. The hottest thing on the air: "Bo Diddley" and "I'm a Man."

We played while we was down there. We played Homer, Louisiana; we played Bo Diddley's hometown, Macomb, Mississippi. And when we got back, Leonard sent Bo Diddley to New York. He was in demand at the Apollo, in New York. He went to New York to stay for one week, and they kept him three weeks.

BEAU: Did any of you go to New York?

BILLY BOY: Not on that trip.

BEAU: Was Clifton James with you then?

BILLY BOY: Clifton went with him later. But when he went to the Apollo the first time, went as a single.

BEAU: With the house band out there?

BILLY BOY: With the house band. A singer. In fact, at that time, if you just had one hit, usually they didn't send you with a band. You worked with the house band. B. B. King did the same thing . . . Chuck Berry. And then after your second hit or your record got big enough, then you got to command your own band.

BEAU: Speaking of Chuck Berry, in relation to this time frame, was Chuck making his move around this same time?

BILLY BOY: Chuck made his move after that.

BEAU: It was after that.

BILLY BOY: Because when we recorded, when Bo did his thing, wasn't no Chuck Berry.

BEAU: Wasn't no Chuck Berry.

BILLY BOY: I guess maybe a year or six months after that, or something like that.

BEAU: He came out with another groove?

BILLY BOY: Chuck's stuff was based really on Jimmy Reed. He was quite a songwriter, good artist. In fact, now, Chuck—the story I heard about Chuck, when he first went to Chess, he went there to sell a song, you know, for somebody else to do, not to promote himself as an artist. And Leonard asked him, "Why don't you do it?" The same way as Percy Mayfield. Percy Mayfield went especially to sell some songs, sell songs, and Leonard said, "Why don't you sing it?" And that's how they got going.

BEAU: Well, going back to Bo. You all started moving, making a move.

BILLY BOY: Well, see, the thing was, I was recording, too. So Bo told me to go to another label, because he didn't think Chess was going to record me. So then I went to Vee-Jay. See, I wrote the second song that went to the second record. It's called "Diddley Daddy."

BEAU: "Diddley Daddy."

BILLY BOY: We was playing it in the clubs. And we did a show with Ruth Brown where we played it. I was singing it, and Bo Diddley was just playing. And Leonard heard it, and Leonard liked it, said, "Tell Bo that should be the next record." So I, you know, I was, you know, I wrote the song, but I was going to let Bo do it, or whoever. But Bo told me that Leonard didn't want me to record. So I went to Vee-Jay, and Calvin Carter said, "Well, why don't you change the lyrics?" That's how "I Wish You Would" was born, right out of that.

BEAU: Born out of "Diddley Daddy"?

BILLY BOY: Well, I was playing the same harp beat on it, but the lyrics was totally different, a totally different song. Because the lyrics that I had for "Diddley Daddy" I changed it totally and made a song called "I Wish You Would." The only thing that was similar was the bop-bop-bop-ba-da-bop-bop.

BEAU: So "Diddley Daddy" took off with "I Wish You Would."

BILLY BOY: That took off with it. Then Leonard wouldn't record Bo in the second session till he got a hold of me. And I was at Universal Studio recording "I Wish You Would," he told Bo to wait for Billy to come. And when I got to the studio, I thought I was just going to, you know, back him up. And Leonard said, "Let Billy sing it." But I had a contract from Vee-Jay, so I thought I wasn't supposed to do that. So then the Moonglows blew out some lyrics right there in the studio with a version of "Diddley Daddy" derived from my version: "She's Fine, She's Mine." And I played the harp on that one. And then . . .

BEAU: You wrote, "She's Fine, She's Mine"?

BILLY BOY: No, Bo did.

BEAU: Bo wrote that one.

BILLY BOY: But I backed it up. But after that, Vee-Jay told me that I need to get my own band, you know, instead of playing with Bo, do my own thing. And they gave us money to buy a mike and a PA system and all that. And they had Shaw Artists as booking agents.

They wanted to book me. So they got me my first gig at the Barrel House. It was a new club opening up called the Barrel House. And they booked me in the Barrel House. And that was my first gig. I had never fronted a band. See, I was a boy; I didn't do no singing, I just played. I didn't know I had any repertory at all, just stuff in my head. It was Little Walter and my band at the Barrel House.

BEAU: So you were a kidman.

BILLY BOY: Well, yeah, because at the time I was a teenager. I wasn't even old enough to play at the club. Everybody in my band was always older than I was. I was the youngest one in the band. The other people were adults, you know, in their twenties and thirties, and I was a teenager.

BEAU: How did you feel being basically a child star with those kind of opportunities? I mean, you leading the band with all these older cats.

BILLY BOY: I never thought about it, and I was doing what I wanted to do. I never was phobic about age or nothing. It didn't make any difference. It takes time to get to where you want to be musically, if ever. I was always appreciative of what I learned from the older guys. I wasn't seasoned like Sunnyland, Walter, and them. Because I was too young. You know, they had experience, years of doing it. But it takes time to arrive at certain spots.

BEAU: Were you pretty impressed with Little Walter?

BILLY BOY: Oh, yeah. He was a genius, I was very impressed with Walter. Like he was the main man. Oh, yeah, he was number one in my book.

BEAU: Did you-all, like, spend time together, like, playing or hanging out?

BILLY BOY: Oh, no, he wouldn't do nothing like that. He knew me, when I was still a teenager, about sixteen. Louis Meyers took me where he was playing, and Louis told him that I could play. And he looked and kept watching me. And he said, "We got a boy in here, he gonna blow the sides off." You know, and things like that. And then when I got up there, I was playing like Sonny Boy instead of him. And that's where he came from originally, too. He was looking at that. And then I talked to him, you know, and he told me how good Sonny Boy was. He said Sonny Boy was the best. He said that Sonny Boy used to tell him that he played too fast. But he said Sonny Boy was good. He said, "Let me tell you, he was really good; he was the best." And it was things like that. And then after I recorded, he came and seen me sort of like a rival. You know, like he saw some things in me that made me stand out. He was really an insecure guy, which he had no reason to be 'cause he stood head and shoulders over the rest of the guys.

BEAU: It's funny how some guys can be that way, when they're the best around.

BILLY BOY: He had an inferiority complex. Maybe it was because he thought he wasn't a good singer or something like that. Or maybe he didn't have any confidence in his ability to endure, you know. I don't know what it was, but he had himself a complex.

But he was a motherfucker. Everything that was going on at the time was going on because of him. I mean, there was guys playing everywhere, everybody was doing his thing.

See, the difference in John Lee Sonny Boy—he was very secure. And he appreciated other artists. At the time when he was barnstorming, he was just like Little Walter. Everybody was calling on him. People was passing themselves off as him. Not only Rice Miller, but people everywhere who could do it, you know, claimed they was him to get recognition.

But he was the type of guy that was well appreciated, he was well thought of, you know, and didn't have any fear of being overexposed, you know. Nobody could've did what he did, because he was a natural. And he didn't seem to have that inferiority complex, like Walter. All of these guys are doing Walter's thing, and instead of Walter, you know, really feeling proud and, you know, really elated about it. . . . I think Walter felt kind of threatened that they're trying to do my thing and outdo me.

BEAU: What about Junior Wells? What was Junior doing at this time?

BILLY BOY: Junior was playing with the Aces at the time. Yeah, with the Aces. He had did his thing with Muddy. Then he left Muddy and went back to the Aces.

BEAU: So the main harp men on the scene were you, Junior, Walter. Who else was on the scene?

BILLY BOY: Well, there was a lot of people on the scene then. Junior was one of the main men. Of course, besides Walter there was Little Mack Simmons, Earl Dayton, Sonny Cooper, P. T. Hays, Blues King, Snooky Pryor, Forest City Joe, Earring George. There were countless guys, guys everywhere. George Smith, he had been on the scene; then he went to LA, but he took Junior Wells's place with Muddy for a while when Junior went to the army. Then Junior came back. I think Junior went with the Aces then.

BEAU: Did you ever take that job with Muddy?

BILLY BOY: I always did my own little thing. After I left Bo, I never played with nobody else.

BEAU: You've always been a front man except for the few years with Bo Diddley?

BILLY BOY: Yeah, well I was—you know, the company told me that's what they wanted me to do to promote my record and blah, blah, blah, blah, blah.

I'm trying to think who else was—Carey Bell was on the scene. I don't exactly remember when Carey Bell came on, but Carey Bell was around—I don't remember what year. I don't know if he came on at that time or not. But he used to play mostly background gigs, so I'd see him around.

BEAU: How long did you keep your thing going?

BILLY BOY: All the way through. I started strumming the guitar when I was, I guess about eighteen. I started strumming on the guitar like that. But I never did use it in clubs up until recently. Then I started playing bass. I played bass with Johnny Young and Charlie Musselwhite. I went on the road with Musselwhite. Then I played bass with my own band, too. Also with Little Walter. Walter was in the same group as us. He asked me, "You quit playing harp?" "No," I said, "I'm just playing bass." We played at the Red Onion and another place. I played some gigs with Muddy Waters Jr. I played with Buddy Guy at Theresa's one night; he needed a bass player. I played a few gigs with Muck Muck.

The reason I started playing bass is because I didn't necessarily have to do the fronting, and I just played with other people 'cause I just liked using and experimenting with different instruments. I was experimenting with piano, guitar, and bass. I never played piano in the club; I would experiment with it. But when I played bass or guitar, I wasn't fronting myself as Billy Boy Arnold.

Then the European thing started coming in. Then I stopped playing bass. I started making European tours and appearances, you know, by myself. And then I never did go back to the bass. I started bringing my guitar to the forefront.

BEAU: Many of your songs have been covered by White rock bands and European artists.

BILLY BOY: Yeah, Eric Clapton and the Yardbirds, David Bowie have done some. As well as Canned Heat.

BEAU: Which tunes?

BILLY BOY: "I Wish You Would," "I Ain't Got You," "Don't Stay Out All Night," "Rockinitis," "You Got Me Wrong." A lot of my tunes have been done by a lot of people, including you and my brother, Julio.

BEAU: Well, let me ask you. Now, I know you sort of withdrew, except for those European tours. Like a personal hiatus.

BILLY BOY: That came about mostly because I didn't have a manager. I didn't want to be local—I mean, if I didn't make a living, I didn't want to do it [play]. Well, the music people declined. Then there was a period when the Blues wasn't as hot as it used to be. It wasn't as widely played in the mid-'70s, as now. But it seems like things slowed down in the industry, you know. Disco took over, and Pop was a different kind of feeling.

I wasn't doing any local gigs around Chicago. I was going overseas two or three times a year. I would work 365 days a year if it had been worth my while financially. But just working locally wasn't for me. I mean, it wasn't enough money to live at the standard that I would like to live.

BEAU: You have other interest including Jazz.

BILLY BOY: Oh, yeah

BEAU: Speaking of Jazz, back in them days when you were coming up, was there much, you know, interaction, hanging out, between Jazz cats and Blues cats? Like at the Jazz sessions that were at the Sutherland Hotel. Would there be an intermingling of cats?

BILLY BOY: No, the Blues crowd, they had their setting, and it was going real strong at the time. And the Jazz artists, they did their thing at the Blue Note or Sutherland, or they had a place called the Bee Hive, things like that. But they wasn't running into me. Because at this time, it was like two different fields, both Black music, you know; there was two separate worlds going. The Blues world, and then there was the Jazz world. And then there was another, like the Gospel world. There was three things going, they were all Black music. And it all had similar roots. But there was people who went for a certain thing. Some crossovers were out there though.

But most Blues guys was playing from feeling and inspiration and like a calling. You know, like somebody say they got a calling to be a preacher. A Blues guy was called. He felt he wanted to do this, or he had a strong burning desire to express himself in that way. Whereas, I don't know for sure, but I think Jazz musicians sort of went to school to learn a form of music, although didn't nobody teach no Jazz in school. Jazz was taught—was derived from Black artists, taking standard form of music and improvising, and doing it the way a Black person would do it. Jazz wasn't wrote in school like Blues wasn't wrote in school. Now you can go to any college or any university and find Blues, Jazz, and everything else. Now you see books and things on Blues as well. There was a time when Blues was strictly a Black thing. Now people are writing books on Blues. Guys with PhDs.

BEAU: Going back to those earlier times, people I've met have always had great things to say about Sunnyland Slim. When did you first encounter Sunnyland?

BILLY BOY: Well, I met Sunnyland when I was fourteen or fifteen when I meet Louis Meyers. I met them up at a club call Sam and Gussie's Lounge on Thirtieth and Cottage Grove. I started hanging around Louis Meyers's house. Junior Wells and Freddie Below would be over there; they'd be rehearsing and exchanging ideas.

How I met Louis and them was one day I was walking buy a pawnshop, and I saw these four guys standing there, and one of them had a guitar. Naturally, when I saw a man with a guitar—I checked them out. I figured it was probably someone I should know. So I walked into the pawnshop, and there was Louis Meyers, Dave Meyers, Freddie Below, and Junior Wells. Junior was buying some harps. I asked them who they were, and they said they were the Aces. They came out of the pawnshop, and I followed them around to Louis's and we went upstairs. I listened to them for awhile . . . and eventually, I got to be a regular hanging around Louis's.

So one day Louis told me about a cocktail party at Sam and Gussie's Lounge that started around two o'clock in the afternoon. Being only fifteen years old, I didn't know if I could get in. So Louis let me put on one of his suit jackets so I would look more mature. At the party, I meet Jimmy Rogers, Sunnyland Slim, J. B. Lenoir, Little Walter, Robert Junior Lockwood, Little Johnny Jones, and others. Little Johnny Jones was the cat I met up at Sonny Boy's, but he didn't remember me. I guess it's because we were just kids.

BEAU: Now you've mentioned only men up to this point. Who were the woman on the scene?

BILLY BOY: Memphis Minnie. I met Memphis out in Robbins, Illinois, when I went out there with Blind John. I sat in with Memphis Minnie then. Now, Robert Nighthawk was on the top at that time, and his wife was a singer, she sang with his band. Memphis Minnie was one of the top stars, she and Big Bill Bronzy. But their names were starting to fade out. Muddy Waters and them had taken over the scene. It was a different scene, a different set.

BEAU: So there were really not a whole lot of women on the set. Big Mama Thornton?

BILLY BOY: No, she wasn't from Chicago, and she wasn't on the scene at that time.

BEAU: How about Otis Spann? When did you meet Spann?

BILLY BOY: The first time I meet Spann was at the Tic Tok at Thirty-sixth and State. Morris P. Joe was playing, and Spann was playing the piano. That was the greatest piano I ever heard in my life. I mean he was cooking—rocking the house. Now at that time, Spann was living with Henry Strong [Pott], Henry Gray, and Jody Williams. They were all living together in a flat at Thirty-sixth and Wabash, a block from the Tic Tok. I saw him up at the Tic Tok a couple of times. This was about a year before he joined Muddy Waters. The next time I saw Spann, he was with Muddy. But he wasn't the same Spann that was at the Tic Tok. When he was with Muddy, he was held in check. They never amplified his piano so he could be kept in check. You know how great Spann sounded on records, but he couldn't be heard in the clubs. When James Cotton joined the band, he fronted the band. I don't believe I ever hardly heard Spann sing. When Spann set at the piano, you could see his hand moving, but you couldn't hear anything. He was held in check.

BEAU: When did you first run into Big Walter?

BILLY BOY: The first time I saw Big Walter was at the Zanzibar. Muddy was playing, and Big Walter was the harp player.

BEAU: When was that?

BILLY BOY: It was right after Junior Wells left. When Junior Wells left, Muddy sent for Big Walter. I don't know whether he was here or in Memphis or somewhere. Big Walter didn't stay with Muddy long. He had the ability to stay as long as wanted. But he was the type of guy that you couldn't control. You couldn't expect him to be there. He liable to take another gig or go back to Memphis or something. You look around, and he done split the scene. The second time I saw him, he was playing with Johnny Shines.

BEAU: He blew one hell of a harp, one hell of a musician.

BILLY BOY: Yes he was. As a harp player, he was second best to Little Walter. The reason I say that is that Little Walter was more melodic. He was faster and quicker with his ideas. He was sharper. Big Walter was solid and powerful. At times, he could be as effective as Little Walter. Little Walter was consistent. Spontaneous. Big Walter could be spontaneous, and then . . . well, he never was mediocre, but sometimes he'd play just a little above average. He wasn't no run-of-the-mill guy. Big Walter was always between above average and spectacular. Little Walter was always spectacular.

BEAU: And Rice Miller?

BILLY BOY: I heard about Rice Miller way before. I heard people mention Rice Miller's name when they mentioned Sonny Boy Williamson that came here from the South. They used to say, "Sonny Boy, you talking about Rice Miller?" He was pretty popular. The first time I heard Rice was when he made "Dust My Broom" with Elmore James and the flip side "Catfish Blues." That was a spectacular record. And they did record it under the name Sonny Boy Williamson.

And I wasn't really impressed by his first record. It was light of touch, you know. But, as far as harp playing, he was consistent at all times. He played a different style than the two Walters.

See, the two Sonny Boys were similar. Both of them, the two Sonny Boys, carried the same name. The two Walters was similar, you know; the two Walters were basically instrumentalists. The singing added an attraction to their performance. The two Sonny Boys were combination men. They were singers and accompanists, accompanying themselves. They were not instrumentalists; the two Sonny Boys never recorded an instrumental. And even if they did do one, it wasn't really an instrumental, let's say, in the sense of an instrumental. But the two Walters were instrumentalists.

But Rice Miller was consistent, like Sonny Boy; he was totally consistent. From his first record to his last, he was top-notch.

The two Walters were more inconsistent, you know; the ability was there. They were actually the greatest of the four as harpists because they were more spontaneous. And that might have came from their inability to sing, you know, and express themselves like the two Sonny Boys. The two Sonny Boys could express themselves. And another thing the two Sonny Boys had in common was they was very gifted writers, very good poets. They were poets extraordinary. So they didn't have to concentrate on their playing 'cause they had a story to tell. Yeah, the two Walters, not being singers and not being gifted poets and writers like the two Sonny Boys, had to rely on their instrumental work. So this might have forced them to be as extraordinary as they were.

BEAU: When did James Cotton come on the scene?

Interview with Billy Boy Arnold 105

BILLY BOY: Cotton. First time I saw Cotton it was with Muddy. He was a young guy, about my age. He was very friendly, outgoing, likable guy, you know. Everybody liked Cotton. He was always very honest, really outgoing and, you know, really expressive. His ability to play wasn't as great as it was now. He was powerful. But what Cotton had, a lot of people don't have, was drive and consistency. And Cotton could sing all kinds of different styles of songs. Cotton was actually a performist. That's why Cotton is successful.

And his powers in the harp was just awesome. He's a powerhouse. He blew out one of my speakers one time, sat in with me on Forty-third. He had much power in his playing; he just ripped the speaker to shreds.

But Cotton's powers and ability lie in his aggressive performances, aggressive harp playing, and ability to sing all kinds of styles, you know what I mean? He doesn't sing one style; he can sing all the styles, any of them, almost any of the records that became current hits. And he stayed on top of what was current. And he could fall back on them down-home Blues, you know, do that as good as he could do anything else. He is dynamic, I mean, as far as his shows. And his ability on stage, he's really what you call an entertainer's entertainer.

BEAU: So many years have passed, and you've contributed so much to our culture. In the mid-'60s you witnessed the arrival of the White man on the Blues scene, not only as promoter or manager, but as player. Suddenly, you had White Blues cats becoming national acts, making national bucks. What was the reaction to Paul Butterfield and some of the others?

BILLY BOY: Well, Paul Butterfield was one of the first. He was, like, I want to play the Blues. And he had the desire and the ability; he could play. And he came in and was considered one of the guys, only he was learning. The difference with Paul Butterfield and the White guys of today was Paul Butterfield didn't have the sound that the White guys have today. They got some White harmonica players out in California that's outta sight. I mean, they got the sound; they got all of it. They got some cats out there that can really blow. And back at that time—well, Charlie Musselwhite was one of the guys who had the sound. Charlie Musselwhite was a more advanced harp player than Butterfield. And I think that's because Charlie's whole being is just the harp, you know.

The harp is his whole existence. And he plays a beautiful intro, man. Charlie Musselwhite can open up an intro, I mean, the baddest intro you want to hear. You just know this is going to be it! He just has that ability, you know. He had that Black sound, you know, that Paul Butterfield didn't have at that time. Charlie had it. He has that real, down-home sound. He is as good as any of the other guys out there playing.

Paul was good, but he was much lighter weight on the harp than Charlie. And he sort of had a different sound; he didn't have the sound that Charlie, Cotton, and everybody else had.

BEAU: But they were accepted?

BILLY BOY: Oh, yeah, they were accepted, yeah, because the Blues has always been the type of music—well, I think that when Paul Butterfield came on the scene a lot of people was sort of shocked at first. And then it made them feel that Blues could be appreciated by everybody, not just limited to one environment.

BEAU: What was the reaction to the economics and political realities of Charlie and Paul being White cats and able to assemble some Black folks and get out here and make them some money, a whole lot more money than any of the others could make?

BILLY BOY: Well, I'd say in Butterfield's case he got some doors to open up for himself, and he started to make some money. But in Charlie's case, I didn't see any doors open up for him, you know. Charlie had to go the whole route. He had to go step-by-step till he got a chance to get a agent or somebody interested in him to back him and blah, blah, blah. I mean with Butterfield, it seemed like somebody just stepped right in and he was set up.

But here is something good that happened, that Butterfield was instrumental in. This happened at Big John's on the North Side.

Butterfield started playing there first. And then one night, when they had to go out of town, Paul Butterfield called me and asked me to bring my band down to take their place. So I went down there with my band; I had Sammy Lawhorn on guitar, Billy Davenport on drums, and Little Bob on bass before he was playing with Koko Taylor. And we started playing at Big John's. Well, the guy, Big John, heard me play and everything, you know, and I was a better singer and harp player than Butterfield. I was

Billy Boy Arnold, second from right holding harmonica, Chicago, circa 1955. Photographer unknown, *OCBA* archive.

playing original stuff, you know. And he said, "Wow, man, where'd this guy come from?" And so he started booking me and my band down there on the weekends. And sometimes two or three nights of the week.

And then Buddy Guy and Louis Meyers came down. Buddy was featured with Louis Meyers's band, not with Buddy's own band. Louis Meyers got the job, and he needed somebody with a name to start. So he got Buddy to come down there and start his band, because Buddy could sing and play and had, you know, a name. And then Louis got J. B. Lenoir to come down. And then I think they had Junior Wells down there a couple of times, too.

BEAU: This was in the '60s?

BILLY BOY: Yeah, '65 or something like that. And dig this: They didn't even know Muddy, who Muddy was. And then somebody told them that there's one guy that's bigger than everybody, the biggest, the giant of them all; you ought to hear him. Anyway, they didn't know who I was. See, Butterfield went in there, took the Blues into Big John's. And he had my brother, Jerome Arnold, on bass and Sam Lay on drums. And they was an overnight success; the place was packed. So Butterfield got me in

Interview with Billy Boy Arnold 107

there by sitting in, you know, playing in his place when he had to go out of town. And so the man said, "Wow, who is this cat?" "Where has he been?" And then when I played there, then next—I don't know how Louis Meyers and, I think, some of the guys started coming down and inquired about jobs. Magic Sam played there only one night. Magic Sam wasn't in the union. And they had Magic Sam down there and the union man came in before Sam could hit a note and refused to let Sam play. A guy named Whitloff was running Big John's at that time.

BEAU: So Butterfield was the key figure in getting the Blues spread to the North Side.

BILLY BOY: Right.

BEAU: Funny, now there's more Blues north than south or west. But that's another story, another few hours of conversation. So what's ahead for Billy Boy.

BILLY BOY: Travel, recordings, growth, and learning. I'm going to be spreading the Blues message.

BEAU: Thanks for your time.

BILLY BOY: You got it.

February 12, 1993, Chicago

INTERVIEW WITH HERB KENT

L. "Chicago Beau" Beauchamp

Herb Kent was the leader of a cadre of disc jockeys that literally held Black Chicago captive musically for more than three decades. From sunrise to sunset to sunrise, Black Chicago slid, grinded, slobbed, hesitated, philly-dogged, Watusied, drank, smoked, patted, thumped, Gouster-walked, Gouster-bopped, and lived to the sounds of Herb Kent the Cool Gent.

At the time of this interview, Herb was carrying the message via Chicago radio station V103. Herb Kent, still master of the airwaves.

BEAU: Herb, hey, February 1st, right?

HERB: February 1st, right?

BEAU: February 1st, 1993. This is how many years in the broadcast business?

HERB: It's hard to say. I would say over forty-five. More than forty-five, because we're talking about me being sixteen, I guess sixteen, first talking into the microphone and having—at WBEZ—having them replay it as a public service on WIND, WJJD, and stuff like that. And I was in high school—they had a big workshop. They took two kids from every high school. And we had to audition, and I won the audition. And that was the start of it.

BEAU: What high school did you go to?

HERB: Hyde Park. There were, at most, maybe five or six Blacks at that time. And the president of the radio was a Jewish fellow, and he was just too strict, plus they were all girls. So they kicked him out and made me president. And I wrote plays and stuff for them. As a matter of fact, I graduated because of this play that I wrote. I was dressed up as the devil with a tail and stuff like that. I took these really fine-looking White ladies and threw them down in a hole.

And at that time, in the '40s, well they just cracked up They had never seen anything like that, all this singing and stuff. And this teacher was gonna flunk me, but she said that when she saw that, she just had to pass me.

BEAU: What was the name of the play?

HERB: Oh, I forget. It was just something I wrote up about the devil

Herb Kent, Chicago, 1995.
Photo by L. Beauchamp.

throwing White ladies in a hole and singing a song. Sometimes we're fortunate to find out at an early age that we got something going. You know what you want, chase it down, and you get it.

BEAU: Are you a native Chicagoan?

HERB: Yes.

BEAU: When did your radio thing really get to be big? I mean, like, when I came along in the '60s, you were the most established figure on WVON.

HERB: From the minute I got in radio, I did all right, you know. When you first got in, you had to sell spots to be in radio. Blacks did, because the only money you made was in percentages of what you sold. You sold one-minute spots, I think at that time, for sixteen bucks. So if you could sell ten of them in your show, that would be a hundred-and-sixty bucks for that day. And then you get 30 percent of that. And if you had two-hour shares, you could really make quite a bit of money. Al Benson made a fortune doing that. And that was a little hard for me to do, but I did it only because I wanted to be in radio. And when I went to WBEE, it really started for me.

BEAU: What year did you make that transition?

HERB: Oh, I'd say in '53, or something. I had been in radio three or four years, and I was not twenty-five at that time. I was twenty-two, something like that. And at WBEE it really exploded. They had a strike. When they broke the strike, I was the best man they had at WBEE. And you understand it was the first time I had made a hundred dollars. And I remember my then-girlfriend threw a party for me when I hit this lofty plateau of making one hundred dollars a day! And it was for like nine-day weeks. You know, you work hard and you learn.

The way they broke the strike was they offered me a job in Chicago, and WBEE then capitulated and accepted the union because they were being hurt, they lost their best man: me. I went to WHFC, and that's when it really exploded for me, with stuff like Rodney Roach and the Grunchens and all the different things. And then WHFC was bought by Leonard Chess; he turned it into WVON, and then it became a twenty-four-hour Black station. And I had the Wahoo Man at the Times Square. It was really huge. We were number one in Chicago and I think the most fantastic station in the nation. I fully expect them to make a movie out of that one day. I think it would be very fascinating. It would be full of lust, [laughing] oh, everything, everything was happening. So that was just only human.

BEAU: So WVON came into existence as Leonard Chess being owner an . . .

HERB: He bought WVON because he used to listen to me on there and I was hot. And he bought that station for a million dollars.

BEAU: A million dollars.

HERB: One million dollars. The first year he grossed clear over three million dollars.

BEAU: And that was a mixture of music, of R & B and Blues?

HERB: On WVON?

BEAU: On WVON, yeah.

HERB: Well that was just Soul, straight Soul station.

BEAU: That was all Leonard wanted was straight Soul?

HERB: Twenty-four hours a day.

BEAU: Twenty-four hours of the day. So when did Pervis Spann "the Blues Man" come to the station?

HERB: Pervis came on—well; see, theoretically, I was the first one he and others came after me. Al Benson came over from GES. GES was going through some changes. Rodney Jones came over. They made him program director. Lucky Cordell came over, and Butterball came over. And they were just generally shifting around until we finally ended up with the crew.

What a crew it was! I'd never seen anything like it, you know.

The bumper stickers you see that are so predominant today, we had one that said "WVON." It was on every car in Chicago. And we'd go out, make appearances and climb inside cars, put it on the inside of windows, on the bumpers. You'd never seen anything like that.

BEAU: All the way live.

HERB: All the way live, you know, Black, White. We were just really big. We were at times as big as WLS, and at times we came in number one and beat WLS out. They [WLS] didn't even know we existed. They called up to find out who the hell we were! Dick Biondi and I were on opposite sides of each other. At the time, we were still friends. One day he would be number one, and the next day I would be number one.

So I have done as well as Biondi and other people. I haven't made as much money because we never did make as much money as they did. But popularity? Yes. When I do my thing at Walter Payton's club—where is he, in Schaumburg? I see many White people come out that I know are listeners. Some will come up and talk; others won't. There was a gentleman who came up, a White gentleman who came up. He smelled mighty—you know he had a nice suit on; he was very meticulous looking; looked like he could have been the vice president of the First National Bank. And he whispered when he went out, "When you get on your show, go way, way back."

BEAU: Way back then. Yeah, yeah, man.

HERB: I might be getting ahead of myself, but it's a very, very colorful career—still is.

BEAU: When I was listening to you at fifteen and sixteen and seventeen, there was a mystique. And I would just love to have a transcript of one of those phone conversations with sexy-voiced chick saying, "Hello, Herb." And you were so blasé with them, finessing them off left and right. And me and my partners would be in the car going, "Damn, man, damn, the Cool Gent got all the ladies!"

HERB: Let me tell you, I was a single fellow at the time. So those ladies would call in and come over to my house later on that night. I lived in Lake Meadows.

BEAU: Uh-oh, that was playland back then.

HERB: That's right. We'd play around, and I'd never see them again. Of course, you couldn't do that today with all the social diseases.

BEAU: No, you can't do that today.

HERB: It was all . . . it was just all life and fun at that time.

BEAU: Tell me about the jargon at the time, the language. You know, like *hammers* and *nails*.

HERB: Well, I started a lot of that. I remember Sid McCoy—I used to look up to Sid McCoy. He was up there with Al Benson. As a matter of fact, he's still on the air today, coming out of California. Really, just a great gentleman and my mentor. And I wanted to sound like him. And it was so strange that years later his daughters used to listen to me. And Sid says—this is the funniest thing—he says, "My kids just think you're king. You're inventing a new language." And I never will forget him saying that. 'Cause that's what I was doing. I was taking CB language and stuff I heard in the street, adding to it, you know, like, *YLs* meant "young ladies," *10–2 double plus* meant "really, really, really good," and *hammers,* I got that from the West Side, which was a name for females. *Fesneckies* I got from some guy that . . . well, we were talking in the dark. I got the idea that he was running from the police. He was an ex-serviceman. And we were all sitting around just partying. And he was on the run from something. But he just felt like talking that night about fesneckies. And I picked up on the term *fesneckie*. I'd go anywhere—at least I used to be able to go anywhere, anyplace, and just talk to people. I found it quite interesting. And I would just react. I would react—I was a big reactor to what was going on in Chicago and what people were saying.

BEAU: I remember a song that had, "There's a new fesnecki in my neighborhood, I've got to know her name."

HERB: "There's a new fesnecki with a mellow fern."

BEAU: With a mellow fern. Uh-oh. That's the whole thing about the language that was just incredible. It amazes me to see, you know, how our language has, like, been extended over to White society. And it's been diluted and homogenized.

HERB: That's true.

BEAU: And they actually think they invented some shit. That's the incredible thing about it. But, you know . . .

HERB: They got our styles and watered them down.

BEAU: Yeah, yeah. The whole language that we have, our movements, dance, everything, they just watered it down and made it acceptable, homogenized it; then the advertising industry turned around a makes a fortune of what we are told is unacceptable language. Black language . . . culture is only acceptable to Whites when they can make some money on it. Suddenly it's cool to be Black-like.

HERB: That's true, definitely true. For instance, when I hear a White chick talk about this dude hit on me, I really still have to turn around and look at her.

BEAU: Trying to imitate us is really humorous.

HERB: That's like trying to imitate the Isley Brothers.

BEAU: Yeah, yeah.

HERB: Which is impossible to do.

BEAU: I want to talk about a movement that seems all but forgotten. An important part of Black culture, urban Black culture: the Gousters.

HERB: Oh, yes.

BEAU: How did they begin?

HERB: Weren't you the one to tell me the Gousters were the first ones with the maxicoats fad?

BEAU: The maxicoats, that's right.

HERB: Oh, let me see. That's—a Gouster. I can remember looking up, thinking there's an English term that is almost analogous to a pimp, a dandy, or a kind of urban gypsy.

BEAU: I don't know if it's in that dictionary there. You probably need to look in a deep English dictionary. But maybe. Maybe it's in there.

HERB: How do you spell Gouster . . . G-o-?

BEAU: I thought it was G-o-u or G-o-w-s-t-e-r.

HERB: Let's see, G-

BEAU: Well, one thing, you know, they were kind of nomadic a little bit. They were cats on the move, you know.

HERB: Yeah. And the way they dressed . . .

BEAU: Nonconformists.

HERB: Yeah, they were nonconformists. They were rough, very rough. They weren't mama's boys at all. They were mavericks. Mavericks, you know, in manner and dress. It was really like a state of mind. Whereas Ivy Leaguers, of course, were more preppy; Brooks Brothers shirts, outfits that you would call preppy. And Ivy Leaguers often weren't as good physically. They took many ass whippings from Gousters. Gousters used to run them home from dances and stuff.

BEAU: People would ask if a set [party] was Gouster or Ivy. If it was predominately Gouster, Ivies were afraid to go.

HERB: For sure. And they actually hung together sometimes. It's a state of mind. And the strange thing about it was the Ivy League ladies fell madly in love with the Gouster fellows. They just adored them! All those rough fellows with the big beaver hats, those long coats, and the sneer on their faces.

BEAU: Clean as the Board of Health.

HERB: That's right. And these ladies really liked them. And that state of mind exists today. Our promotion guy who puts all of our spots together is White. He'd call them greasers. The White term is greasers. Some Black dudes in Philadelphia, they had a term for them, they call them Toughies. Black Gouster, Toughies. See, it's a state of mind that exists still somewhat today, I think.

BEAU: You know, it would be wonderful to get some documentation, photographs from the Gouster era. I've had no luck in my search.

HERB: It's a good thing about the job I have now, I come to care about what I do. And I get involved in these projects, and one is really to get into the Gouster/Ivy League thing. The people were really serious about that. Some guys from the West Side who are politically in power now used to be stone Gousters, you know, years ago. 'Cause years ago, like as you were saying in the '60s, you really had to just about declare what you were. Some guys, it would be either one depending on where they were in the neighborhood. And then some guys were just dyed-in-the-wool Ivy League guys, and some were dyed-in-the-wool Gousters. Some Gousters have become doctors, and, on the same hand, some Ivy Leaguers have done well. And on the other hand, some Gousters and Ivy Leaguers have ended up in jail.

BEAU: Yeah, well, there were some hard Ivies out there.

HERB: Hard Ivies that chased a few Gousters.

BEAU: Yeah. I knew a couple of them. This cat they called R. T., he was a hard Ivy that would bust a Gouster's ass. Some of them cats could do that.

HERB: Remember we used to have them Lochinvar social clubs?

BEAU: Yeah, Lochinvars. How do you spell that?

HERB: I don't know.

BEAU: I never knew how to spell that.

HERB: Put it down phonetically. I believe they're still going today.

BEAU: Lochinvars. That was an Ivy club.

HERB: And there were a few other Ivy clubs like that.

BEAU: I was a Gouster; we didn't have social clubs like that, but we went to the clubs on the street, like the Peps.

HERB: OK, the Peps. You'd see more Gousters at the Peps, places like that.

BEAU: And Budland?

HERB: The Bud, see the Budland was the first place that really, that kind of youngish, not underage, that people could go and listen to the music that we were playing, like "T Mambo" and stuff like "Stand By Me" by Ben E. King, and drink.

For some reason, Budland got more exposure than the Peps. The Peps has always been there. But these were places where you could go and drink. I was doing the teen thing. These teens would leave my place and go, maybe, to the Peps and go to the Budland and do their thing. The Budland didn't have that big connotation of achievement. They didn't have fights and stuff that the Peps did. But the Budland in kind of way was a smoother operation. They had more of a to-gether kind of thing. Rodney Jones and them were bringing shows down from the Regal, like Aretha Franklin and stuff like that. But I had them, too, also, at various places. I used to date this man's daughter just recently that owned the Peps, she was telling me—while we were still on good terms, she was telling me about the place.

BEAU: Here's another thing about the Gousters. They had their own dances: the Gouster Bop, the Gouster Walk.

HERB: The Gouster Bop, the Gouster Walk, and the Dip.

Another good Gouster place was the Persian Ballroom. I had Gouster Sunday there, let me tell you. It was the biggest crowd I ever had. And these guys came in little packs, like eight guys, two guys, four guys. And they'd all come in together, you know. And they were clean, with the beaver hats and long coats and everything.

And I believe it was 10:00 p.m. when somebody gave the signal, and all hell broke loose. We just kept playing records, you know, but I was ducking down behind the thing. And these guys fought out of—I never will forget it—they fought—are you familiar with the Persian?

BEAU: Yeah.

HERB: They fought down the steps of the Persian, fought down Cottage Grove down to Walgreens on the east side of the street, crossed the street, fought over to the Tivoli Theatre, fought all in the lobby of the Tivoli, fought all the way back to the Persian, up the steps, and back into the ballroom! I talked to some guys that were in there back then, and we just marveled at that, boy!

BEAU: Cats could duke it out. Humbugging was what it was all about back then.

HERB: Not a shot was fired. I imagine there were some black eyes and some cut lips, but not a shot was fired.

BEAU: It was all about the finesse of the fist, man.

HERB: All about who was the best Gouster at that time.

BEAU: That's it.

HERB: And I just don't understand today. I guess I do understand. Because I was watching last night—if you watch any given day on TV, they have AK-47s, machine pistols, the most powerful handguns; it's a damn shame. The same Gousters we're talking about, if they'd been exposed to that, perhaps they would fall the victim to it, too.

BEAU: Well, one good thing about it was in those days—I mean, like, Forty-seventh Street was flourishing—I mean, survival was not as difficult because the buck went a lot further. A cat with a few dollars in his pocket, man, you know, he'd go to Jew Town and get semiclean and go to Forty-seventh Street and get his shit made, you know. And if you had twenty dollars, man, in your pocket on a Friday night, where the beer wasn't but sixty cents in the bars . . . your shit was happening.

HERB: Go get your shoes shined with the white stitches and put the peroxide on there, take the brush and go around there and whiten up the stitches. Now, they have pistols. They have little nickel-plated .38s and stuff like that.

BEAU: Nothing like now, man. No, they weren't in the trade. The cats peddled reefer, something like that, but nobody was in the crack trade.

HERB: You could still ride the bus at night, you know, always at night you wandered. But I remember doing stuff at the Guys and Gals as late as '69, '70. And standing outside one day at two o'clock in the morning, and a bus pulled up and twenty people got out. To go to a nightclub off a bus! Could you imagine them doing that today on Sixty-ninth Street?

BEAU: No, man, no. Because I remember stuff like that. I remember taking a bus up to the Toronado and then over to the Doll House, then take another bus up to Fran's Illumner Lounge and ride back down to Budland, and then end up at the Castle Club on Seventy-first and East End.

HERB: Or walk from Sixty-third Street and Stony Island trying to get to Cottage and drop in these little places and drinking. If you could stay sober enough, you might make it at two, three o'clock in the morning without any fear. I remember that. So times have changed, really colorful times. It was places. It was Chuck's place on Cottage Grove. It was Budland. It was the Toronado. It was the Peppermint. Of course, then I had the Times Square. It was the Regal, the Tivoli. It was the Metropolitan Theater, they did a couple of things around there. It was the Rhodes theater. Many American Legion halls up and down Cottage and Forty-seventh Street. There were just tons of places that you could rent, the Parkway Ballroom and the YWCA.

BEAU: I mean the fact that you could go out—I mean, my phone started ringing on Wednesday telling me where the sets was, you know; basically who was stepping where and where you could get down at. And it was like by Saturday night you would be like, whoosh—you'd be partying hard, man.

HERB: You could buy a suit of clothes for eighty-five bucks, pretty decent. You could get a suit made for under a hundred dollars.

BEAU: Do you know what was, like, the basic price for a tough Gouster jacket from Cherry the tailor?

HERB: I think that you could get one, a plain one, for about twenty-eight dollars. A little plaid—they had green plaid, red plaid. You could get an all-white one with brass buttons and stuff like that. Cherry the tailor was really something. He was an old-line pimp.

BEAU: An old-line pimp?

HERB: Yeah. The girls who were sewing for him were going to bed with him. Then there was Smokey Joe. See, part of my reason for success was the sponsors that I had and the commercials I produced for these guys. I set them up with the Supremes, and I wrote the commercials and stuff like that. That all goes back to my thing. I've just been totally 200 percent involved into radio, and I guess I still am. You talk about this R & B, that's all part of it. People could come out and see you and be with you. I would make my gimmicks come alive, like the Wahoo Man.

BEAU: What did the Wahoo Man look like?

HERB: He's hideous. He's patterned after a man that really existed. He had some kind of runny sores on his face and wore an old brown hat, carried a broomstick, wore a long coat, and was very, very mean. He just scared the shit out of everybody.

Yes, sir, we created him. We went to the Art Institute, had a rubber mask made, and we got makeup that seemed like pus and sores. We got a casket from A. R. Leak. Ladies fainted. Kids peed on themselves publicly on stage.

BEAU: How would you bring him out?

HERB: All kind of ways. Usually in a casket. I would go into a place with the casket closed, and they would dance and everything. And all of a sudden, we would stop the dance and dim the lights and start playing Bach's Fugue in E—you're aware of that, you know, it's a most tremendous song.

In today's radio, we don't have the flexibility that we once had. We used to sit up here and talk, call on the phone, play records on the turntable, and just carry on. Today, it's less talk and more music. You don't have that amount of time. And the radio station wants me to be Herb Kent, but they put me within a framework to be Herb Kent. And that's what I work with. So it's very difficult to bring a lot of that stuff back. I can do it partially in a contemporary way.

BEAU: You know Gerri's, Gerri's Palm Tavern around there?

HERB: Sure.

BEAU: That's the last thing that happened on Forty-seventh Street.

HERB: She's still open over there?

BEAU: She's still there, yeah.

HERB: Oh, no, there's another club—this other club is still there, the one next to Gerri's, the 113 Club or something like that.

BEAU: That's still there?

HERB: That's still there. Those two are still there. Also, on Fifty-first Street, the Brown Derby is still there. I think that's about it. I think they're just hanging on.

BEAU: The eradication process is almost complete now. It's a removal of people, often forced out. Gentrification. You know what I mean? When I look up the West Side and the South Side and I see Realtors that I know are basically North Shore Realtors with signs stuck in houses up and down Warren Boulevard and King Drive.

HERB: You know Madison Street was a good strip at one time. They had the Red Top. They had the Speakeasy. They had the Lion Room, which might still be there. They had tons of nice places that were happening on the West Side at the time, too. All that is gone. I don't know . . . things change.

BEAU: You know, but do we have a community anymore, a visible community? Do we have a community, something that's vibrant, with a center, a focal point, a culture, a history?

HERB: Well, it's deep because the family thing is not what it used to be. How many people really sit down to dinner with the family every night?

BEAU: Very few.

HERB: And then, too, on the same hand, high tech has given us movies at home, hi-fi at home. You can, instead of going out to these clubs, you can have a party at home and be out late, too. So, it's a whole new ballgame.

BEAU: We don't have clubs, we don't have shops, basically, you know. We don't have services for each other the way we had them, so the music was like part of the cohesiveness. I mean, the music was like magic, it was, like, spiritual.

HERB: The way we control a lot of folks was through music, I don't care who it is. Even today, they like that music. The hardest, toughest person likes his music. I noticed that back in '65, '70, some of the most hard-core criminals liked some of the most beautiful songs. They had a feeling; they had a feeling for some of the really nice music. I really remember one guy stayed in jail, he was a Blackstone Ranger, he liked "Scarborough Fair" by Wes Montgomery, he liked "Hurt So Bad" by Little Anthony and the Imperials, really nice music that these rough guys liked. They really related to that. And that's something they liked that you don't think about today.

BEAU: Like you say, Blackstone Rangers, some of those cats, I remember a lot of those cats were street-corner poets. A lot of cats were poets. I mean, because you had to be able rap up on what you wanted anyway. You know, ladies, some sex, whatever. You couldn't just be walking around talking about "gimme some." You had to have something to say back in them days, you know. You had to have a rap. Ladies dug a smooth rap, and dudes used to practice their raps. Sometimes modeling after the Temptations or others.

HERB: Yes, it was a different ballgame.

BEAU: What about Gousterettes?

HERB: Oh, the Gouster girls . . . and Ivy League girls. I talked to them on the phone on Sundays, and I'm going to start doing that again with the ladies. I haven't done that in a long time. The ladies describe what they're wearing. You know, like the favorite dress of an Ivy League lady was a peppermint shirt with button-down collars. And the Gouster girls were telling me what they were wearing. Most of the time it was, you know, high-style stuff I think, all of these pleats and things that the Gouster dudes were wearing. I get the feeling that a Gouster dame was a rough dame, and an Ivy League dame thought of herself as a more refined and sophisticated dame. That's a feeling that I get because I think that, overall, the overview of that stuff, that's what it is. Even though the Gouster dudes don't admit it, but they were gang-type dudes.

BEAU: Well, I mean, like the Ivy Leaguers, if you go down to Brooks Brothers and buy you some clothes, you know, you're acquiescing to a whole European ethic, in a sense.

But when you're a Gouster, you rejecting—I mean you wear European-type clothes . . . we're in the West, but you're rejecting the norm. And you got the whole philosophy to go with it. I mean, like you said, cats fighting all the way out and around the corner.

HERB: Sure. I talked to a police commander I'm acquainted with. I said, were you a Gouster or an Ivy Leaguer? He gave me a hard look, and then he said, "I was an Ivy Leaguer." And I didn't believe it. I didn't believe it for one minute. I says, "Man, I ain't going to tell nobody."

BEAU: Would you like to give me some closing thoughts on a couple of things? What happened to cats, man, or the deep poetry of cats like Donald and the Delighters, people like that? I mean, they had songs, man, that was like sagas.

HERB: "Elephant Walk."

BEAU: Yeah.

HERB: So what happened to them?

BEAU: Yeah, I mean that style, you know.

HERB: Sure. Basically it was the Doo-wop groups like the Spaniels, the El Dorados, the Wrens, the

Sparrows, etc. Business things forced the lead singers, like Donald Jenkins and the Delighters, to go out on their own. The Delighters, or so-and-so, and Diana Ross and the Supremes and these things. When this thing started to happen, sooner or later the lead singer ultimately made it on the big switch and went solo, and the group generally died. And the groups ultimately just faded. Matter of fact, it still happens today, like the Commodores. On the rare occasion, the group will continue on when the lead singer goes, but it's very rare. I don't know what's going to happen to Kool and the Gang. Kool and the Gang is very good, but they got this J. T. that's the most amazing fellow I think I've ever seen. I mean he just sings everything, just sings so smooth . . . just right. I have a feeling that he needed them, too, as much as they needed him. 'Cause I hadn't heard that much of him, you know. But that money pressure bit, the pressure of money that causes the change of times and stuff like that.

BEAU: What's the typical pattern for successful albums for R & B?

HERB: Well, what I found out for Black albums is that the magic number is three. A good example would be the Ohio Players. Their first one was *The Ohio Players in Person,* then they got that *Fire* album, and then I think they had *Sweet Sticky Thing,* and that was about it. They had a couple of others, but I don't think they really sold. So they do about an album a year, so you're looking at a three- or four-year run for a group, and then it's over with. There's a lot of pressure, sometimes internal pressure, like with the Temptations; Barry Gordy split them up. It was friction from the beginning between Otis, Melvin, and Eddie. And Barry Gordy was the recipient of all that unhappiness. They're on the road making 500 dollars a week each, and Barry's making all the rest of the money. They couldn't stand each other. It's a wonder they stayed together as long as they did. I was the last one to interview Eddie Kendricks before he died, and he hated Motown. He hated them with a passion for what they had done to him. I asked him, "What about your royalties?" He laughed, "What royalties!"

BEAU: Who would you call the connecting artists between the Blues and R & B? I like to try to bridge things together so that people won't lose sight of our music.

HERB: Tyrone Davis, Johnny Taylor, Garland Green; a lot of them came out of Chicago. Chicago was the headquarters for this. O. V. Wright, Bobbie Bland—who had a Jazz thing happening, too. And Albert King, who was really hard-core Blues, sometimes took the edge off, like, in "The Very Thought of You."

BEAU: Give me your message to the young Black folks about how to preserve and cherish this music? Give us some pearls of wisdom?

HERB: Be interested in more than one kind of music. There's good music everywhere. There's some good Soul music, good Blues music, and you might even find a good Rock thing, you know. Try to get a message out of the music and don't take literally what you hear in the Rap music. Realize that these are just people behind a microphone, almost like a soap opera; they're just acting, making a picture of stuff that's not real. Don't get off the true course of what's happening. And above all, save all your records; they'll be valuable twenty years from now.

BEAU: Thanks, Herb.

HERB: Thank you

February 1, 1993, Chicago

THE BLUES ARE A PEOPLE WHO ARE FINALLY GOING TO TAKE CARE OF BUSINESS

David Whiteis

It's been a rough year in Chicago Blues. As outlined elsewhere in this issue, we've lost several of our most beloved and treasured artists; others are in shaky health. On a more global scale, political atrocities from Los Angeles to Somalia to Bosnia have put a pall over the human spirit throughout the world, and at least some of that international sense of catastrophe and dread has necessarily filtered down into the local consciousness. There's a jaunt missing from our step: Things ain't what they used to be, and our Wang Dang Doodles don't roar all night long with quite as much reckless abandon as before.

As usual, the community has come together in moments of grief to help and support its own—it's characteristic of both the music and those who love it that we've managed to create some healing rays of light in the midst of the darkness that's threatened to overtake us this year. Benefits have been held, sympathies extended, memorial concerts and Blues family reunions have helped ease the pain.

Even more encouraging: In the truest spirit of "bring me my flowers while I'm living," we've managed to overcome the unfortunate human tendency to sit on our generosity until only memories can be honored. A benefit for guitarist Lefty Dizz filled the cavernous room at Buddy Guy's Legends just before Christmas; Dizz responded by rallying miraculously from the cancer that had seemed determined to sap his spirit and his life. He's back out there playing again, rocking houses and delighting fans with his gut-level emotionality and musicianship as well as the riotous good humor of his stage act. More recently, a group of entertainers ranging from Otis Clay, Tyrone Davis, and Mavis Staples to Alvin "Twine Time" Cash presented an old-fashioned Soul revue at the New Regal Theatre to benefit Kitty Neely, a well-known Chicago radio personality who's in danger of losing her home due to hospital and health care costs.

But death and devastation have raised some issues that can't be palliated by star-spangled shows or charity events. Dizz and Ms. Neely are doing fine, but it's no secret that some of the other people we've lost and some of those we seem to be on the verge of losing were and are in the throes of drug and alcohol addiction. It's also no secret that the absence of health insurance, financial management skills, and simple guidance has left many artists vulnerable to the vicissitudes of fate, poverty, and the dealings of the unscrupulous leeches who populate the "business" end of show business.

There've been benefits where the intended recipients never saw any of the money; other acts of alleged support have left a vile taste in the mouth of everyone who knew the real story. Certain clubs have repeatedly splashed the names and faces of deceased artists all over their advertisements to publicize "tributes" that weren't sanctioned by the artists' families and had little to do with anything but the clubs' revenues.

Sometimes the very people who help bring artists to their destruction dance in the flames of their funeral pyres, still raking in the profits from death. In at least one instance, an artist whose demise had been precipitated by a heartbreaking drug-related decline in health and career was feted at a memorial presented by a local club owner notorious for his "hands-off" (and, perhaps, "pockets-full") attitude toward the drug dealing that goes on every night in and around his establishment.

That kind of thing is beyond cynical or even unconscionable. It's obscene, and it's been going on for years. They did it to Jazz musicians in New York in the 1950s; they did it in the '60s to visionary and vulnerable young artists like Jimi Hendrix; they're doing it in Chicago in the '90s.

I'm not naive: I realize that Bluesmen and Blueswomen are adults, responsible for their own behavior. But I also know that handfuls of money can do strange things to a person who's never had any, and I know that the allure of the fast life has shot down more than one promising career. You can't babysit anyone, but you can make damn sure that your own business—nightclub, record company, whatever—does nothing to propagate the destruction.

There are some encouraging stories—not everyone in the business is a bloodsucker. One young guitarist, fresh from the West Side, possessed with visions of glory and superstardom, went through several confrontations with cocaine before he finally broke free—his record company stayed with him throughout his ordeal, paying for his rehab, assuring him that he wouldn't be abandoned. A veteran performer, finally free from a years-long addiction that almost destroyed him, is currently being helped by his agent and producers to the extent that they've hired security guards to keep the vultures away from the man's dressing room when he's on tour.

But we can't rely on the beneficence of the bosses to keep the scene clean. First and foremost, of course, as the Staples reminded us years ago, we have to respect ourselves and each other. Veteran Blues artists must counsel their protégés in more than just music, and everyone has the responsibility to act, well, responsibly. Even more important, though, we can't allow the twentieth-century Western capitalist myth of "individual responsibility" to obscure the social and political overtones of what's going on here.

Individuals must own up to their own behavior and weaknesses, but make no mistake, the same people who control the money and the gigs also control the drugs—maybe not always the same individuals under the same roof, but definitely the same economic, class, and cultural interests. (I'd like to add "racial" to the list, but it's a tragic fact that some moneyed, self-interested African Americans are as ready as the most voracious White genocidist to fill young bodies with poison and then laugh all the way to the Cadillac dealership.)

Quite simply, it's time for us to do on the streets, in the nightclubs, in dressing rooms and union halls what I can't do on paper for fear of lawsuits: name names, give addresses, pull coats.

I know that gigs are hard to come by, and no one should have to give up a well-paying job for the sake of righteousness. But if word really got around that no musician of repute would support a businessman of disrepute— someone who allows or encourages the sale or use of destructive substances in his club, someone who keeps artists and others strung out and beholden with "loans" to support a habit, someone who revels in the stereotypical and racist "sleazy Blues club" image to the detriment of the dignity of music and musicians alike—that club just might find itself unable to compete, and some of the lowlifes who propagate the destruction around here might have to clean up their acts or get out of town.

It's not just drugs, of course. The legion of Blues masters who've died in penury, ripped off and exploited for their whole careers, would fill all of the various Blues Halls of Fame currently battling for supremacy in Chicago, We seem to have fallen into a fatalistic trap: That's the business, that's the Blues, the bosses are going to exploit the servants whether either is White or African American.

We can't afford that attitude any longer. The music community should join others—people of color, single mothers, gays, those discriminated against on the basis of physical appearance—and demand legal representation. We should be out there agitating for an increase in the funding and availability of Legal Assistance Foundation lawyers to represent the oppressed in an increasingly corporate-dominated, exploitative world.

Again, I don't want to paint with too broad a brush: There are scrupulous Blues labels out there. Even some of the larger ones, the ones we grumble about because of their putative stranglehold on the business and their bull-in-a-china-shop turf wars, have honorable records in terms of fiscal honesty and payment. But it's a commentary on how vile the recording industry is that we feel compelled to praise simple decency—honoring contracts, being loyal to an artist who's made a lot of money for the company—as something exemplary and unusual.

It's up to us to up the ante. These companies have lawyers; it wouldn't hurt them to present a series of workshops on the legal basics of career management—how to read a contract, what to look for, how to cross out an offending clause so it won't come back to haunt you, how to deal with releases and permission to tape performances. These workshops should be given pro bono and should be open to all performing artists (not just Blues musicians) who feel the need to attend. It would be a small price for a successful company to pay, to have its lawyer give a few weekends back to the community from which they've reaped their profits. It can happen, but only if we demand it.

Finally, I want to say a few words to myself and my own colleagues—the journalists and writers who also make our livings from the artists who play the music. We have a major responsibility, and we don't always meet it. I know that in the past I've written things that weren't as well researched as they might have been because I knew the artist I was writing about couldn't read or would never see the article. My intentions were good—to add anecdotal color, to fill out a character portrait—but my methods were wrong. We've all got to be more careful not to take the easy way out.

I've read alleged onstage "quotes" and on-the-scene accounts from some writers that I know were fabricated, because I was at the event and it didn't go that way at all; other times I've seen articles that were so condescending and insulting I thought I was reading a discarded page from the script for *Birth of a Nation*. If writers can't write the truth—and perhaps more important, if writers can't get outside their prejudices and preconceived notions to see the Blues culture in all its diversity and dignity—then they should be writing about something else.

These days there's a new breed of journalist out there: the taper. Video cameras seem to be sprouting on archivists' shoulders like second heads; these twin-cranium'd beings have been spotted lurking around stages all over Chicago, soothing artists' misgivings with promises that "it'll never be used commercially" or "it's just for a student project." Well, my CD rack is filled with live performances, on major labels, that someone originally taped fifteen or twenty years ago for "private" use; I've already begun to see bootlegged copies of videotaped performances making the rounds.

Anyone with any kind of recording device—audio or video—should be in possession of a legally verifiable document promising that any and all royalties and proceeds from the performance, including copyrights of songs not yet published, will return to the artist. The artist must be guaranteed a copy of the tape. I don't care if the person doing the taping is a student, a journalist, a hobbyist, or a boyfriend or girlfriend of the performer—no contract, no recording. No release, no taping—no ifs, no ands, no buts. If the artist feels uncomfortable with any part of the arrangement—no go.

Some veteran musicians may be uninformed or naive about written contracts; many of these elders have young sidemen who must take on the responsibility to act as "instant agents," advising their mentors and helping keep the tapers and filmers in line. I know it's not always possible—and some bootlegging is probably inevitable—but again, we've got to pull together and help one another as much as we can. At the Chicago Jazz Festival, performers have been known to stop in midshow to demand that cameras be lowered. As an MC at the Chicago Blues Festival, I've personally interrupted a performance and waited until the police could escort illicit tapers out of the park.

I could go on forever, but I think my point is clear: The best way to honor the memory of those who've gone before is to make sure that the pitfalls and oppression that have dragged too many down will not devastate future generations. The only way I know to do that is to change things so that sufficient power rests in the hands of those who make the music.

The title of this article comes from *Ringolevio,* a remarkable book by a 1960s-era street radical named Emmett Grogan. He understood, and lived by, the truism that liberation and freedom are taken, never given: You don't get anywhere asking the powers that be for favors. The late Bluesman Jimmy Reed understood the very same thing: "If you want it done right," he sang, "you've got to do it yourself."

FROM THE *ORIGINAL CHICAGO BLUES ANNUAL*

Issue Number 6

OCBA number 6 is dedicated to Gwendolyn Brooks, Randall Robertson, Katherine Dunham, and Nelson Mandela. We praise and honor Mandela for securing freedom for his people after years of struggle and for his rise to the presidency of South Africa. I have been asked many times by self-anointed Blues purists, "What does Mandela have to do with the Blues; he's not even an American?" My usual reply has been that it doesn't matter on what side of the ocean apartheid is taking place. The pain and suffering of Mandela and his people are the same as ours here. The music of Black South Africa reflects a brutal condition and tradition, as does ours; out of the misery, it provides a counterbalance to the menacing behavior of the White establishment, in the present and in the past. I wish there was a Mandela here. For those who ask that question, Blues is seemingly nothing more than a carnival or minstrel show played out in saloons and musty nightclubs around the country to White audiences. And some of these very people organize themselves into Blues societies yet know little, if anything, about the Black experience in the Americas and elsewhere and live their day-to-day lives far from the conditions that brought about the music and other elements of a Blues life.

INTERVIEW WITH CHICAGO BEAU
A Conversation between Old Friends

Julio Finn

Whoever is part of whatever civilization helplessly loves some aspects of it, and some of the people in it. A person does not lightly elect to oppose his society. One would much rather be at home among one's compatriots than be mocked and detested by them. And there is a level on which mockery of the people, even their hatred, is moving because it is so blind: it is terrible to watch people cling to their captivity and insist on their own destruction. I think Black people have always seen spinning above the thoughtless American head, the shape of the wrath to come.

—James Baldwin, from *No Name in the Street*

JULIO: Tell me something about how you as a young child and today, forty-five years later, came to be a seeker of knowledge?

BEAU: There are people who at an early age seem to have a sense about who they are and who they can become. When I was around ten years old, I remember I had done a chore for a neighbor and got paid a hefty ten dollars. I took the money and bought two books: *Great Essays in Science,* and *Great Essays in Philosophy.* I may not have understood what I was reading entirely, but I had the desire to learn something and was intrigued by the subject matter. My mother was concerned that I would be perceived as an egghead if I took those books around when we were together. You know, like at the beauty parlor or shopping. It's interesting to think now about how the thinking was. Parents wanted you to have an education, but there was a fear of not being accepted if you were perceived as being too smart. So being average was the norm; that was acceptable. Being something other than average had and has a negative connotation. Also part of her concern was a result of her experiences with White folks. The thing in the South and North was that Whites didn't like no "educated, uppity, smart-ass nigger," so in her own way she was kind of protecting me from the vicious reprisals inflicted by White people, which both she and my father had witnessed. But even still she always encouraged reading. She always bought my sister and me books. And my father is a reader. When he was around on weekends, he was also the homework overseer.

JULIO: It's always tantalizing and inspirational to meet someone engaged in discovery. The things I know that you're involved in, you don't have to do them. They certainly don't make you any money, any big money. Correct me if I'm wrong, but you haven't been paid for being the first Black person to create a journal about the bedrock of Black culture in America.

BEAU: The remuneration for this type of effort is not instantaneous from a monetary standpoint. The reward is in the accomplishment, which is getting the message out there, touching others, and then again, being touched. That's inside of me, and that's what I live with.

JULIO: That's a type of reward that most people are not satisfied with. Most people want to see something tangible from their work: a car, a bank account. It's intriguing to come across someone like you whose interest goes beyond the material.

BEAU: When you are building a foundation for yourself, and at the same time contributing to an already existing foundation that consists of the ages, energy, the blood, and sweat of our Black ancestors, ultimately the reward you get is knowing that you have contributed to the broadening and strengthening of that existing foundation for those who are to follow. Here in the West, especially in America, that concept is considered abstract and damn near insane. Another reward is a paragon like Snooky Pryor telling me last year in San Remo, Italy, that he was proud of my work and that Black artists and the masses in general should take heed. Hearing that from a senior elder like Snooky is an exceptional reward. Snooky is wise in many ways and understands fully the nature of individuals who attempt to commandeer our culture. Euroamericans, if you will, are for the most part interested in our culture for self-serving reasons. I'm not saying all of them think the same way, absolutely not. I'm saying there is a trend afloat for four centuries, and there are some folks at the helm with bulging pocketbooks and vapid souls.

JULIO: One of the things I appreciate about your *Blues Annual* is that you have created a platform for Black commentators and writers and many Blues people to voice their feelings about their culture. Correct me if I'm wrong, but this is something that's never been done before, even in the other Blues publications. It seems all the writers contributing to these journals are White. Strange isn't it that no one that's a part of the subject being dealt with has an opportunity to voice their comments.

BEAU: What I see in some other Blues publications are policies that exclude any Black that may challenge the self-appointed positions of the publishers and editors. I've spoken with a few of them who not only haven't a clue about Black life or history but also see Blues as something anybody can do: a bandwagon on which any bored, lifeless, cultureless, soulless grunt can jump on and make a name and a living for themselves.

JULIO: That's their arrogance. And it's selective. They wouldn't dare attempt to preside over Chinese culture. You don't see these people in Chinatown telling them what it is to be Chinese. But because of this stage of our evolvement we are easy prey. What's the word for these kind of people?

BEAU: In this case, *parasite* fits. It's true almost anybody can learn anything, including Blues music, technically. And certainly, anyone can appreciate, love, and respect other cultures. But a person is who they are: The Jewish experience is theirs, as with the natives of America or anyone else. We can all appreciate, emulate, copy, and pay tribute to one another, but we cannot fraudulently replace each other. Anybody can play the Blues, but only Black people are the Blues. Which is why I refute and detest the sayings "Blues is American music" and "Blues is an indigenous American art form." Euroamericans are so willing to claim cultural kinship with us when it's convenient. We are one big happy family when we can fight their wars or make them some money. But still our children get the worst education, the prisons are full of Black males, and a great percentage of us are jobless and living in poverty; and they continue to pump guns and dope into our community. The Blues is not American music. The Blues is the music of Black people who were enslaved and colonized everywhere and are still held captive, in a manner of speaking. The most annoying thing is to hear a Blues artists say their music is American, while America kicks he and his people's ass every day. My music is not American; it belongs to and is from the entire Black diaspora. Yet it is not selfish; it serves as a catalyst for expression for anyone that embraces it. Think about this: Just a short time ago, Blues was widely called (and still is by some) the devil's music by *good* Christians from this "one nation under God." Now the same people, the same White God-fearing culture of Madison Avenue and across the country, are raking in the bucks from books, recordings, films, advertising, and so on that is Blues oriented or directly from it. Every syllable of Black slang has a price, but the beneficiaries are rarely Black. Who's in league with the devil? Who, then, must become the caretakers?

JULIO: There is only one vehicle for Black people to put across their ideas on the bedrock of our culture which is the Blues, and that's the *Original Chicago Blues Annual*. It takes a lot of work and a lot of courage, and you are due all praises for that.

BEAU: Thanks. Now here's something. You take the Blues Foundation in Memphis. We have been doing the *Blues Annual* for six years along with our other publications. To this day, they have not acknowledged the existence of the *Blues Annual*. I believe it's because there is free Black expression in our pages and we do publish writers of merit who write from the inside of the culture. They've assembled themselves into a collection of misfits, with a few Black "yeah boss" types giving credence to their arrogance. And to further their arrogance, they give out Blues awards in the name of W. C. Handy—best this, best that. And that whole process is saturated in the petty politics of record companies. I really don't care to be recognized by them because I don't see them as anything other than what I've already said. Sadly, Black Blues artists go for this kind of circus, which results in a zero increase in how much money they can command. They're still playing for peanuts in those foul-smelling dumps in Chicago like Kingston Mines, which is really a labor camp, and other joints which have a mutually agreed salary cap to be sure Blues artists are always underpaid and on the verge of desperation.

You really have to understand what the real message is coming from many Whites, not all, in the Blues business. And I must add, there are a few Black rascals out there that are collaborators and legmen for their masters or even more exploitive than the Whites have been. They are like Black slave catchers who betrayed their brothers and sisters who were trying to escape the horror of slavery.

But ultimately, if wrongs are to be corrected and a new straight-ahead course taken, the responsibility lies squarely on the shoulders of Black people.

JULIO: Propaganda. You've managed to circumvent theirs and to propagate real Black thought.

BEAU: To certain Whites in the Blues business, a Black doing anything other than being part of the carnival they've created is unnerving. I mean, I've spoken with people that were rude, made racist comments, and suggested that if this was a Black publication it must be inferior, wouldn't last, or must be full of dissident rhetoric. We've outlasted all those that started when we did, plus we've added *Blues World Digest*. On the other hand, I'm appreciative of the support the *Blues Annual* has received from a number of local and international businesses, including the City of Chicago, that recognize the importance of the publication in a broader sense: that of business and culture. The *Blues Annual* is sold all over the world and is multilingual. The *Blues Annual* is good business. And that's the sad thing about some diehards. They are so blinded by their hatred and fear, they can't see what's in front of them. So after six years, we have managed to identify a number of those individuals and companies who are hopelessly lost in ignorance. Now we have a good foundation of contributors and advertisers that are involved for cultural and/or business reasons, and some, political. And our whole concept is to be inclusive. Our contributors have not been limited to Blacks or those who share my point of view. We have had the good fortune to have had Chicago writer David Whiteis, a regular contributor to the *Chicago Reader* newspaper, write for the *Annual*. His writing is always informational and stimulating, and he deals with the issues straight on. His article that appeared in the 1993 *Blues Annual*, "Taking Care of Business," was a gem. And there's Jacques Lacava, Isio Saba, and Rosanna Cassano. These individuals contribute greatly to the overall identity of the publication.

JULIO: For some people, just the idea of a Black Blues publication must be kind of a nightmare.

BEAU: Well, the role that's been assigned us, especially in entertainment, is to entertain. Insofar as images created in media for public consumption, that has in every area been controlled by Whites. We are not suppose to go eyeball to eyeball with them or perpetuate images that we want—images and portrayals that are ours, not stereotypes. I have to call them on that all the time. Sadly, many of us think that success is ensured if we play the nut role and comply with the stereotype. It's the "don't make waves" approach many Black people and other so-called minorities have. I think that attitude is as tired as the people they are trying not to upset or offend. We have to realize that most people that hate us, and who are trying to control things, will give up anything anyway when confronted in the right way: with power (the only thing they respect in all of its forms), intelligence, and time. Why kiss ass hoping to get a few crumbs thrown at you. But by presenting writers like Quincy Troupe, Henry Dumas,

Kalamu Ya Salaam, Hart Leroy Bibbs, Eugene B. Redmond, Deitra Farr, Elaine Moore, Raymond Patterson, you and others, we are offering our readers an insight into the wholeness and aesthetic of the Blues as culture. I see Blues artists coming into the fold of "cultural wholeness" more and more. I feel the shuffling, compliant, bootlicking stereotype will soon be an image and practice of the past. A broad awakening is on the horizon.

JULIO: It's people like Robert Palmer, Nat Hentoff, Pete Welding, Sam Charters, Bob Thiele, and others who have proclaimed themselves as the great White authorities of a culture that to which they are not only alien but also hostile towards. They have created these stereotypes. And their arrogance knows no bounds, and it's based on what?

BEAU: That's right. And the work none of them speak about is the one they should relentlessly venerate, and that's Amiri Baraka's book *Blues People*. Furthermore, they have absolutely nothing to do with the Black continuum. That is why we have to continue to elevate and make visible writers like Maya Angelou, Henry Dumas, Toni Morrison, and Baraka. And these writers and others must engage their responsibility with more vigor and become more approachable by the masses.

JULIO: Amen.

BEAU: Well, the book you wrote, *The Bluesmen,* is written from within, from within the culture. And you have some fans of all colors and backgrounds who really appreciate your work. I run into them when I'm touring and lecturing. There's one thing they all say. Why doesn't this book get more coverage? The answer is simple. You, like me, are one of the few Bluespeople who play the music, and can articulate without reservation, our history and social and economic condition. And that is a threat to those who for years have been lying, perpetuating false history, and creating images of Blacks to enrich themselves and at the same time attempt to convince us that we are who and what they say we are. Your book is the "Muhammad Ali-ism" of Blues books.

JULIO: Speaking of books, Peter Guralnick's book on Robert Johnson has got to be the silliest rehash of material on Robert Johnson since there has been material on him. It contains no new insights and no attempt at interpreting Robert's situation. In fact, the book seems to praise all those who have written about Robert Johnson. This book simply uses Robert's name as a commercial prop.

BEAU: Well, you have the Peter Guralniks and Steve LaVeres who collaborate with one another, loot Black estates, and proceed to mythologize and write their own Black history. My old friend Johnny Shines once told me he has sent many of them on wild-goose chases looking for all kinds of things that he made up. Praise be onto that ancestor.

But you know there are the internal issues among our people that have to addressed. There are Black nationalists, Black bourgeois, the Black intellectual elite, the Black educators, and on and on. Some of them are highly critical of what the others represent, but from what I can see, a very few of these people are interested in being curators of the Blues element of the culture. And if any of them pursued as vigorously the preservation of our culture as they do Gucci purses and fake kente cloth made in Indonesia, we probably wouldn't be having this conversation. The fact is, what is done is done. We cannot extract any part of our history, or present, and deny its existence; and that is what some of us are trying to do. And then there are those from all backgrounds who have toiled to preserve the Blues and not augment its meaning or relevance. I take my hat off to those people and institutions which exist all over the world: in Italy, Nigeria, America, Senegal, France, Brazil, all over. But it is incumbent on our people to play a major role in the preservation and education. I have to extend praise to harp player Billy Branch for his work in the various Blues in the Schools programs, which I believe originated in Chicago. In fact, Chicago is at the vanguard of authentic Blues education for all youngsters. And you have Amina Dickerson over at the Chicago Historical Society, who has made great strides in preserving and educating—now and when she was president of the DuSable Museum of African American History.

Speaking of the DuSable Museum, here is an incident that happened a couple of years ago that is a perfect example of White folks trying to control the actions of Black people, and right in the confines of a Black institution. Benson and Hedges cigarette company came to town [Chicago] and sponsored a Blues festival. Now, among the events that were held was a discussion group and poetry reading at the DuSable, with the moderators and poets being me and Sterling Plumpp. The topic was "The Return of Blacks to the South." Well, it was a Sunday afternoon, and the place was full of mostly Black people genuinely interested in participating. Of course, one cannot talk about the migration of Blacks, or the condition or lives of Black people, without the discussion being political. In fact, not just Blacks, but the same applies to any group of human beings on earth. So the discussion group became a forum for discussing a broad range of opinions relating to the condition of Black folks in the North and South. Overall, it was a good, healthy afternoon. When it was all over, this little White lady, an ugly hag, Jane something, from Benson and Hedges, flew into a rage about how improper we were to become political, that her company did not sponsor political events. And how they had had a very successful gathering of Black people in Atlanta at the Martin Luther King Center and nothing political or militant in tone had transpired. I mean, here we are in the Black community, in a Black museum with slave shackles on exhibit and a room full of Black people and we are to be censured and regulated by these people just because they threw out a few hundred token dollars to position themselves to sell more cigarettes. I told her that maybe those people in Atlanta needed money so bad they were willing to be compliant to get it. Maybe that's the Christian way. After all, the last time I was in Ebenezer Church down there, they had a White Jesus ten times bigger than life above the pulpit. I don't bite my tongue. So the point is that these people have to be held in check. And we do that by conducting our own forums. Be it a museum, a street corner, or the *Original Chicago Blues Annual*. The *Annual* is a forum for what has just been said. I'm exposing the true nature of those people who were arrogant and bold enough to come into our bastion of history and try to dictate what we should speak about—the Benson and Hedges cigarette company.

JULIO: Well I'm sure they've got you blacklisted, literally. I want them to put me on there, too.

BEAU: You know we're lifetime listees anyway.

JULIO: Right on. So the *Blues Annual* is a coming together of people . . . no matter Black, White . . . to make this Black cultural outlet a reality. This a great example of unity and love toward the Blues by the contributors. So the whole magazine becomes a contribution to the world by these people.

BEAU: Exactly. And here I have to mention Eugene B. Redmond, who has made himself unselfishly accessible. Eugene is poet laureate of East St. Louis, Illinois. In all of my publishing endeavors—*Literati Chicago, Literati Internazionale, Blues World Digest,* and the *Blues Annual*—he has contributed many hours, talent, and information. And he is one of those scholars that dwell among the people, physically and spiritually. He is a frontline fighter, griot, and great friend. Praises.

And then there is A.-C. McGraw, whose talents have contributed greatly to my ideas becoming reality and the success of the *Annual*. There's such an enormous amount of work that goes into this kind of project that the principals involved really have to be dedicated team players. As I said earlier, the remuneration doesn't come in the form of money. A.-C., like me, has put in countless hours working on the *Annual* as well as other projects. I am deeply appreciative of her effort and contributions.

I'm in contact with writers, run the advertising sales, PR, and international affairs. Besides all of that, I'm touring playing the Blues, I write and lecture about the Blues— I'm living out my Blues dream.

April 12, 1994, Montparnasse, Paris

JULIO: If I remember correctly, Memphis Slim played a major role in your development.

BEAU: Memphis was great influence and a great friend. I would say he performed his duty as elder to the highest degree. You and I knew him around the same time . . . so this is really for our readers because you already know. This is good though, because you and I haven't talked about Memphis for a long time.

Memphis, recognizing us as two cats cut from the Blues fabric, and also from the fabric of survivors and preservationists, was willing to share with us certain tools of the trade he couldn't share with others. The first thing that comes to mind about Slim was his generosity; he set an example of generosity, information gathering, and sharing. Through him, we got our first Musicdisc recording sessions, which resulted in *Black Gipsy* with Archie Shepp and *Certain Blacks* with the Art Ensemble and others. I mean, he gave us that contact. How we managed it is a different story. He turned us on to countless promot-

Memphis Slim at the Ritz Hotel, Paris, 1980. Photo by Eric Fienblatt.

ers, press people, etc., and he even recorded with us. He was vital in helping us begin our careers. He taught us the ropes of survival in France and Europe, which could be applied anywhere. He sat our minds right in this business. He conducted himself like an elder, older brother, griot, all in the same person. He shared the esoteric knowledge, the unwritten knowledge. What we call "the Book." And it's pitiful that when you say "the Book" to young Black people today, they ain't got an inkling about what you are talking about. But Memphis did what we will do—pass the knowledge onward and upward to future generations.

And besides of all that, Memphis Slim knew how to live. He was a big guy anyway, around six feet five. He was big and his life was big and dignified. His Rolls Royces, Lincoln Continentals, and tailored suits were not symbols of a vain and materialistic man. They were proper for the enjoyment of he and his family after he had paid over thirty years of heavy dues in the United States. When he died, I read an evil obituary in one Chicago newspaper. The writer said something to the effect his music had become less authentic since he moved to Paris.

JULIO: Jealous dog.

BEAU: Exactly. Memphis was independent of these people, the club scene, and the politics. And to be that, and arrive at greatness and wealth, is contrary to a Blues existence. You can only be what they want you to be. Memphis was able to see through the bullshit. And he garnered for himself and family—a sweet season.

JULIO: Another person that influenced you greatly in your Paris days was James Baldwin.

BEAU: Right. Well, Baldwin had an affect on my life years before I met him. In 1965, I was attending Mount Carmel High School in Chicago. There were only a handful of Blacks in the school, and they were there primarily to participate in sports. When I took the entrance exam, which I didn't want to take, I randomly filled in the dots in the multiple choice questions. The test was suppose to last five hours; I was finished and out of there in one hour. Within a week, I got a letter of acceptance and a call from the football coach inviting me to try out for the team. Well I didn't make the team. Primarily because I couldn't stand the coach, some White man, barking out insults, which questioned one's sexual orientation and/or complexion. But even back then I was hip to the resident inadequacies in these men which causes such behavior.

Alright. I so much disliked the whole physical fitness program at this school, because of the screaming and ethnic slurs, that I devised a way not to go to gym at all. I claimed an allergy to the chorine in the shower water and had my doctor write a note stating that. This got me a free period, which I usually spent in the library reading selections I had brought with me from home. One day I was reading Baldwin's *Another Country*. The disciplinarian, a priest named Jordon Rooney, who spent most of his time administering beatings with a huge belt or a tennis shoe to bare-assed boys or gazing at boys in the shower, crept up behind me and snatched my book from me. He broke into a tirade about the filthy contents of the book and Baldwin's mind. About how hopeless my situation was in the eyes of the Almighty. And how he could not allow my presence in the school any longer. I protested this wretched invasion of my person and his attempt to censor what I was reading. I got sent home. I was elated. Well, my parents made some sort of deal so I might finish out the school year. The following year, my parents tried to get me into other schools with no success. The Mount Carmel people put in my records that I was a real problem student who brought dirty books and pornography to school. Them Catholics really wanted to blackball me—or, in fact, whiteball me—embarrass my parents, and stifle any advancement or improvement in a Black person's life. They were exactly like the times—like now.

Thanks to Baldwin, in a way, I had my first real experience with impassioned race hatred. Rooney was mostly outraged because he knew Baldwin knew the truth about "the White lie," and if I was reading Baldwin, I was getting an education.

When I told Baldwin this story at the Café Mabillon, he said that, "It's good you were awakened early; your eyes will see more and more as time goes on." I was twenty-one at the time.

So I used to chat with Baldwin from time to time in different Paris cafés. I learned a lot from the man as he related his observations and experiences. He talked a lot about his former Paris days, about the French attitude toward colonialism and their aggression in the colonies, in Indochina, and about our people. He spoke about a mutual friend, painter Beauford Delaney, who had become seriously ill. And whom Baldwin held in great respect and admiration.

The last time I saw him was down in the south of France, in St. Paul de Vence, with journalist Ray Frost, who was writing for *Jet* magazine at the time.

He was aloof yet intense. He was saturated with knowledge, and it was as if he wondered to himself, would time allow him to say all he needed to say. I believe at the time, among other work, he was tightening up *No Name in the Street*. To me, he is our greatest philosopher and essayist.

JULIO: You were twenty years old. There were a lot of great people in Paris during this time. The Art Ensemble of Chicago, Reverend Frank Wright, Bobby Few, Famoudou Don Moye, Archie Shepp. What was it like for you to find yourself in such a brotherhood, such a range of people.

BEAU: Well, it was pretty powerful. Especially when I sit back and realize what was really happening. All the people that you mentioned always had a positive approach to living. And today those that are still with us are just as vibrant. And we're talking twenty-five years ago. Back then, we all had artistic and political reasons for not wanting to be in the States all the time. We all had the same idea at the same time: to be somewhere else. So in our community there was a real spirit of sharing. Everybody did projects together, and most of us tried to help each other and cut each other *into* possibilities. And there was a confluence of many elements of the culture. African dancers, poets, Blues artists, Jazz artists, you name it, we all did projects together. One project that comes to mind was Hart Leroy Bibbs's play *Blue's Dream* at the Théâtre du Ranelagh. We all came together: Blues, Jazz, French, Algerian musicians, set designers, actors, poets. I wish it were that way today.

And Archie Shepp, like Memphis, was very helpful in helping us get things going. Remember, Archie called us in for our first recording session. Think about that. We worked with Jeanne Lee, Malachi Favors, Dave Burrell, Philly Joe Jones, and Archie. That was August 16, 1969. That's the day I consider the beginning of my professional life in music.

That period was a major contribution to music history, and our culture, from all of us. And it was such a beautifully formative time. We were beginning to be what we would become. And we had great adventures. You better believe it. There were women, abundant times, intolerably lean times, babies born, losses, success, and disappointment. I remember Lester Bowie had his whole family over here. Fontella Bass was singing and Lester was playing with Art Ensemble of Chicago. They all lived in a house in Saint-Leu-la-Forêt.

Then there is my friend Famoudou Don Moye. He was wild. We all were. He has emerged as one of the most genuine and spiritual men I've ever met. I could easily write a book on the Moye philosophy. And I can tell you that he has played a major role in the success of many of may endeavors. And the Art Ensemble of Chicago as a group were the first to support my publishing ventures. I'm talking, spiritual and monetary. You know, this past summer we had a kind of reunion. We did a three-month tour: the Art Ensemble of Chicago and the Chicago Blues Tradition. Besides the Art Ensemble, was Herb Walker, Amina Claudine Meyers, Frank Lacy, James Carter, and me. It was really a creative high point. And Lester Bowie and me had our sons working with the group. They were a part of the experience, thereby helping the continuum play on. They are basically the same age as we were back in Paris.

JULIO: If I'm reading you right, you're talking about the capability of loving. You could break bread with these people. We really have to give thanks to those who help open the door for us.

BEAU: I would really like to see that kind of energy in the Chicago Blues Community. You know creativity and survival were central to our existence. We were not dominated by petty rivalries to get gigs or the whims of club owners. We were not apolitical, we were not afraid. The word was Great Black Music . . . on our terms.

April 13, 1994, Montparnasse, Paris

JULIO: What about your productions with GBW records in Japan?

BEAU: Well, I have wanted for a long time to produce Blues as homogeneously as possible. Blues produced without input from people outside of the culture. So that when the musicians are playing, they are playing for themselves, from memory, and for the ages. They don't have to worry about if they got it right for a non-Black somebody trying to construct a sound for a particular market and labeling it Blues. I wanted my GBW projects to be Black music production and expression.

But here's how things got going. Famoudou Don Moye and I had a similar vision on this. He introduced me to couple of business contacts back in 1989, and we had several meetings over the next couple of years in various parts of the world. Finally we agreed to proceed.

The result has been some previously unrecorded artists getting their music out there; like the Burnin' Chicago Blues Machine, Shirley King, and Kay Reed. Then there were veterans who hadn't had anything new out in a while: Billy Branch, Junior Wells, and Valerie Wellington. And I got a couple of new sides out myself, *My Ancestors* and *Having a Fit over Your Love*. And there was a live recording party that had Deitra Farr, Tommy McCracken, Jim Conley, and Willie Kent that was the first project. These recordings are not being promoted in the same way in the U.S. as in Japan, and there are not billboards of the artists on Sunset Boulevard in Hollywood, but I hope that those I have recorded can use their project as a stepping stone towards the advancement of their careers.

JULIO: It's a wonderful thing those records you've done. Are you the only Black producer in Chicago?

BEAU: No, there have been a few over the years. Big Bill Collins, Cadillac Baby, Vee-Jay records, and others. I'm not certain whose doing what at the moment. But I wish that there was more activity among Black producers and Black Blues labels.

JULIO: And you did some other projects in Iceland and Sardinia.

BEAU: Yes, those were really a lot of fun. That's what I call a collaboration of two cultures with Blues as the catalyst. We made live recordings with Pinetop Perkins, Jimmy Dawkins, and me. And my partners Dori and Julia, of Reykjavík, put on a concert series over a couple of years that included Shirley King, Billy Boy Arnold, Tommy McCracken, Deitra Farr, Jimmy Dawkins, Pinetop Perkins, and myself. The Icelandic connection has been and continues to be very rewarding. And I took the Iceland show on the road to Sardinia, where I am the artistic director of the Sardinia Blues Festival. That's another collaboration which has yielded several tremendous positive experiences.

JULIO: How do you see the future for yourself, Chicago Beau?

BEAU: Well, I have a lot of work to do. I have a couple of literary projects in progress at the moment; one is a memoir and the other is a research piece. I have decided to accelerate my performance schedule in order to support some more dreams I have. I love to cook. So something along those lines is in the cards in the very near future. All of these things require cash and time. So hard work is what is ahead, that's the way it's always been.

JULIO: Thanks for this time together.

BEAU: Thank you, my brother, thank you.

April 14, 1994, Château Rouge, Paris

INTERVIEW WITH E. PARKER MCDOUGAL

L. "Chicago Beau" Beauchamp

E. Parker McDougal and Jay J. Peters cofounded Chicago Hardcore Jazz, a school of Jazz defined by them as "a swinging, no-gimmicked, no-nonsense approach to modern saxophone artistry."

I met McDougal the first time at Club Montmartre in Copenhagen, Denmark, in 1971. He made a guest appearance on a Ben Webster/Dexter Gordon set; we have been friends since then.

E. Parker McDougal can be heard on several albums, including his LP *Initial Visit,* on Grits Records (GR2001), along with other Hard Core artists Jay J. Peters on tenor sax, Willie Pickens on piano, Dan Shapera on bass, Fred "Bud" Hudson on piano, Henry El on bass, and Jim Cottrel on drums.

He can also be heard on my CD *My Ancestors,* playing on the tune "Chi-Groit Chanson/I the Blues."

CHICAGO BEAU: Mr. E. Parker McDougal, where are you from?

E. PARKER MCDOUGAL: I was born in Gary, Indiana. My father was born here. So, actually, I've been in the Chicago area all my life. I went to McCosh Elementary School and Englewood High School.

BEAU: And beyond?

E. PARKER: I dropped out of Wilson Junior College. I got a scholarship to North Carolina behind the segregated system they had.

BEAU: Not the University of North Carolina?

E. PARKER: No. That was all White. I went to North Carolina College in Durham. They had a two-tier system. The White kids went to one school; we went to the other one. The White kids drank out of one fountain; we drank out of the other one. I had never seen anything like that before.

BEAU: What years we talking about here.

E. PARKER: We're talking around '44.

BEAU: Well how old are you anyway, man?

E. PARKER: Well, I'll be seventy on August 6. I was born in 1924. I've lived through some scenes.

BEAU: How long were you in North Carolina?

Left to right: L. "Chicago Beau" Beauchamp and E. Parker McDougal on Beauchamp's front steps, Chicago, 1994. Photo by L. Beauchamp.

E. PARKER: I was there four years. I got a bachelor's degree, with a minor in physical education. My major was sociology, and I was a basketball player. Then I came back here and went to Chicago Teachers College, and I got my psychology major together. Then I had a double major.

BEAU: When did you start playing the horn?

E. PARKER: In Gary. We was all in the band. You ever heard of Morris Lane and Thomas "Chew" Crump? They worked with Lionel Hampton when Bird was there. I was playing clarinet then. Then when I went to school, I was playing with Blues bands in the South. That's all you were basically playing. So when I came back here [Chicago], I had the experience of traveling around. Playing around in little towns. Towns too small for B. B. King and Buddy Johnson.

BEAU: Who were the big Blues stars at that time, in your college days?

E. PARKER: In the '40s, the big singers was T-Bone Walker, Winnone Harris; a harmonica player named Rhythm Willie was big. I saw him at the Rum Boogie here in Chicago.

BEAU: How would you describe the Jazz scene of the '40s?

E. PARKER: Well, you had a crossover. You had bands and big bands. The Rum Boogie was a nightclub, but you had a band in there of twelve or fourteen pieces. And they played the acts. Sugar Ray Robinson's wife had an act in there: Edna Mae Holly. That was before she married Sugar Ray. Then they had a chorus line and a comedian; they would always have a big show. And the

Blues act was part of the show. It was all going on in the same joint.

BEAU: Who was on the scene in those days?

E. PARKER: Ethel Waters was in Chicago. She had a joint out on Sixty-fourth and Cottage Grove Avenue; it was called Cabin in the Sky. She was in the motion picture called *Cabin in the Sky*. Billy Holiday was here, but I didn't work with her until 1951. I worked with her over at the High Note here in Chicago at 450 North Clark Street. They brought in acts like Anita O'Day. And they had Charlie Mingus in there. Mingus came in there with a White guy; let's see, his name was Red Norvo. He played vibes and marimbas. He could deal.

You talk about Jazz in the '40s. The bands would come through. They'd play the Savoy over by the Regal Theater over there. Now they done tore all that down. Ain't nothing over there now.

BEAU: What year did you come back to Chicago?

E. PARKER: 1949.

BEAU: That's the year I was born.

E. PARKER: Well, we was both babies. We both got here at the same time.

BEAU: Well, back in those days it was a different scene, I'm sure. People wasn't knocking each other in the head like now.

E. PARKER: No, no. It was a different scene. People went and took care of their own thing. I mean, you didn't know everyone around, but the people took care of their thing. If you lived in a kitchenette apartment building, you may not know who was next door; each crib was considered a house. The doorbell might be set up for three rings for me or two rings for somebody else. That's how it was set up. You had a shelf in the back for your food . . . that kind of thing.

BEAU: Yeah, man. When I first left home, that's what I had—a kitchenette in Boston.

E. PARKER: Now from there I meet the guy who was at the union. We had two unions. We didn't get integrated until 1966. We had Local 208, that was the Musicians' Protective Union, as opposed to the Musicians' Union. We was blocked from working downtown. You could work down there if you was Louis Armstrong, and they wasn't gon' keep him there but for two weeks anyway. Every now and then, you'd get a "single"; Dorothy Donnigan and them worked down there.

BEAU: Was she a Chicago lady?

E. PARKER: Yeah. She went to DuSable High School. She living out there on Forty-ninth and Vincennes.

BEAU: What was the scene like at the Sutherland Hotel?

E. PARKER: They used to bringing groups. Groups like Miles Davis was in there. I know Coltrane was in there with him. Cannonball was in there. They'd bring in cats like Chico Hamilton. Yeah, the Sutherland was cool, but the one who done the most bringing in was McKies over on Sixty-ninth and Cottage Grove. And further down was the Pershing. That's where Ahmad Jamal was. Down from there was the C and C on Sixty-fifth, where Gene Ammons and Benny Green and all of them would be hanging out.

Anyway, in the '50s there was Nob Hill and the Bee Hive. The Bee Hive brought in Lester Young, Coleman Hawkins, and Charlie Parker. They'd bring them in as a single with young local cats playing behind them. McKies was more eclectic. They'd bring in Miles Davis, Muddy Waters, and me in the same week. Also, there was a place called the Tracadero at Forty-seventh and Indiana in the basement. That's were you could catch a lot of the Blues cats; cats from Ray Charles's band would come up in there and jam when they were in town. Up the street was Theresa's; that lady that just died.

Now of course, the West Side was always a home for the Blues. Sylvios over on California and Lake; over on Madison was the Big Squeeze.

BEAU: Were you doing much playing with Blues cats at that time?

E. PARKER: I played with J. B. Lenoir, and I played with Memphis Slim down at the Tracadero. I went on short tours with Willie Mabon. We were on the bill with Chuck Berry out there in Iowa, Wichita, that sort of thing. I worked with Sonny Thompson; he had a hit out with Lulu Reed.

BEAU: You have been primarily a musician most of your life?

E. PARKER: Yeah, well, the '40s and '50s, primarily. The bottom fell out of the business, so to speak, in the '60s. Cats went to Europe, California, the penitentiary, or wherever. They weren't here in the '60s. The whole vibe changed. It was real slow for Jazz with the Beatles and all that. So I went around for awhile doing covers: James Brown, whatever was commercial. Then I had chance to get a foreman's job over at the Illinois Department of Labor that came through in a nick of time. Good thing I had that background with school and all, so I knew something about what was happening.

Interview with E. Parker McDougal

BEAU: How about the arrival of the cats like Pharoah Sanders and Albert Ayler and who were your main boys and influences during the '40s?

E. PARKER: When they [Albert and Pharoah] came in, I was already established in the way I was going. I fell more into the line of Don Byas, Coleman Hawkins, Lester Young, and of course Charlie Parker. They came in on the top of Charlie Parker primarily. The only one which was really different was Archie Shepp. He came in the same way I started, with the Ben Webster–type tone. With the full tenor sound. Everybody else was Stan Getzin' it. They were trying to get like Prez, but they weren't really, they were more like Stan Getz. But it really wasn't but two schools: Lester Young and Coleman Hawkins. Coleman Hawkins, they called him the "Bean" and the "Hawk."

BEAU: Yeah, and they called Sonny Rollins the "Newk." Why the "Newk"?

E. PARKER: The first Black baseball pitcher was with the Brooklyn Dodgers was a cat named Don Newcomb. He was a strong right-handed pitcher. Sonny Rollins looked like him. That's why they put the "Newk" on him.

BEAU: Why did they call Hawkins the "Bean"?

E. PARKER: I don't know, but he's been the "Bean" for a long time. They called him "Hawk" because the White people on the radio and the TV would say the Hawk was really blowing. That came from Coleman Hawkins. We used to stand on Fifty-fifth Street and here Coleman Hawkins coming out of White's Emporium, which was on the other side of the el [elevated train]. You could here him all the way across the street; and that's a double boulevard. That's how people started talking about the weather as the "Hawk." Came from Coleman Hawkins.

BEAU: Where does John Coltrane fit in for you?

E. PARKER: Trane came out of the Hawkins/Dexter school. But he had his own sound. Didn't nobody sound like Trane. But Prez was the one that had no vibrato, a straight sound. I like Prez. But there are two ways of playing: vertical and horizontal. Vertical means you in the chord changes. The melody is there, but you on the changes. Horizontal is like the melody and you can turn them around some. When you put them both together, you come out with Dexter and Trane. Bird used a combination also. Now Von Freeman, he's out of the Lester Young thing.

BEAU: What are your thoughts on the AACM [Association for the Advancement of Creative Musicians].

E. PARKER: I was established to a degree in the Chicago area when they started. And some of the guys that started it played with me: Muhal Richard Abrams, Jodie Christian, and Malachi Favors. I think that what they had to do is what they did. They went to the people, and they had their own music. They didn't make it playing no Stardust. They didn't make it playing Charlie Parker. Charlie Parker had Charlie Parker covered. So they went their own way. Either you dug it or you didn't. Out of that group came the Art Ensemble of Chicago, Henry Threadgil, and Lester Bowie.

BEAU: How would you evaluate your life as a musician?

E. PARKER: Well, the older I got, I started to realize that the time and energy I spent in other disciplines, like studying psychology, administration of physical education, and sociology, I could have spent more in the music. I'm talking about the ultimate in music: orchestration, arranging, composing, and teaching. Had I been more focused, I would have been better off. I made a living alright, but that ain't the ultimate. That would have accomplished everything. Look at Quincy Jones and Nelson Riddle. It's good to know how to deal if you want to. That's what I would suggest to somebody getting into the business. Go on and be a soloist, but learn these other things. Look at Lester Young. He waited all his life, then ended up doing Lester Young and Strings, but he never learned how to do it [arranging] himself.

BEAU: Some cats maybe reached certain levels and didn't continue because their survival depended on them making money quickly.

E. PARKER: A lot of them had some support. Charlie Parker had a mama in Kansas City. He had somebody to go home to. Dexter's father was a doctor. He treated Lionel Hampton and Duke Ellington, two of the most famous people in the world. And Dexter got on [playing] with Lionel Hampton. That was his first band. And Miles Davis, his father was a dentist. What I'm saying is some of them had middle-class background and the money. Some of them had the background and no money. Miles's folks sent him money to go to Julliard before he got to be a junkie. What it adds up to is if you're lucky to have some money behind you in this business, you got a better chance, because this business is flaky.

BEAU: But basically, you've enjoyed your life.

E. PARKER: For a Black man, I don't know what he could do to be in a better position than a Jazz artist, a bandsman. First of all, you already got the situation of males and females. Then you got the alcohol already built in. You got a spotlight that's on you. And usually you got a uniform on. You got you little bow tie and jacket on. That means to some of them ladies that you got a job. And because of that, you meet people, and sometimes you get picked. The women pick you up. She made the choice whether she gon' go with you or not before she let you hit on her. A lot of guys don't know that. They think they did, but the woman is smart enough to give them that ego trip. You got groupies. Now you can take the *town* side of it. Some towns are sax towns; others are piano or trumpet player towns. Cats talk all that shit. Groupies in them towns go for a certain kind of cat. Cats in New York used to say they were going to Montreal because it was a tenor player's town. Now if you married, this life breaks up a lot of marriages. First place, you got no home. Then if you want to do right, you probably ain't all the time. But you shouldn't be married if you can't do the right thing. Don't make no sense to be out there messing up somebody's life.

And you have to make decisions. Which group you gon' go with, because you know some of them are sniffing or something. I remember I was in New York at the Roseland. A cat came and said, "Are you shooting, drinking, snorting, sniffing, or smoking, or do you want a pill. I got everything." So you got to make decisions. So anyway, that's my opinion on the life. Everybody does they own thing. But that side of the life never computed with me.

BEAU: In closing, do you have some words for the up and coming.

E. PARKER: Well, like Von Freeman told me: "Stay healthy and keep out of jail, then you got it made." That's a simple way of putting it. But whatever you set out to do, you got to focus on it. And get as much formal education as you can.

February 21, 1994, Chicago
E. Parker McDougal,
August 6, 1924–July 18, 1994

BLUES FOR ZAZEN

Joseph Jarman

Did you ever sit down
on a pillow that's round
and discover that you belong there.
That your hear and your soul
yes they are truly bold
you can live your life straight
as an arrow.

You are right to the mark of the target
All the love in your heart it is pure
You are free in yourself as the air is!

Then you discover Blues for Zazen.

Yet you go on your way
living day after day
knowing all you need do
is sit down.
Everything that you feel
is a block in your path
and your reason for living is sorrow.

And tho' no one speaks
as you go there
to the quiet place that's inside
you are all at One with the Heavens.

Even the Hell Gods let you pass by.

If you never sat down
on a pillow that's round
you may just be missing
a great pleasure.
Tho' it's hard when you start
to just simply sit down
you'll discover a joy
in your being.

Let the demons come
you'll destroy them.
Let the terror grip
on your soul.
Let the joy of life
enfold you!

Then you discover Blues for Zazen
Then you discover Blues for Zazen
Then you discover Blues for Zazen

FROM THE *ORIGINAL* CHICAGO BLUES ANNUAL

Issue Number 7

Great Black Music—Ancient to the Future! The proclamation of the Art Ensemble of Chicago. This means no boundaries, anything can be included in their presentation of the journey of Black music from Africa to the present: field hollers, preaching, screams, arias, chain rattling, costumes, face paint, whiskey, hip-hop, reefer, zoot suits, overalls, washboards, nudity, rituals, speaking in tongues, slave narratives, and more. The Art Ensemble appears on the cover of this issue, and the magazine features a special Art Ensemble section that includes an essay by Mike Hennessey.

From day one, like no others, the Art Ensemble of Chicago has been a major factor in the progress of *OCBA*, providing various elements of support and, most important, deep and profound *bloodhood*.

Changes in the music business and the increasing global economic struggle made continuing the *OCBA* in its current form nearly impossible. The Internet, music downloads, and cheap CDs at big box stores began to hurt many of the smaller players in the music business, many of whom had been at the core of our advertising strategy. Small businesses and art organizations began hurting from prevailing economic conditions, and predictions of future gloom, which have come to pass, soured our chances of growth without a huge influx of cash.

My *OCBA* dream had been realized just as I had dreamed it—and beyond. I seriously contemplated an issue number 8 but decided to leave that to the future. Maybe someday, in some other form, the *OCBA* will rise again to be a voice for Blues people.

Blessings to everyone.

INTERVIEW WITH JOHNNY SHINES
L. "Chicago Beau" Beauchamp

Johnny Shines's life and music swept out of the Mississippi Delta, through the urban gateways of the North, and into the concert halls of the world. Johnny passed into ancestorhood in 1992; he was born in 1915. He was a dear friend and mentor.

CHICAGO BEAU: Johnny, where did you come from this time?

JOHNNY SHINES: We come up from Tuscaloosa, Alabama, my wife and I. We like it better down there; gonna stay down there.

BEAU: I was happy to see you on this year's Blues Festival. What do you think about today's Blues players?

SHINES: Well, it was hectic days back when I was coming up. That's why I tell everybody, "How in the hell you goin' to play the Blues if you ain't never lived the Blues?" You don't know what the Blues is about if you ain't never lived them. People can train you to drive a car, people can train you to play a guitar, but who the hell is going to train you how to feel? If you don't feel nothing, ain't nothing happening. I can drink all day, goddammit; if I don't get high, I don't know I drinking. The purpose of singing the Blues is to feel the Blues. You feel them and let the people feel you and understand what you're doing. If people can't feel you, they don't know what you're doing. That's like sitting on your doorstep looking into somebody else's house across the street. You see the mouths and hands moving and everything, but you don't know what the hell is going on over there. These people tell me that they Blues players and ain't never had the Blues in their damn life. How the hell you gon' have the Blues when you ain't never been hungry or slept in cow shit or had to live outdoors; you understand what I mean?

BEAU: Tell me about you and Robert Johnson.

SHINES: Robert was a good man but didn't know it. He thought he was a dirty son of a gun; he tried to be, he just couldn't be.

BEAU: Was he that way with women?

SHINES: Yeah, kinda. That's what killed Robert. Success killed Robert. See, Robert was very successful, he was a nice-looking boy, and he played very, very well.

Johnny Shines, Davenport, Iowa, 1989. Photographer unknown.

BEAU: How old were you when Robert died?

SHINES: Let's see. Robert died in 1938, and I was born in 1915; I was about 23.

BEAU: How did you and Robert meet?

SHINES: I was playing guitar with a fellow named M & O, and M & O wanted me to meet Robert because he thought Robert was beside himself. He didn't figure Robert was as good as he thought he was. So he wanted me to meet Robert and put him in his place because I could sing and play pretty good. He keeps trying to get me to go to Helena, Arkansas.

BEAU: Where were you at the time?

SHINES: Hughes, Arkansas, and Robert was in Helena. One day we finally jumped a train and went on down there. I ran up on Robert. I went down there to cut Robert's head, and vice versa, he cut my head.

BEAU: He got down on you?

SHINES: He sure did. Did me pretty bad, too. I mean, the man was playing everything I thought I wanted to play. Playing like I thought I wanted to play and everything else. The thing about Robert is that he never did have to learn how to play nothing. Robert could hear it once and start playing it. He didn't have to practice. I ain't never seen Robert practice nothing in my life. He'd sit down and listen to a song and learn it right off the bat. Robert would sit down talking just like you and me now with the radio on. Robert would stop talking to you, grab his guitar, and play whatever was on the radio—note for note and word for word. I didn't' say *learn* to play it; he'd just play it. I never saw him try to learn a song; he could play what he heard. Now me, I had to learn songs. I'd put twenty-five cents in the vendor and play a song five times to learn it, or maybe more than that. But Robert learned a song the first time while it was playing.

BEAU: A lot of people talk about Robert making a hoodoo pact at the crossroads. There have been movies made and stories told about this pact. Did Robert make a pact?

SHINES: Heck no, man! The man was gifted. He was a born musician. Ain't nothing to that talk people talk. Me and Robert traveled together to Canada once on freight train. Everywhere we went, people loved Robert's playing and singing. They liked me, too, but Robert was special. He was gifted; he didn't need to make no pact.

BEAU: You were the best of friends?

SHINES: For sure!

BEAU: What about hoodoo in general?

SHINES: Things have happened [makes a deep sigh]. I had an auntie that had a rodent over her shoulder blade. They say it was meant for her heart. This thing would run from one side to the other. He was supposed to be under her shoulder blade; if he had been, he would have struck her heart. My cousin, her daughter, was messing around squeezing this bump on her shoulder. Finally, that thing came out of her and ran across the room. She had been told by a hoodoo doctor seven days before that it was going to happen like that, and that three days later the woman that had done it to her would come by her house.

BEAU: This rodent was a kind of a mouse living under her skin?

SHINES: That's right. It looked like a mouse when it ran out. So anyway, the hoodoo doctor had told her that she could tell the one who did it to her by the way she was acting. She would start scratching her eyes and shout loudly, "whoo! whop! whoo!" three times. Well, this woman came by to see my mother, and all of a sudden her eyes started blinking, she started scratching her eyes, then started shouting, "whoo! whop! whoo!" My auntie got up and chased that woman out into the streets.

Here is something else that happened. I was a boy when this happened. I went over to see my auntie at John Gaston Hospital in Memphis; she was a cook there. They brought a man there in a wheelchair. The man was hollering, "There it go, there it go again." Something was in his stomach, then it would go up to his chest. You could see it zigzagging across his chest under his skin. About ten minutes after they brought him in there, a tall Black fellow showed up and shouted, "Where's he at?" Then a woman pointed him out, and the man said, "I come after this man." The hospital doctors asked him who he was. He said he was a hoodoo doctor from Louisiana, then he showed them his credentials from a hoodoo school in New Orleans.

BEAU: He was certified hoodoo doctor.

SHINES: That's right. Well, after the other doctors had looked at his credentials, they told him to go ahead and see what he could do for the man. The hoodoo doctor said he had to get the serpent out of the man to make him well. So he mixed something in some water, and the man drank it. Then the sick man started hollering and carrying on; then in a few minutes, the snake came out of the man.

BEAU: How did it come out?

SHINES: It came out through his chest, fell down on the floor, and tried to crawl away, but the doctors caught it before it got away. They say that snake was meant for the man's heart. I guess they still got that snake down there at John Gaston Hospital.

BEAU: The man recovered?

SHINES: Yes. About three weeks later, he was back working his horse.

BEAU: Fascinating stories.

SHINES: You know, hoodoo is like anything else; there's good and there's bad. Some woman made a man's balls swell up so large he couldn't close his legs, and then a hoodoo doctor came along and reduced his balls to normal, which is the right thing to do. But I believe somebody got to have something on you for hoodoo to work on you. If you're a good person and have good things, you'll be all right.

BEAU: Good things like a mojo hand?

SHINES: Yeah, and just keep good thoughts. Treat your fellow man right, keep a job, and keep playing the Blues, and everything will be all right.

June 5, 1987, Chicago
Johnny Shines,
April 26, 1915–April 20, 1992

INTERVIEW WITH BARRY DOLINS
L. "Chicago Beau" Beauchamp

The Chicago Blues Festival is the largest free Blues Festival in the world. The person on whose shoulders lies most of the organizational responsibility is Barry Dolins of the Mayor's Office of Special Events. He is often the target of harsh criticism as well as lavish praise for his efforts. The following interview gives some insight into the skill, depth, and motivation of Barry Dolins.

BEAU: I've worked with you for so long that it seems odd to be asking you questions that I should know the answers to, but in many cases I don't, and maybe not our readers, so here goes. Are you a native Chicagoan?

BARRY: I was born in Chicago; I grew up working in the Maxwell Street Market. In the stall on one side of me was Johnnie Johnson, a Blues butt who sold records and tapes out of the trunk of his car—everything from Howlin' Wolf to Horace Silver. On the other side was Blind Arvela Gray. That experience sort of indoctrinated me into the music side of things.

Academically, I was going to DePaul University and getting a master's in history. My first thesis was going to be on the migration of Russian Jews into Chicago. Then through friendship with piano player Erwin Helfer, my brother and I started a record company. We recorded an album called *Heavy Timber* with Sunnyland Slim, Willie Mabon, Erwin Helfer, Jimmy Walker, and Blind John Davis. I changed my thesis. It was on "House Party Piano Underground Music in Chicago from 1913 to 1927," which was labeled Boogie-Woogie by Pinetop Smith. I did a lot of coverage of people like Mama Yancey and Sunnyland Slim showing how the Blues community had its earliest generation at the turn of the century with the migration of African Americans out of Mississippi into Chicago. And how the Blues as a folk music became a part of the recording industry back in 1921, and how Chicago became capital of independent record production with labels like Paramount and Black Swan before the war. Then around World War II, there was Chess, Vee-Jay, JOB; and after the war, Delmark and the independent labels out there today.

BEAU: How old were you when you started on Maxwell Street?

BARRY: I started in 1962; I was thirteen years old.

BEAU: What were you selling?

BARRY: My dad's friends had the drugstore at Thirteenth and Halsted. In the summer we'd put up a stand and sell shades. I'd be hawking them: "Pick 'em up, try them on, I got all types, all colors, all sizes."

BEAU: Moving on to your approach to the Chicago Blues Festival.

BARRY: Well, I was teaching public school. I retired from a tenured position in the East Maine Township School District, finished my master's thesis, and started my record company called Sirens all at the same time. Then in the mid-'70s, I went off to Philadelphia and went into folklore and folklife at the University of Pennsylvania. I finished my course work in the PhD program, and basically I was semi fed up with the academia. So I came back to Chicago and was teaching an adult education class at Loyola University called Chicago Blues: An Urban Experience, which included a lot of volunteer busing down to the Checkerboard and a number of other clubs. I wrote grants to bring in a number of performers who played and told their histories. I got grants through the Illinois Arts Council and the Carnegie Mellon Foundation. Then I had a grant from the National Endowment of the Arts to fund a series of six mini Blues festivals in 1983 and 1984. A third of that became the publicity event for the first Chicago Blues Festival as well as the first neighborhood festivals.

BEAU: Did you get your grants independently?

BARRY: No, I was working through Loyola as the fiscal agent.

BEAU: Was the first Chicago Blues Festival in 1984 a difficult sale to the city?

BARRY: Basically, the Mayor's Office of Special Events started it after seeing the success of the Blues Stage at Chicago Fest and the success of the Jazz Festival. And since the Jazz Festival ended the summer, they decided to start something to begin the summer. I wasn't really at that original planning committee. They told me they had enough White people there— that was the excuse that was given to me. But Lois Weisberg had faith in me to troubleshoot the first festival and work with the neighborhood festival program.

BEAU: Who was mayor then?

BARRY: Harold Washington.

BEAU: Who was mayor during Chicago Fest?

BARRY: Well, Michael Bilandic founded it; I helped bring some Blues to that. I brought in Little Brother Montgomery, S. P. Leary, and Erwin Helfer to do the first Chicago Fest, and then I worked with Blind John Davis as kind of rode manager driving him around . . . like to Juneteenth in Houston and around Texas.

BEAU: What was your actual function in the first Chicago Blues Fest?

BARRY: I got them to document everything for the archives on audio; I was a troubleshooter dealing with problems on sight.

BEAU: Were you actually working for the special events office?

BARRY: I was on a voucher, independent contractor, at that point in time. They used part of my grant in conjunction with the six mini Blues festivals I was doing that year. The first was in January at the Chicago Cultural Center with Little Brother Montgomery, Barrel House Chuck, and Blind John Davis. This was Little Brother's last live performance. He played a Bosendorfer; it was basically a Boogie-Woogie celebration. In February, I did a program at Truman College which was a Delta guitar workshop, with Homesick James and Honey Boy Edwards.

Then there was the Memorial Day Gospel Blues Bazaar; I was working with Barbara Jean Wright-Homes and the Mac Newberry Center and a church in the Maxwell Street. In terms of Memorial Day, it was actually a tribute to Snooky Pryor and Homesick James, who met at Okinawa in World War II. The following week was the Blues Festival, and later that summer I created another neighborhood festival for DuSable Museum around Bud Billiken Day and had Blind John Davis as in his original band, which was called Big Johnny Davis and the Original Music Masters. They re-created that jump style for that event. On Labor Day, which is around Sunnyland Slim's birthday, we did a tribute to Sunnyland down by the Water Tower. In October we did a tribute to Mama Yancy at the Chicago Historical Society with a lot of Blueswomen.

BEAU: That's a lot of work. A great grant.

BARRY: At the same time, I was working in the office on a voucher and doing my own events, doing neighborhood festivals, and working with those organizations.

I helped to develop the neighborhood festival program. That year,

1984, was the original year for the neighborhood festival grants. Then I basically helped develop the neighborhood festivals for '85 and '86. By 1989 under Mayor Daley, I was named the director of Neighborhood Festivals.

BEAU: By this time, you had become a bona fide employee of the City.

BARRY: Right.

BEAU: That seems to have been quite an arduous transition.

BARRY: I take pride in my work. I feel that we've done a great job for the Blues community and the neighborhoods. Helping them put on events that best depict their community.

BEAU: Chicago is such a multiethnic, yet divided, place. I think these festivals really help smooth out that situation. And the international festivals certainly reflect the diversity of the citizens.

BARRY: Celebrations have the atmosphere of coming together. People can see their similarities and their differences. People get to appreciate those things in a festive atmosphere. The significance of festivals was heavily stressed in my folklore background.

BEAU: What is your real motivation, the inner force that says, "Barry do this"?

BARRY: A lot of this is the education background. Deep down, the idea is to teach. To teach people how to do events or how other people live or have the events teach people. Well, Blueswise, at one time Blues was a pretty nasty word . . . derogatory. Now it's become fashionable, and everybody is a Blues lover nowadays. As Mama Yancy said, "Blues is letting your hair down and having a good time." But it's really an ethnic folk music; how a folk music develops in modernity is that it does cross racial barriers.

BEAU: It has its origins and roots. And it does cross barriers, economic ones. The Blues business is a multimillion dollar business. I don't know of many Bluespeople getting rich, but Blues culture has certainly made a good living for some people.

BARRY: When I started my fledgling company and Earwig and Alligator Records all around the same time, I don't think anybody had the vision that it could be a business that supports presidents of companies, publicists, shipping clerks, marketing directors, whatever.

BEAU: In terms of the Blues Festival and festival planning, I'm sure our readers would like to have an insight into the mechanics; I mean, what goes into the largest, most successful Blues festival in the world. Also, there are so many opinions that I've head over the years with regard to the politics of the festival, etc. I believe many people would like to hear from you on that, just to clear the air.

BARRY: Well, it has developed into a formula. If it were a simple formula, you'd think the job would get easier, but it doesn't. We sort of go with the old cliché that two heads are better than one. We have an ad hoc committee, and I've created a balloting process that allows some two dozen people to have some input philosophically and otherwise into the programming and direction of the festival. I've taken a look at it since 1991, when we celebrated Robert Johnson's eightieth birthday. You know, as a historian you like to celebrate such benchmarks. So we've celebrated T-Bone Walker, Lightnin' Hopkins, Big Bill Broonzy, the Bessie Smith centennial the last couple of years. Then we can really put the living legends in context. Such luminaries who live or have lived in Chicago should be celebrated. This year, 1995 celebrates the generation of 1915. People such as Memphis Slim, Josh White, Billie Holiday, and Muddy Waters were all born in the same week. And there are living legends that are out there: Robert Junior Lockwood, Honey Boy Edwards, Floyd McDaniel, Brownie McGhee, who I have been trying to get to come out of retirement in Oakland to come and celebrate his life at our festival. We're looking at doing a West Side guitar thing with Eddie C. Campbell, Luther Allison, and Otis Rush, maybe with a closing jam at the end. That would be a great ending to Saturday night.

BEAU: What do you think about doing some roots type of presentations? Out of Africa, the Blues tradition, and the continuum.

BARRY: This is very important. In fact, at Navy Pier one year we did a whole African Village. And it's unfortunate that the three days of the Blues festival only allow for thirty sets. It would be great to celebrate this thing a lot longer. But that's why we do create a month of activities leading up to the festival. Independent organizers and entrepreneurs can get involved by presenting or sponsoring events during Blues Month. The Center for New Horizons, headed by Ralph Metcalfe Jr. is looking to do a series of Saturday afternoons leading up to the festival to pay tribute to the memory of Theresa Needham.

BEAU: What's the future in your eyes in terms of upcoming artists, events, etc.?

BARRY: I believe the city will continue to be the Blues capital of the world. Not only is there a world-class festival, but the Chicago Blues Archives is in the process of writing a National Endowment for the Humanities grant, "Rock My Soul: The rise of Blues and Gospel in Chicago." This should help document the role Chicago has played in the development of African American culture.

Also, with the work of a number of individuals, cultural events are developing all over. From Willie Dixon's Blues Heaven Foundation at 2120 South Michigan Avenue, to the Theresa Needham Blues Center at Theresa's old location, the celebration of the Blues tradition will live on.

February 1995, Chicago

JUKE JOINT VOICES
James Otis Williams

Otis Williams performs at Nyumburu Cultural Center, University of Maryland, 1992. Photo by L. Beauchamp.

At night during the summers of my youth as I lay in bed waiting for sleep to replace the lingering heat, I could hear the vibrating sounds of tree frogs singing and dogs barking. I also heard the soothing sounds of the Blues coming from Hollis Denton's juke joint up the street. We were living in the little shotgun house on Pearl Street where I was born. I had listened to juke joint Blues sounds float into my room like lazy rain clouds over late-night breezes for as long as I could remember. You could hear the jukebox playing the Blues night and day.

The jukebox later became my friend. As I grew older, it drew me like a giant magnet into Bell Sykes Cafe whenever I had money in my pockets. You could play one record for a nickel and five for a quarter. It may sound like a very dull existence, but it was exciting to me at that time. Listening to that great Seeburg jukebox sound was almost like being at a live set.

The music captivated me. I sometimes played one tune over and over again. It seemed to penetrate my soul almost like the spirituals in church. But it was different. The Blues made me want to travel to the big city to check out the bright lights and see the great musicians playing in swank nightclubs and juke joints. I wanted to catch the northbound train to glory, know what I mean?

I got to know them (the musicians) through their voices on the jukebox. I would feed on their soulful musical energy, often singing along with the record. There were times when I would sing all of the parts, vocal and instrumental.

I grew up with the sounds of these voices, and I couldn't wait to get to see some of them in person. However, they came to the small town where I lived only on very rare occasions, if ever. However, I was fortunate enough to see some of them onstage in later years. But they could always be heard on the jukebox in the local juke joints.

I picked cotton at three dollars per hundred pounds to get money for a ticket to see B. B. King for the first time. I hated picking cotton, but it was worth the pain. At the dance, B. B. came out in this orange-colored suit for the first set. He changed to light green on the last set. It was a boss show. He sang tunes like "3 O'Clock Blues," "Blind Love," "You Upset Me Baby," "Please Love Me," and "You Know You Didn't Want Me When You Fell Down across My Bed."

Even though B. B. King was coming from Memphis only 100 miles north on highway 51 (55 wasn't built yet), it was like he was from heaven. I became a lifetime fan of B. B. King. My two all-time favorites of his tunes are "Please Love Me," a medium shuffle number with a guitar roll introduction that can be traced back to Elmore James, and a smooth ballad/love song, "Darling You Know I Love You." I first heard it on a jukebox in a little joint in Durant, Mississippi. It was simply beautiful.

I managed to see a few other artists in my hometown, including Ivory Joe Hunter. But the well-advertised and anticipated Battle of the Blues between Clarence "Gatemouth" Brown and Aaron "T-Bone" Walker never happened. The promoters "went South" with the ticket money. So I had to depend on the jukebox to listen to the T-Bone shuffle.

One of my most profound jukebox experiences took place one spring Sunday afternoon. I was sitting in Bell Sykes Cafe with this nineteen-year-old young lady.

She was fine and brown with eyes that sparkled like ebony emeralds in her pretty head. Her body had more curves than a Mississippi country road. I was wild about her and a little surprised that she took the time to spend some time with me a mere sixteen-year-old.

We were listening to Blues on the jukebox when this man (whom I never liked) came in and offered to drive her, along with her sisters, to an evening of partying in a Mississippi Delta juke joint called the Brass Rail.

So she left me alone and blue with only my friend the jukebox to keep me company.

I put fifty cents in the box and punched Little Walter Jacobs ten times. The song that I played was:

This is a mean old world
To have to live in by yourself
Can't get the one you love
Have to use somebody else

The jukebox wrapped its soulful arms around me like shucks on an ear of corn and let Little Walter do the crying for me. Springtime was in the air. So was the Blues. Hello, Blues.

There are many pleasant jukebox memories in my mind. Along with cultivating a great ear for the Blues and what was known as Rhythm and Blues, I also learned to dance by the music on the jukebox. I thought I had one of the coolest Jitterbug styles in the state of Mississippi. My slow drag step was slower than the shuffle of a Jimmy Reed tune.

"What kind of music is that," she asked.

"Blues," I said, staring into her deep brown eyes like I was looking into her soul.

Speaking of dancing, I'm reminded of a weeknight with several new friends in this small Arkansas city. I was new in the area, and some of the guys had invited me to accompany them to this little juke joint call the Hall. There were two very attractive young ladies in the party. One of them captured my heart on the spot, and she didn't even know that I existed. Anyway, she was with one of the guys who had invited me to come to hang out with them.

When I discovered they had Blues on the jukebox in the back of the club, I stood around and punched up some Muddy Waters, Eddie Boyd, Lowell Fulson, Howlin' Wolf, Guitar Slim, and others. To my surprise, the young lady that I liked stopped to chat with me on her return from the powder room.

"What kind of music is that?" she asked. "The Blues," I said, staring into her deep brown eyes like I was looking into her soul. "How do you like it?" "It's OK, I suppose," she said smiling.

And then I asked her if her friend would mind her dancing with me. "He's too busy running his mouth," she said. So we danced very slow on five straight records. They never even noticed us.

Words began to flow from my mouth as soon as I caressed her to dance. I simply couldn't help it. I told her that she was the most beautiful woman that I had ever met. (She was twenty or twenty-one; I was twenty years old.) She laughed. I kept talking, and the voices on the jukebox kept singing the Blues. I told her that we were destined to be together and I was prepared to dedicate my life to the accomplishment of that goal. She stopped laughing and asked me a bunch of questions. I answered as our bodies moved closer and closer together in unison and rhythm with feeling. My feet hardly moved. I was losing my heart in the magic of her innocence and the fresh jasmine honeysuckle fragrance of her smell. The tenderness of her softness made me want to hold on forever. The voices on the jukebox, my allies, kept right on singing in our ears. "See you later, Blues," she said as she walked back to the table.

I remained in the back of the room with my friend the jukebox and the voices of the Blues. She had not agreed to meet me the next day. She had not said no either. I was at peace.

Before we left the club, the other young lady slipped a note into my hand and asked, "What did you do to my friend? She has lost her mind." I smiled. The Howlin' Wolf was singing in the background. It sounded louder than it really was . . .

Oh stop your train
And let a po boy ride
Oh don't you hear me crying
umm, oh umm

I could tell you story after story about this relationship between the juke joint, the Blues, and me. It's the voices that have always spoken to me. And they speak through me in my poetry and songs, in the classroom when I teach my students, even in my stories and speeches. Like a true friend, they seem to be there when I need them. I remember hearing Joe Turner sing:

I use to live across the street from a juke joint baby,
all night long they played the blues

The juke joint voices sang to me and nurtured me. They brought me from a mighty long way. And they are still with me, some living and others gone to another place. They live in my heart and on records, CDs, audio and videotapes, and jukeboxes. Juke joint voices keep on singing . . . Muddy Waters, Howlin' Wolf, B. B. King, Sonny Boy Williamson, Bobby "Blue" Bland, Bessie Smith, Little Junior Parker, Mississippi John Hurt, Billie Boy Arnold, Denise LaSalle, Solomon Burke, the list goes on and on.

Listen and you can hear golden-voiced Bobby "Blue" Bland moaning like a sanctified preacher on the jukebox in the Log Cabin, Hole in the Wall, Bucket of Blood, or any juke joint USA:

There's a stranger in my house, woman,
and I don't know what to do
ordinarily I would call the police
But the stranger is you.

ART ENSEMBLE OF CHICAGO
The Band That Has Given a New and Totally Musical Significance to the Term *Black Power*

Mike Hennessey

In August 1966, the twenty-six-year-old Chicago multi-instrumentalist Roscoe Mitchell recorded the album *Sound* for the Delmark label. In his sextet at the time were trumpeter Lester Bowie, from Frederick, Maryland, and thirty-nine-year-old Chicago bassist Malachi Favors.

Nobody—not even the musicians themselves—had any intimation of it at the time, but the album planted a musical seed that was to flourish and flower into one of the most uniquely enterprising groups in the history of Black music: the Art Ensemble of Chicago.

Recalling the album, which appeared at a time when the Jazz movement was in something of an avant-garde turmoil as Jazz musicians energetically, stridently, and anarchically looked for new directions in which to take the music, British writer Graham Lock observed: "Just when one wondered how Jazz could go any further without smashing itself to pieces on walls of febrile noise, Roscoe Mitchell—practically unknown outside his native Chicago—reasserted the elementary values of space and silence. His *Sound* and *Conglipitous* LPs (the latter recorded for Nessa Records in March 1998, with Bowie, Favors, and drummer Robert Crowder) signaled a new attitude in the music; it stopped screaming and began to breathe. *Sound* floated in and out of silence; cries and whispers would swell and fade in a complex ensemble dynamic."

In between those pacesetting albums, Bowie, Favors, and Mitchell joined forces in the Lester Bowie Quartet for another Nessa date in August 1967, producing *Number 1/Number 2*. Completing the quartet was twenty-nine-year-old instrumentalist Joseph Jarman, from Pine Bluff, Arkansas. These four men were the founding fathers of the Art Ensemble of Chicago—a group title foreshadowed by the name of the unit: the Roscoe Mitchell Art Ensemble.

Art Ensemble of Chicago and the Tradition of Chicago Blues Tour, Rostock, Germany, 1993. Back row, left to right: Famoudou Don Moye, Herb Walker, Roscoe Mitchell, Frank Lacy, James Carter, and Malachi Favors Maghoustus. Front row, left to right: Amina Claudine Meyers, Lester Bowie, Joseph Jarman, and L. "Chicago Beau" Beauchamp. Photo by DonAlonzo Beauchamp, *OCBA* archive.

Since those pioneering days, the Art Ensemble of Chicago (AEC) has become a major force on the Jazz scene, expanding from a quartet to quintet when drummer and percussionist Don Moye joined the group in Paris in 1969. Not the least impressive aspect of the remarkable AEC story is that it has survived and prospered with the same personnel for three decades—an astonishing and unprecedented achievement for a co-operative group, which speaks volumes for the musical, mental, and moral compatibility of its members.

As British writer and musician Ian Carr noted: "The Art Ensemble showed a way out of the cul-de-sac of abstraction and became one of the key groups of the 1970s and 1980s. Its inclusive, pluralistic music fused elements from Free Jazz and the whole Jazz tradition, going back to New Orleans, and there were also strong ethnic— particularly African—ingredients. Their performances also presented the music with brilliant theatrica."

Lester Bowie says, "All the members of the Art Ensemble have special areas of expertise—so between us we can operate over a wide range of music. We have five different people with five different lives and sets of experiences, which are brought in to make up the music. This isn't a band where the leader dictates the way everything should be done."

In the course of its three decades of existence, the AEC has produced a richly varied pantheon of recorded music: more than forty albums. Not counting the growing catalog of bootlegs. The legitimate repertoire includes two seminal albums for ECM, *Nice Guys* and *Full Force,* and other landmark sessions for Delmark, Atlantic, Freedom, and, more recently, the Japanese DIW label.

But the full impact of the Art Ensemble can only be experienced in live performances, with their colorful costumes, their tribal war paint, and their immense panoply of percussion instruments.

The AEC has always proclaimed its repertoire as being "Great Black Music: Ancient to the Future." The fact that the ensemble came into being in the mid-1960s, at a time when the United States was in the throes of a civil rights upheaval, when Malcolm X's Black Nationalist movement was mounting a militant challenge to institutionalized racial discrimination, meant that the band was frequently identified with the Black Panthers and its members portrayed as angry, White-hating, politically motivated renegades.

But, as Don Moye has observed, "All political agitation of the '60s is contained in part of who we are. They tried to involve us politically with slogans and rhetoric, but none of us had any background in the bullshit of politics. Our training was as musicians—we wanted to make strong statements about our identity and heritage. We wanted to make strong declaration of who we were, regardless of the social climate—we never got involved in politics."

British writer Valerie Wilmer succinctly identified the AEC's positioning in the hierarchy of Black American music when she wrote, "The Art Ensemble are a long way from being revolutionaries in any political sense, and yet their music represents another interpretation of Black Power. Although the dedicated bunch of Chicagoans are artists first and foremost, they come closer to realizing that slogan more than some of their brothers do, simply through playing the people's music."

NOW MOTHER OF TIME

Hart Leroy Bibbs

Now mother of time
    The family weeps
Now mother of time
    The coffin creaks
Now mother of time
    Black night speaks

Vertiginous music rising
    Realities brushed on drums
Personalities emphasizing
    The man and his horn have gone

Horizontally now he defies his tunes
Way way behind the dark stage
Where bass auras are written
Spirals of green, amber and blue
And spirits is now his home
His soul's silver reflection
Music no more shadowed by essence
    And the sympathetic look
Of written love
    In a black book

This page is readable by all
Whose lifestyles write rhythms
Of repeated past shimmering—
The tower's strength
    And the flame of his beauty
Then the sun rises once more, once more
    Now mother of time
Black night speaks
    Now mother of time
A coffin creaks
    Now mother of time
A family weeps

Afterword

As this book goes to press, I am compelled by the extraordinary events of our epoch to write an afterword that reaches beyond closing thoughts solely on the best of the *Original Chicago Blues Annual*.

On January 20, 2009, an African American was inaugurated the forty-fourth president of the United States and moved into the White House, which is, in part, a house built upon the suffering and displacement of others. A house whose foundation, brick, mortar, and marble are fused with consanguineous DNA from the labor of the *unfree* through blood, saliva, sweat, flesh, vomit, tears, and death. It is my hope that the spirits of those who endured the whip and worse, and those removed from their ancient lands in Africa and America, and the pantheon of orishas, both peaceful and wrathful, will swirl, hover, dance, sing, scream, and rejoice in a joyful haunting of the White House, celebrating their vindication and inspiring Barack Obama in his work and challenges. In many ways, more than I could possibly mention here, the White House has been a House of Blues, from its construction, to policies and declarations that have emerged from it, to the great Black artists who have performed there, to the occupancy of Barack Obama and his family. Alas, time has done what it does so well: brought about change.

The *Original Chicago Blues Annual* focuses on the reality of Blues life and music through interviews, writings by those from within the Blues experience, and contributions from those outside of it who have a deep respect and sensitivity toward Blues people, Black people. Over the course of seven years, without homogenizing our pages, the *Blues Annual* remained definitive and uncompromising in its identity and yet delivered a clear message of multiculturalism and inclusion—a message shared by many and that is gaining momentum and bringing about changes in this world that just a short time ago were thought impossible.

As editor of the *Blues Annual,* my philosophy is never to forget our history but be not shackled and hampered by it. Do not hold responsible those who have no responsibility, and do not let off the hook those who do. The old White House, like the Berlin Wall and apartheid in South Africa, has crumbled under the weight of time; however, the residual bitter dregs of the past will certainly take decades to dissolve. Today's Blues messenger must be a griot of truth about our past and a beacon lighting the way toward a bright future filled with possibility in every area of life without severing the Blues connection that has brought us to this point.

The *Original Chicago Blues Annual* serves as a messenger from Blues generations past and present. It is rich with the voices of those who are a greater part of the bedrock of America's cultural identity and, by extension, are a major influence on popular music and lifestyles across the globe. And now, the son of a Kenyan father, who, like his ancestors, suffered under the brutal yoke of British colonialism, and a White American mother whose ancestors gave us the Blues has moved into the White House with his wife, a descendant of African American slaves, and their children, whose ancestry is profoundly defining of where many have come from.

The Blues message remains. The most visible Blues messenger is occupying the White House. He must be watched with eyes wide open, and we must never forget that he is human.

Contributors

L. "CHICAGO BEAU" BEAUCHAMP is a writer, editor, and musician. Beau is founding editor of the *Original Chicago Blues Annual, Literati Chicago,* and *Literati Internazionale.* Among his books are *Art Ensemble of Chicago—Great Black Music, Ancient to the Future* and *Blues Stories.* He has made numerous recordings, the latest being *Last of the Saboom Boom Gypsies.* Beau appears as MC in the Billy Cobham documentary *Sonic Mirror.* At present he is working on a memoir.

BARBARA BAREFIELD has been a presence on the Detroit Black music scene since the early 1970s. Her photographs have been included in publications around the world, as well as on the covers of numerous records and CDs. A collection of her work has been presented in *Jazz Space Detroit,* a photo book with commentary by author Herb Boyd. Her photos can be viewed at the Detroit Public Library's E. Azalia Hackley Collection. Over the past three decades, she has worked with her husband, jazz guitarist Spencer Barefield, in presenting Jazz, Classical, and Creative music in Detroit and internationally, including a thirteen-year award-winning series at the Detroit Institute of Arts.

DONALONZO BEAUCHAMP is a photographer, record producer, and artists' manager. He is founder of Katalyst Entertainment, a resource for multicultural music presentations. He is also a great son.

HART LEROY BIBBS generally resided in Paris, France. He was one of the leading Black poets/philosophers/essayists of the 1960s, 1970s, and 1980s and is highly regarded as a no-nonsense man of letters who survived through his craft and wits. Among his books are *Diet Book for a Junkie, Poly-Rhythms to Freedom,* and *Hey Now, Hey!* He also was an accomplished photographer of Black musicians and a playwright. February 6, 1930–August 31, 1994.

DEITRA FARR is one of Chicago's "top female vocalists," according to *Living Blues Magazine* (May 1997). She is a graduate of Columbia College in Chicago, with a bachelor of arts degree in journalism. Deitra has recorded many of her own compositions and has written articles for the *Chicago Daily Defender, The Original Chicago Blues Annual, il Blues* of Italy, and *Living Blues Magazine.* Deitra currently resides in Norway.

ERIC FIENBLATT says, "I've taken portraits as long as I've taken pictures. And though for years I've combined images on my computer screen, I always seem to return to the basic low-tech portrait. I guess it has something to do with what happens between two people face to face."

Eric's photographs have graced the pages of *Marie Claire, France; Vogue, France; Vogue, Germany; HG, USA,* and *Le Ministère de La Culture, France.* Many of his portraits are in the permanent collection of the Bibliothèque Nationale in France.

JULIO FINN was born in Chicago and now resides in Paris, France. He comes from a family of Blues artists that includes Jerome and Billy Boy Arnold. Julio has recorded several albums over the years, including collaborations with Linton Johnson, Archie Shepp, and Chicago Beau. He has written several important works, including the following books: *The Bluesman: The Musical Heritage of Black Men and Women in the Americas, Voices of Negritude,* and *The Poetry of the Cigar.*

JAMES FRAHER'S photographs have appeared in many publications, including on the covers of *The Original Chicago Blues Annual, Living Blues* magazine, and on more than one hundred music recordings. He is the author of *The Blues Is a Feeling, Voices and Visions of African-American Blues Musicians,* published by Face to Face Books in 1998. James has collaborated with writer Roger Wood to produce two books published by the University of Texas Press, *Down in Houston: Bayou City Blues* (2003) and *Texas Zydeco* (2006).

James's photographs and posters are in the permanent collections of the Smithsonian Institution, the Chicago Blues Archive at the Harold Washington Library Center, and the University of Mississippi Blues Archive in Oxford, Mississippi. He currently resides in County Sligo, Ireland.

JOAN HACKETT is recognized internationally as one of the world's leading photographers. Chicago-based Joan brings to her work the trained eye of a graduate anthropologist from the University of Illinois at Urbana-Champaign with an advanced degree from the School of the Art Institute of Chicago. Joan's wide-ranging and diverse assignments include documentary, photojournalism, portrait, music, performance, and aerial and underwater photography. She has photographed world leaders and been official photographer to many, including Mikhail Gorbachev; the presidents of Ireland, Liberia, and Mexico; the king of Jordan; Barack Obama; and Madeleine Albright. Photographing celebrities Oscar de la Renta, Christopher Reeves, Gwendolyn Brooks, Spike Lee, Bill Murray, Philip Glass, and Luciano Pavarotti have been among Joan's assignments.

Joan's diverse body of work includes photographing voodoo rituals and social conditions in Haiti, Frida Kahlo's home and garden, Day of the Dead celebrations in Mexico, Chicago steel mills, and urban community gardens.

Joan is widely published and has been exhibited in numerous museums.

MIKE HENNESSEY was born in London, England, on February 25, 1928. "The family was musical, my mother played piano and had a good contralto voice, and my brother took up drums as a hobby and still plays. I wound up learning to be a teleprinter operator in the RAF [Royal Air Force], prior to being given the opportunity to beat the system by becoming a musician and writer," says Mike.

Mike's books include *Some of My Best Friends Are Blues,* with Ronnie Scott; *Klook,* a biography of Kenny Clarke; *Tin Pan Alley,* a book about the British music business; and *The Little Giant: The Story of Johnny Griffin.*

JOSEPH JARMAN was born on September 14, 1937, in Pine Bluff, Arkansas. He is a jazz musician, composer, and a Shinshu Buddhist priest, and he holds a rank of Godan, fifth-degree black belt, in aikido. He is perhaps best known as one of the first members of the Association for the Advancement of Creative Musicians and the Art Ensemble of Chicago.

JACQUES LACAVA, originally from Paris, France, now resides in Chicago. He is a writer, songwriter, filmmaker, and translator. He contributed regularly to *The Original Chicago Blues Annual* and is a correspondent for the French music magazines *Soul Bag* and *Jazz Hot*. Jacques is also founder of Le French Link, a translation and interpretation service dealing with the Francophile international, business, and diplomatic communities.

GUY LERNER, formerly of Chicago, is a physician practicing medicine in Kentucky. He has an enthusiastic appreciation for the Blues—the musicians, the lifestyle, and the art form. As a writer, Guy has published numerous articles on Blues and is founder of TheTechnicalTake.com, a Web site that offers content, commentary, and strategies for investors and traders. Guy has a bachelor of arts degree in literature from the University of Pennsylvania, and he attended medical school at the University of Pittsburgh School of Medicine. His formal training is as a pediatric anesthesiologist, and for the past twenty years he has worked in some of the top universities and hospitals in the United States.

JULIE PARSON NESBITT is author of the poetry collection *Finders* (West End Press). She received the Gwendolyn Brooks Significant Illinois Poet Award and holds a master's degree in fine arts in creative writing from the University of Pittsburgh. Her poetry has been published in numerous journals and anthologies. She is coeditor of *Power Lines: A Decade of Poetry from Chicago's Guild Complex* (Tia Chucha Press). She previously served as executive director of the Guild Complex, a cross-cultural literary arts center, and is currently a grant specialist for the University of Illinois at Chicago and cochair of the board of directors for Young Chicago Authors.

EUGENE B. REDMOND is an emeritus professor of English at Southern Illinois University at Edwardsville and the editor of *Drumvoices Revue*. He is an active voice in the local writing community as well as in national and international circles. As a founder of the Eugene B. Redmond Writers Club (1986) in East St. Louis, Illinois, he continues to be instrumental in the lives of novice and experienced writers across the globe.

His awards include a National Endowment for the Arts Creative Writing Fellowship, the Lifetime Achievement Award from Pan-African Movement USA, a Pushcart Prize Best of Small Presses, a Tribute to an Elder from the African Poetry Theater of New York City, an American Book Award for *The Eye in the Ceiling: Selected Poems* (1993), and writing fellowships from the California, Illinois, Louisiana, Missouri, and West Virginia arts councils.

OSCAR ROMERO was born in Mexico City in 1954. He was one of nine children in an artistic family. Oscar's art is steeped in the myth, ritual, and cultural memory that emerges from his heritage in Mexico and also reflects his present life. As a partial descendent from Mayan, Toltec, and Olmec people with a trace of Spanish heritage, he incorporates many traditional symbols into his work. The "magic" Usumacinta River and the Aztec capital of Tenochtitlán are part of Oscar's memories of place and time.

KALAMU YA SALAAM is founder of NOMMO Literary Society. NOMMO is a New Orleans–based creative writing workshop whose members are published in national anthologies such as *Dark Eros, Kente Cloth, Catch the Fire,* and *360°: A Revolution of Black Poets*. He is also a founder of Runagate Multimedia, which focuses on New Orleans and African-heritage cultures worldwide.

Salaam is the leader of the World Band, a poetry performance ensemble that combines poetry with Blues, Jazz, and other forms of music. Salaam's work includes the spoken-word CD *My Story, My Song* (AFO Records) and *What Is Life: Reclaiming the Black Blues Self* (Third World Press).

QUINCY TROUPE, poet, performer, and editor, was born on July 22, 1939, in St. Louis, Missouri. His books of poetry include *Transcircularities: New and Selected Poems* (2002), *Avalanche: Poems* (1996), and *Weather Reports: New and Selected Poems* (1991). Other works include *Miles: The Autobiography* (1989), which received an American Book Award; *James Baldwin: The Legacy* (1989); and a memoir, *Miles and Me: A Memoir of Miles Davis* (2000). He has taught at the University of California at San Diego and Columbia University. He was the first official poet laureate of the state of California.

DAVID WHITEIS is an independent scholar living in Chicago. His writings on the Blues have appeared in many publications, including the *Chicago Reader, The Original Chicago Blues Annual,* and *Living Blues;* he has written a book titled *Chicago Blues: Portraits and Stories* (University of Illinois Press).

JAMES OTIS WILLIAMS founded and was first director of the Nyumburu Black Cultural Center at the University of Maryland. He hails from Granada, Mississippi, where his daily life growing up was surrounded by the poetry of Blues as lifestyle. He authored several volumes of poetry, including *The Natural Truth, Hootchie Kootchie Man,* and *The Blues Is Darker Than Blue*. Williams was also a singer and performance poet. He taught Black music studies at the University of Maryland. James Otis Williams became an ancestor on April 4, 1997.

DAVID WITTER is a Chicago-based freelance writer and photographer. His writings on Blues have appeared in *The Original Chicago Blues Annual, Living Blues Magazine, New City, The Bay Area Music Magazine, Gambit,* and *Buddy Guy's Bluesletter*. His work has also been featured in the *Washington Post,* the *Chicago Tribune,* the *Chicago Reader,* and the Copley newspapers. He is the author of *Oldest Chicago,* a book of prose and photographs (Lake Claremont Press).

Index

10–2 double plus, 111
113 Club, 114

AACM (Association for the Advancement of Creative Musicians), 51, 134
Abidjan, Côte d'Ivoire 75, 76
Abrams, Muhal Richard, 51, 134
Africa/Africans, 15–16, 31, 36, 53, 65–68, 70, 71, 75–77, 126, 137, 144, 150, 153, 154, 157
African Diaspora, xiii, 38, 95
Ahmad Jamal's Alhambra, xii
Alitalia Airlines, xiv, 71
Alligator Records, 54, 81, 144
Allison, Luther, 37–38
American Ace Harps, 75
Angelou, Maya, 126
Another Country, 129
Arnold, Billy Boy, xii, xiv, 33, 95, 97–107, 130, 155
Art Ensemble of Chicago, xiii, xiv, 13, 15, 47, 51, 129, 130, 134, 137, 149–51, 156
Asim, Jibari, xiii
Atlantic (Records) 150

Baldwin, James, 123, 128, 157
Baraka, Amiri, 126
Barefield, Barbara, 71, 90, 155
Barrel House Chuck, 143
Barry, Gordy, 150
Bass, Fontella, 51, 129
Baze, George, 73
Beale Street, 10, 25, 32
Beauchamp, DonAlonzo, 155
Beauchamp, Lincoln "Chicago Beau," xii, 123–30, 155
Beauchamp, Lincoln Sr., xii

Benson, Al, 110, 111
Benson and Hedges, 126, 127
Bey, Amir, xiii
Bibbs, Hart Leroy, 9, 27, 126, 129, 155
Biondi, Dick, 111
"Black Dilemma," 9
Black Gipsy, 127
Blackstone Rangers, 78, 115
Blue Flame Blues Club, xii
B.L.U.E.S., 82
Blue's Dream, 129
B.L.U.E.S., etc., xiv
Blues Foundation, 125
Blues Heaven Foundation, 145
Blues in the Schools, 126
Bluesmen, The, 126
Blues People, 126
Blues World Digest, 125, 127
Bowie, Lester, 47–53, 150
Boyd, Eddie, 9–12, 148
Branch, Billy, 27, 126, 130
Brooks, Gwendolyn, xiii, 121, 156
Brooks Brothers, 112, 115
Brown Derby, 114
Brown, Sterling, xii
Brutus, Dennis, xiii
Bud Billikin Day, 143
Budland, 113, 114
Burnin' Chicago Blues Machine, 130
Burrell, Dave, 129
Butler, Jerry, 51

Cadillac Baby, 130
Calloway, Cab, 92
Camus, Albert, xii
Carpentier, Alejo, xii, xiii
Carr, Ian, 150

Carter, James, 130
Carter, Nell, 93
Certain Blacks, 127
Charters, Sam, 126
Checkerboard, 73, 77, 143
Chess, Leonard, 144
Chess Records, 6, 20, 51
Chicago Blues Festival, 1, 8, 9, 37, 28, 74, 120, 142, 143
Chicago Historical Society, 126, 143
Club Georgia, 11, 99
Collins, Big Bill, 130
Conglipitous, 149
Conley, Jim, 130
Crawford, Pete, xiv
Crisis, The, xiii

Dallas, 78
Da Nang, 110
Davis, Blind John, 142, 143
Davis, Miles, 94
Davis, Sammy Jr., 77
Davis, Tyrone, 77, 116, 117
Dawkins, Jimmy, xiv, 55, 56, 130
Dip, The, 113
Dishrag, 10, 11
DIW Records, xiv, 45, 150
Dolins, Barry, 142–45
Doll House, 114
Donald and the Delighters, 115
Donleavey, J.P, xiii
"Don't Mess Up a Good Thing," 51
Du Bois, W. E. B., xiii
Dumas, Henry, xiii, 125, 126
DuSable Museum, 126, 143

Earth, Wind & Fire, 51

East St. Louis, Illinois, 48, 127, 156
Ebony magazine, xiii, 50, 76
ECM, 150
El Dorados, The, 115
Ellington, Duke, 10 13, 16, 88, 134

Farr, Deitra, 62, 126, 130, 155
Favors Maghoustus, Malachi, xiv, 129, 134, 149
fesnecki, 111, 112
Fienblatt, Eric, 155
Finn, Julio, xii, 33, 97, 155
Fire, 116
Forty-seventh Street, xii, 113, 114
Fraher, James, 156
Franklin, Aretha, 91, 113
Fred Robinson, the Great Baby Boy and Party Makers, 18
Freedom Records, 150
Frost, Ray, 129
Full Force, 150

GBW Records, 130
Gerri's Palm Tavern, 114
Gousters, 109, 114, 115
Gray, Blind Arvela, 142
Great Black Music, 13, 130, 137, 151, 155
Green, Garland, 116
Green Gables Hotel, xii
Guralnick, Peter, 126

Hackett, Joan, 156
Hagedorn, Jessica, xiii
hammers and nails, 111
Handy, W. C., 125
Having a Fit Over Your Love, 130
Hayes, Willie, 73
Heavy Timber, 140
Helfer, Erwin, 142, 143
Hennessey, Mike, 137, 156
Hentoff, Nat, 126
hoodoo, 26, 31, 43, 77, 83–87, 140, 141
Hooker, John Lee, 24, 60, 81
Hope, Bob, 77
Hopkins, Linda, 92
Horne, Lena, 92
Hound Dog Taylor, 57, 80, 82
humbugging, 113
Humphery, Hubert, 75, 76, 77
Hunter, Alberta, 91
Hurston, Zora Neale, xii
Hutto, J. B., 55, 80–82

Iceland, xiv, 30, 130
Iglauer, Bruce, 54–61
Illinois Arts Council, 143
Ivy Leaguers (Ivies), 112, 113, 115

Jack Harris and the Invaders, 50
Jagger, Mick, 78
Jamal, Ahmad, xii, 133
James, Elmore, 3, 18, 80, 82, 105, 147
Jarman, Joseph, xiv, 149, 156
Jenkins, Donald, 116
Jet magazine, xiii, 129
Johnny Davis and the Original Music Masters, 143
Johnson, John H., xiii
Johnson, Robert, 31, 88, 126, 139, 144
Jones, Philly Joe, 129
Jones, Rodney, 111, 113
Jordan, Michael, 79
jukehouse, 20

Kendricks, Eddie, 112
Kent, Herb, 109–16
Kent, Willie, 130
King, Albert, 48, 51, 95, 116
King, B.B., 18, 32, 81, 101, 132, 147, 148
King, Martin Luther, xii, 127
King, Shirley, xiv, 130
Kingdom of this World, A, xiii
Kingston Mines, 5, 125
Kinsey, Big Daddy, 17–21
Kool and the Gang, 116
Koren, Gabriel, xiii

Lacava, Jacques, xiii, 125, 156
Lacy, Frank, 130
Lane, Pinkie Gordon, xiii
LaVere, Steve, 126
Leak, Lafayette, xii
Lee, Jeanne, 129
Lee, John (Sonny Boy Williamsom), 9, 103
Lerner, Guy, xiii, 156
Lincoln University, 50
Lion Room, 115
Literati Chicago, xiii, xiv, 127
Literati Internazionale, xiii, 45, 127, 155
Little Brother Montgomery, 55, 143
Little Milton, 35, 48
Littlejohn, Johnny, 82
Lochinvars, 113
Locke, Sharese, xiii
Locket, James, 74
Love, Willie, 75

Mabon, Willie, 133, 142
Madison, Tamara, xiii
Malcolm X, 151
Mama Yancey, 142
Maxwell Street, 24, 25, 142, 143
McClure, Bobby, 51
McCoy, Sid, 111
McCracken, Tommy, 130
McDougal, E. Parker, 131–35
McGraw, A.-C., xiii, 1, 127
mellow fern, 146
Memphis Slim, 37, 127, 128, 133, 144
Metcalfe, Ralph Jr., 144
Metropolitan Theatre, 114
Meyers, Amina Claudine, 130
Miller, Henry, xiii
Miller, Rice, 31, 75, 103
Mirikitani, Janis, xiii
Mississippi, 9, 10, 18, 20, 21, 23, 29–33, 36, 43, 55, 88, 101, 139, 142, 147, 148, 156, 157
Montreal Jazz Festival, xiii
Moore, Elaine, 126
Motown, 38, 116
Mount Carmel High School, 128
Moye, Famoudou Don, xiv, 13–16, 49, 71, 129, 130, 150, 151
Musicdisc, 127
My Ancestors, 130, 131

National Endowment of the Arts, 143
Nice Guys, 150
Nicholas, Marta, xiii
No Name in the Street, 123, 129
Number 1 / Number 2, 149

Obama, Barack, 153, 156
Ohio Players, The, 116
Ole Miss, 21
Original Chicago Blues Annual, xiii, xiv, 1, 27, 45, 71, 95, 121, 124, 127, 137, 153–57

Palmer, Robert, 126
Paris Review, xiii
Parson Nesbitt, Julie xiii, 71, 156
Patterson, Raymond, 126
Pepper's, 55, 78
Peps, 113
Perkins, Pinetop, xiv, 29–36, 130, 142
Pershing, 133
Platonic Records, xiv
Plumpp, Sterling, xiii
Pryor, Snooky, 99, 124, 143

Rabearivelo, Jean-Joseph, xiii
Red Top, 115
Redmond, Eugene B., xiii, 1, 26, 44, 126, 127, 156
Reed, Ishmael, xiii
Reed, Jimmy, 18, 19, 21, 24, 101, 120, 147
Reed, Kay, 130
Regal Theater, xii, 113, 114, 117, 133
"Rescue Me," 51
Rhodes Theatre, 114
Rolling Stones, 53, 78
Rolling Stone magazine, 6, 58
Romero, Oscar, 157
Russell, Jacob, xiii

Saba, Isio, xiii, xiv, 125
Saigon, 76
Sain, Oliver, 36, 48, 51
Saint-Leu-la-Forêt, 52, 129
Salaam, Kalamu Ya, 27, 126, 157
San Remo, Italy, 124
Sardinia, xiv, 71, 130
Shepp, Archie, xii, 127, 129, 134, 155
Shines, Johnny, 31, 105, 126, 139–41
Shyvette, xiii
Smith, Pinetop, 29, 31, 142
Sound, 149
Spaniels, The, 115
Spann, Lucille, 93
Spann, Pervis, 111
Sparrows, The, 116
Speakeasy, 115
SS *United States*, 52

St. Paul de Vence, 129
Sugar Blue, 27
Sullivan, Ed, 78
Sunnyland Slim, 1, 55, 104, 142, 143
Sweet Sticky Thing, 116

Taylor, Johnny, 116
Taylor, Koko, 3–8, 90
Temptations, The, 115, 1162
Théâtre du Ranelagh, 129
Theresa Needham Blues Center, 145
Thiele, Bob, 126
Thornton, Big Mama, 94
Times Square, 110, 114
Tivoli Theatre, 113
Toronado, 114
Troupe, Quincy, 27, 125, 157
Two Gun Pete, xii

United States, 14, 20, 21, 77, 128, 151, 153

V103, 109
Vee-Jay, 55, 101, 102, 130, 142

Wahoo Man, 110, 114
Walker, Herb, 130
Walker, Jimmy, 142
Walker, Margaret, xiii
Wallace, Sippie, 90
Waterman, Dick, 75, 78
Waters, Muddy, xii, xiv, 3, 18,19, 20, 23, 29, 32, 34, 38, 70, 78, 80, 88, 100, 104, 105, 133, 144, 148

Waters, Muddy Jr., 103
WBEE, 110
WBEZ, 109
Welding, Pete, 126
Wellington, Valerie, xiv, 62, 95, 130
Wells, Junior, xiv, 3, 56, 71, 73–79, 103, 104, 105, 107, 130
West Memphis, Arkansas, 74, 75
Wheeler, Big "Golden," 27
White, Maurice, 51
Whiteis, David, xiii, 1, 95, 125, 157
Wilkins, Joe Willie, 31, 75
Williams, James Otis, 157
Williams, Lil' Ed, 80–82
Williams, Pookie, 80, 81, 82
Williamson, Sonny Boy, 9, 31, 75, 98, 105, 148
Wilmer, Valerie, 151
Wilson, Jackie, 51
WIND, 109
Witter, David, xiii, 157
WJJD, 109
WLS, 111
Wolf, Howlin, 24, 32, 70, 78, 101, 142, 148
Wrens, The, 115
Wright, O. V., 116
Wright, Richard, xii
WVON, 110, 111
Wyman, Bill, 79

Young, Johnny, 9, 12, 103

THE UNIVERSITY OF ILLINOIS PRESS
IS A FOUNDING MEMBER OF THE
ASSOCIATION OF AMERICAN UNIVERSITY PRESSES.

COMPOSED IN SCALA AND SCALA SANS PRO
BY JIM PROEFROCK
AT THE UNIVERSITY OF ILLINOIS PRESS
DESIGNED BY KELLY GRAY
MANUFACTURED BY SHERIDAN BOOKS, INC.

UNIVERSITY OF ILLINOIS PRESS
1325 SOUTH OAK STREET
CHAMPAIGN, IL 61820-6903
WWW.PRESS.UILLINOIS.EDU